BUENOS AIRES TRAVEL GUIDE

Captivating Adventures from Tango Rhythms, Latin American Charm, Landmarks, Hidden Gems, and More

Welcome Aboard, Discover

Your Limited-Time Free Bonus!

Hello, traveler! Welcome to the Captivating Travels family, and thanks for grabbing a copy of this book! Since you've chosen to join us on this journey, we'd like to offer you something special.

Check out the link below for a FREE Ultimate Travel Checklist eBook & Printable PDF to make your travel planning stress-free and enjoyable.

But that's not all - you'll also gain access to our exclusive email list with even more free e-books and insider travel tips. Well, what are you waiting for? Click the link below to join and embark on your next adventure with ease.

Access your bonus here: https://livetolearn.lpages.co/checklist/

Or, Scan the QR code!

TABLE OF CONTENTS

INTRODUCTION

Do you want to experience the best of South America's Argentina? Then you should book a ticket to Buenos Aires, the country's massive cosmopolitan capital city. The city sits majestically beside the western shore of the Rio de la Plata with a crooked finger, inviting travelers from around the world to get drenched not in water (except if you wish to go swimming) but by its electrifying culture and a never-ending stream of captivating experiences. Buenos Aires has a charming blend of past and present that promises to leave you spellbound and wanting more.

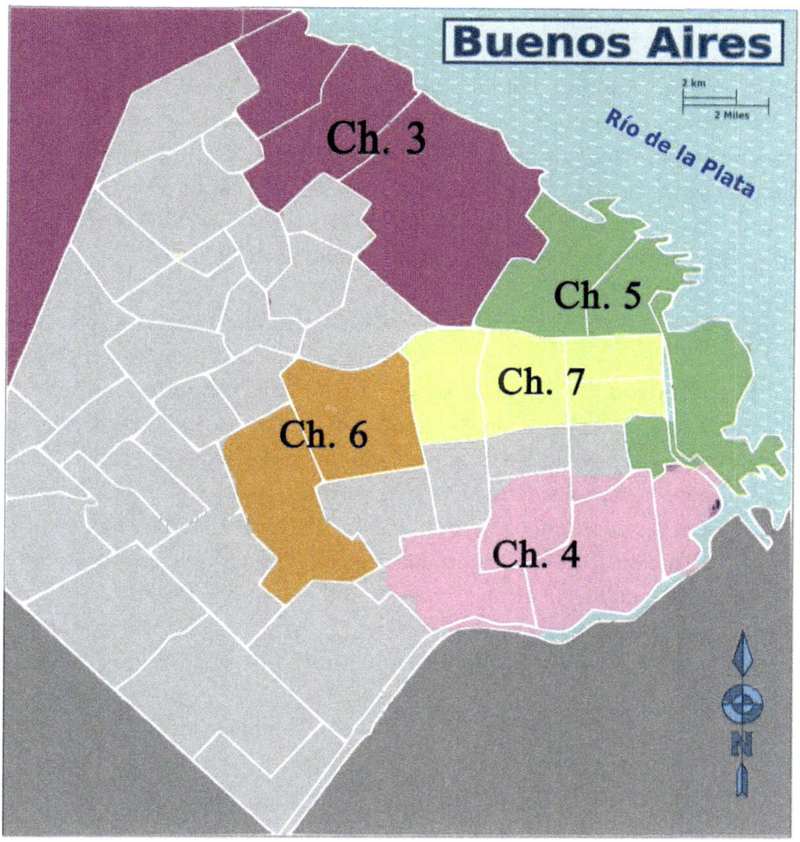

Districts mentioned in the book.[1]

Are you already picturing yourself stepping off the plane and into the bustling metropolis where energy crackles in the air? You are not the only one. Travelers worldwide often visit Buenos Aires for time away from home to adventure in the home of the sultry tango. However, as someone visiting a new place for the first time, you need all the advice to visit the city and enjoy a carefree holiday. Don't worry. Everything you need to know about Buenos Aires is within these pages.

This book is written explicitly for first-time visitors like yourself. The information is in a clear, easy-to-understand format. So, whether you're a history buff, a foodie, or a culture enthusiast, this guidebook equips you with knowledge and insider tips for an unforgettable Buenos Aires experience. Unlike other travel guides that leave you searching for additional resources, this one provides everything, from planning your trip to navigating the city and its environs.

The book begins with an introduction to the city of Buenos Aires, getting familiar with its geography, history, and people. Next, you'll be taken through the city's main airports, learning how to get around each airport when you arrive and how to travel to the different districts. Then, explore the mosaic of neighborhoods in the city, from the western to the southern, northern, eastern, and central districts, each with its distinct personality.

Explore Palermo, a neighborhood with rows of cafes and boutiques lining its streets. A short distance away, you'll run into Caballito, the district with elegant architecture and delightful parks. Buenos Aires is a city that ignites the senses. Close your eyes for a moment and picture La Boca, a neighborhood bursting with sparkling colors. Here, the famous Caminito street comes alive with the rhythm of tango, and its brightly painted houses are a backdrop for passionate dancers and talented street artists. A stone's throw away is Barracas, an artistic haven with amazing galleries showcasing local talent. Experience the city's rich cultural heritage by visiting the majestic Teatro Colón, one of the world's grandest opera houses. The rest of Buenos Aires is here for you to explore. The city is known as the "Paris of South America," so keep reading to discover why.

Buenos Aires, - "the Paris of South America," is famous for its colorful beauty and lush green scenery. The city has a European feel, with architecture resembling anything in Paris and Rome. It is commonly called "la Reina del Plata" and is translated to "The Queen of the River Plate" because of its strategic location. Buenos Aires is a fun place to visit. It has a grand opera house, the Teatro Colón, and gorgeous scenery that looks like a film set. Argentina's capital is a cultural center that is booming with plenty of live music and dance, especially the famous Tango Argentino. So, if you want a beautiful, exciting city to explore, Buenos Aires should be on your travel list.

Buenos Aires is the Paris of South America.[2]

GEOGRAPHICAL LOCATION AND STRUCTURE

Buenos Aires sits on the coast of South America by the Rio de la Plata estuary. It stands out as a hub for politics, culture, and commerce in Argentina. The city's location was significant in its history as a port city that welcomes trade and diverse communities. Its design reflects past and modern influences, showcasing a grid layout established during colonial times. It is split into 48 neighborhoods (barrios), each with a distinctive charm and historical importance. The bustling Microcentro area is the administrative core, housing government buildings, businesses, and financial institutions. The Plaza de Mayo stands at the center, surrounded by landmarks like the Casa Rosada palace.

Moving north from Microcentro takes you to Recoleta, a neighborhood known for its architecture, luxury shops, and the renowned Recoleta Cemetery, where famous figures such as Eva Perón rest in peace. Next to Recoleta is Palermo, a neighborhood known for its green areas, hip cafes, and lively nightlife. Palermo splits into Palermo Soho and Palermo Hollywood, each catering to various preferences and hobbies.

On the city's east side, San Telmo offers a peek into Buenos Aires's roots with its old-fashioned streets, vintage stores, and traditional tango bars. It is one of the oldest neighborhoods and a favorite spot for history and culture enthusiasts. La Boca is recognized for its buildings, artistic community, and La Bombonera Stadium, where the Boca Juniors play.

The city's southern side includes neighborhoods such as Barracas and Villa Lugano, which have more of a working-class heritage. These regions are being transformed through upliftment initiatives and residential developments.

Buenos Aires is bordered by the Rio de la Plata, which provides views and plenty of leisure opportunities. Its extensive waterfront is home to the Costanera Sur reserve, which has many walking paths and a variety of bird life for those who love birdwatching. The transportation network in Buenos Aires is well-established, with a public transit system linking neighborhoods. The city is known for its parks and squares, where locals and tourists have many areas to unwind and savor the lively city atmosphere.

HISTORICAL OVERVIEW

Buenos Aires has had a complex past that has molded its character into an urban center. The city was founded in 1536 by the explorer Pedro de Mendoza. Due to ongoing threats from indigenous groups, the settlement was eventually deserted. Buenos Aires was reestablished in 1580 by Juan de Garay, marking the beginning of its permanent presence.

Buenos Aires was part of the Viceroyalty of Peru before becoming the capital of the Viceroyalty of the Río de la Plata in 1776. This transition boosted the city's importance as a trade and immigration center thanks to its strategic location on the Rio de la Plata. Over time, Buenos Aires became a melting pot of cultures, with waves of European migrants - mainly from Italy and Spain - arriving in the late 19th and early 20th centuries. This cultural blend impacted Buenos Aires's identity through art, architecture, and culinary customs.

Buenos Aires was at the forefront of Argentina's struggle for independence from Spain. The May Revolution of 1810 in Plaza de la Victoria, today known as Plaza de Mayo, marked a turning point that eventually paved the way for Argentina's independence declaration in 1816.

During that time, Buenos Aires thrived as a hub of groundbreaking ideas. It influenced the broader movement for independence throughout Latin America. After gaining independence, Buenos Aires went through times of discord and internal conflict, with centralist and federalist factions often at odds. It was named the capital of Argentina in 1880. The 19th and early 20th centuries saw growth and modernization in Buenos Aires, and the city developed majestic boulevards, theaters, and public edifices, earning it the nickname "Paris of South America."

The 20th century brought about political and economic transformation in Buenos Aires. The city underwent industrialization and urban expansion accompanied by political movements. In the 1940s and 1950s, a notable figure, Juan Domingo Perón, significantly impacted the city's political landscape, ushering in a new era focused on labor rights and social welfare initiatives. Buenos Aires grappled with economic uncertainty and political upheaval, including a period of military rule from 1976 to 1983 characterized by widespread human rights violations. The revival of democracy in the 1980s sparked an optimism and cultural renaissance, leading Buenos Aires to embrace its lively character once more.

Nowadays, Buenos Aires is a beacon of strength and flexibility, embodying a past marked by colonization, revolutions, immigration waves, political turmoil, and cultural evolution. The city's convoluted history has molded it into a cosmopolitan hub that draws individuals from all corners of the globe.

COMPARATIVE URBAN RELATIONSHIPS

Buenos Aires is a major world city in South America, with qualities setting it apart from other major cities worldwide. Buenos Aires has long been a city where trade, culture, and politics come alive. While it shares traits with other global cities, it retains many characteristics deeply rooted in its Latin American heritage. The city is often compared to Paris and Madrid primarily due to its architectural styles and interesting cultural scene. The metropolis has expansive boulevards, majestic theaters, and refined buildings that showcase influences from the late 19th and early 20th centuries when European migration significantly shaped the city's landscape that became Argentina's capital.

Its role as an epicenter can be seen and felt in the flourishing arts community attracting visitors worldwide. The esteemed Teatro Colón is regarded as one of the world's premier opera houses, further cementing Buenos Aires's cultural importance. The local music scene thrives on tango; tango clubs and events draw crowds from across the globe.

Buenos Aires' landscape reflects its Latin American essence, influenced by a history marked by populist movements and military interventions. The city's association with Peronism created a fusion of nationalism, social equality, and workers' rights. This distinct political backdrop sets Buenos Aires apart from cities in stable regions. It functions as the commercial hub of Argentina, hosting the Buenos Aires Stock Exchange and major corporate entities. Unlike other Latin American urban centers, Buenos Aires boasts a diversified economy with robust finance, media, technology, and tourism sectors. Its strategic positioning along the Rio de la Plata historically positioned it as a port city facilitating trade and bolstering its prominence.

Unlike many Latin American cities, Buenos Aires is renowned for its lively street culture, public gathering spots, and booming nightlife. Each neighborhood, from the Palermo districts to the historic allure of San Telmo, offers diverse experiences that distinguish Buenos Aires from other cities.

PORTEÑOS

Buenos Aires residents are called "porteños," translated as "the people of the port." They form a distinctive community with a cultural background shaped by the history of living in a major Argentinian port. "Porteño" signifies the city's roots, reflecting its blend of European, American, and indigenous influences that have converged over time to create a dynamic population. The people are known for their nature and expressive demeanors. This vibrancy is palpable in the streets, where individuals participate in discussions at cafes, public transport, or local markets. Their sociable disposition fosters unity and hospitality, defining Buenos Aires' essence.

At the heart of porteño culture is a profound attachment to tango - as a style and a dance tradition. Originating in the working-class districts, the tango has evolved into an essential component of the city's identity. Tango represents more than music for porteños. It embodies emotions such as passion, nostalgia, and love. Tango clubs, known as "milongas " are popular with the locals and where the port's people come together to dance and socialize.

Tango originated in working-class districts.[3]

The café culture in Buenos Aires is a part of the porteño lifestyle. Traditional coffeehouses, "cafés notables, " have been gathering spots for generations.

People meet here for lively discussions on politics, literature, and art that can last for hours. Iconic cafes like Café Tortoni and La Biela are emblematic of the city's vibrant intellectual and artistic community.

Porteños are deeply passionate about football (soccer). They show unwavering loyalty to their teams, Boca Juniors and River Plate. Football matches transcend sporting events. They are spectacles uniting people and instilling pride and belonging. The fierce rivalry between Boca Juniors and River Plate, famously known as the "Superclásico," is among the most intense in world football, showcasing the love porteños have for the game.

Another integral part of porteño culture is the "Asado" tradition, a gathering centered around grilling meat. Asados are held on weekends and holidays, bringing families and friends together to savor food, music, and conversations. The tradition illustrates how vital community and family are in society. Their love for tango, soccer, social events, and their community bond adds to the city's warmth.

CULTURE, ARTS AND CUISINE

Buenos Aires is famous for its mix of music, dance, art, literature, theater, and cuisine, which were influenced by European migration, indigenous customs, and broader Latin American traditions. One essential element of Buenos Aires culture is tango dancing, which originated in the working-class neighborhoods during the 19th century. This passionate dance combines African and indigenous styles and is globally popular. The city has numerous tango dance halls called milongas, where locals and tourists come together to enjoy tango music. The annual Buenos Aires Tango Festival and World Tango Championship draw participants from all corners of the globe, reinforcing its reputation as the tango capital.

Theatre is also essential in the Buenos Aires cultural scene. The Teatro Colón stands tall as one of the world's opera houses known for its exceptional acoustics and magnificent architecture. Buenos Aires has a thriving theater scene outside the mainstream, with numerous intimate venues spread across the city presenting an array of shows ranging from experimental performances to classic plays. The Buenos Aires International Festival of Independent Cinema (BAFICI) highlights an active film industry with significant appeal for filmmakers and movie enthusiasts.

If you are more into visual arts than performing arts, Buenos Aires has something for you, too. The city's visual arts scene is home to numerous museums and galleries. The Museo Nacional de Bellas Artes (MNBA) is an art institution housing a collection of European and Argentine artworks, including pieces by acclaimed artists like Diego Rivera and Antonio Berni. The city's streets come alive with fantastic artwork transforming into an open-air gallery. Residents' contributions are seen in the colorful murals decorating neighborhood buildings like Palermo and San Telmo. Guided street art tours have become popular among visitors seeking to immerse themselves in the exuberant Buenos Aires expression. The city is renowned for its literary community, with many authors and poets who have left their mark on Argentina's cultural landscape. A well-known literary figure, Jorge Luis Borges, is closely linked to Buenos Aires, and the city honors its tradition in the many bookstores and literary gatherings.

Buenos Aires does not joke with its porteños stomachs. The city emphasizes meat dishes, particularly beef. They have a tradition dedicated to it, the Asado, synonymous with barbecues that involve grilling various cuts of meat over burning embers. Empanadas - a pastry filled with meat or vegetables - also holds a special place in the Buenos Aires food court. Other local foods include Locro, Pastelitos Criollos, Dulce De Leche, and Choripán. In the cafe scene, fashionable coffee shops are meeting spots for thinkers, creatives, and locals seeking a moment of peace with a cup of coffee and a medialuna (pastry).

SPORTS AND LEISURE

You'll quickly discover that sports and leisure are as vital as arts and culture in Buenos Aires. Among all sports, football (soccer) is the most popular pastime with devoted fans. Whether you root for Boca Juniors or River Plate, the city's football clubs, everyone in Buenos Aires has a team close to their heart. The rivalry between these two teams, known as the "Superclásico," is one of the hottest battles in football. To feel a tangible atmosphere with thousands of fans cheering, singing chants, dancing, and waving flags, attend a match at these two stadiums: La Bombonera or Estadio Monumental.

However, football isn't the focus of sports culture in Buenos Aires. Argentina is a leading nation in polo, with clubs where top-level matches are played. Among these is the Argentine Polo Open held in Palermo, which attracts polo lovers from across the globe. Another popular sport in the city is tennis. The city has nurtured tennis stars like Gabriela Sabatini and Juan Martín del Potro. If you're a tennis fan, check out the Buenos Aires Lawn Tennis Club, home to the Argentina Open, an ATP World Tour tournament. It's a chance to see players from around the world compete in a laid-back and welcoming setting.

For those who enjoy leisure time, Buenos Aires has plenty to offer. You can spend time in the city's parks and green areas like Parque Tres de Febrero in Palermo. You can rent a paddleboat, run, or picnic by the lake. If cycling is more your speed, Buenos Aires has a network of bike lanes and a bike-sharing program allowing you to discover the city at your pace.

Buenos Aires will give you a beat if you are passionate about dancing. You don't have to be a professional dancer to attend a milonga, a traditional tango dance venue. You can take lessons, watch the experts perform, and test your dance moves.

NOTABLE FIGURES FROM BUENOS AIRES

It's impossible not to think about the individuals who have made an impression on the city and beyond. These notable personalities come from diverse backgrounds, including sports, politics, literature, and entertainment, adding to the cultural fabric that sets Buenos Aires apart.

EVA PERÓN

- **Date of Birth:** *May 7, 1919*
- **Died:** *July 26, 1952*
- **Place of Birth:** *Los Toldos, Buenos Aires*
- **Zodiac Sign:** *Taurus*
- **Occupation:** *First Lady of Argentina*

Eva Perón, affectionately known as Evita, is a significant figure in the history of Buenos Aires. You're probably familiar with her story if you are interested in history or musicals. As the wife of President Juan Domingo Perón, she symbolized justice and empathy. Her advocacy for workers' rights and women's suffrage endeared her to Argentinians. When you visit Recoleta Cemetery, you'll come across her grave, where people still pay tribute to her memory.

ALFREDO DI STÉFANO

- **Date of Birth:** *July 4, 1926*
- **Died:** *July 7, 2014*
- **Place of Birth:** *Buenos Aires*
- **Zodiac Sign:** *Cancer*
- **Occupation:** *Footballer*

Alfredo Di Stéfano was a superstar football player from Argentina who played for Spain. Many people believe he was one of the best. He is remembered for playing for Real Madrid, a famous Spanish team, and helping them win many championships in Spain and Europe in the 1950s. He made Pelé's list of top 100 players in 2004 due to his excellence.

Alfredo Di Stéfano.[4]

JORGE LUIS BORGES

- **Date of Birth:** *August 24, 1899*
- **Died:** *June 14, 1986*
- **Place of Birth:** *Buenos Aires*
- **Zodiac Sign:** *Virgo*
- **Occupation:** *Writer*

Jorge is an Argentinian literature figure. You should read his works, as his influence goes beyond the Buenos Aires borders. His stories and philosophical reflections have earned recognition worldwide. You can experience his connection to the city by visiting the National Library he once headed or wandering through the streets that inspired his writing.

ASTOR PIAZZOLLA

- **Date of Birth:** *March 11, 1921*
- **Died:** *July 4, 1992*
- **Place of Birth:** *Mar del Plata, Buenos Aires*
- **Zodiac Sign:** *Pisces*
- **Occupation:** *Musician*

A musical giant in Buenos Aires. Piazzolla transformed tango by blending it with jazz and classical elements to create "nuevo tango." His compositions are musically significant, and his impact on the Buenos Aires music scene is profound. If possible, attend a performance at a tango venue to witness the vibrancy and creativity Piazzolla infused into the genre.

NICOLAS OTAMENDI

- **Date of Birth:** *February 12, 1988*
- **Place of Birth:** *El Talar, Buenos Aires*
- **Zodiac Sign:** *Aquarius*
- **Occupation:** *Professional Footballer*

Nicolas Otamendi is a famous Argentinian soccer player. He helped Argentina win the Copa America in 2021 and played in two World Cups. He won two Premier League titles and one FA Cup with Manchester City. Previously, he won three consecutive league titles with Porto in Portugal.

These individuals represent a fraction of the artistic figures linked to Buenos Aires. Whether you have a passion for sports, politics, literature, or music, Buenos Aires is a tapestry of narratives and traditions waiting to be discovered. Each personality has added to the city's essence, turning it into a destination worth exploring and comprehending.

TRANSPORTATION

Exploring Buenos Aires can be quite an adventure. Thankfully, the city boasts a mostly dependable transportation system. You may observe the hectic traffic on your arrival, but the public transport network simplifies moving around the town.

Traveling by Subte: This is the city's subway system. There are six lines designated A through H, each connecting various areas of Buenos Aires. Although it can get crowded during peak times, riding the Subte is usually cost-effective for navigating Buenos Aires.

Taking Budget-Friendly Buses: Buses, known as *colectivos* in Spanish, are another choice for getting around town. With routes spanning across Buenos Aires, buses can take you anywhere. You'll require a SUBE card to use the colectivos, which is valid on the Subte and certain trains. The buses operate 24 hours a day, so a bus will take you home even if you're out late. Getting around in Buenos Aires involves some tips for choosing the bus route. Handy apps and maps will help you navigate to your destination.

Taxis and Ubers: Plenty of taxis are easily recognizable by their black and yellow colors if you prefer this transport mode. You can flag one down on the street or use ride-hailing services like Uber or Cabify. Taxi fares are calculated using meters, so you don't have to negotiate prices. However, having cash on hand for rides is advisable.

Biking/Cycling: Buenos Aires offers an expanding network of bike lanes known as "ciclovías" for those who enjoy exploring on two wheels. The city features a bike-sharing initiative called EcoBici, which lets you hire a bike for a specific time and return it to designated stations.

Traveling by Train: If you plan to go beyond the city limits, Buenos Aires provides commuter trains and long-distance buses as part of its transportation network. Trains link you to the outskirts and surrounding regions, whereas intercity buses depart from Retiro Bus Terminal, transporting you to locations within Argentina and neighboring countries.

USEFUL WEBSITES/RESOURCES

Here are websites that could be useful for planning your trip to Buenos Aires:

TRAVEL PLANNING

- *https://secretsofbuenosaires.com/*
- *https://www.cntraveler.com/destinations/buenos-aires*
- *https://solsalute.com/buenos-aires-travel/*
- *https://sologuides.com/buenos-aires/*
- *https://www.travelocity.com/Buenos-Aires.d178242.Destination-Travel-Guides*

ACCOMMODATION

- https://www.travellerspoint.com/accommodation/argentina/buenos-aires/
- https://www.expedia.com/Buenos-Aires-Hotels.d178242.Travel-Guide-Hotels
- https://ba-h.com.ar/en/accommodation-in-buenos-aires/
- https://www.vrbo.com/vacation-rentals/south-america/argentina/buenos-aires
- https://guests-house.com/buenos-aires/

ACTIVITIES

- https://www.expedia.com/Things-To-Do-In-Buenos-Aires.d178242.Travel-Guide-Activities
- https://secretsofbuenosaires.com/things-to-do-in-buenos-aires/
- https://turismo.buenosaires.gob.ar/en/recorrido/must-see-attractions
- https://www.tripadvisor.com/Attractions-g312741-Activities-Buenos_Aires_Capital_Federal_District.html
- https://www.getyourguide.com/buenos-aires-l1/

INVITATION TO EXPLORE

Get ready for a fabulous experience if you consider visiting Buenos Aires. The city is full of surprises, from treasures to exciting seasonal festivities that can make your visit unforgettable. Once you've seen the landmarks, it's time to delve deeper and uncover the essence that makes Buenos Aires so lively.

- *Picture yourself strolling along the cobblestone streets of San Telmo, where vintage stores and cozy cafes line the pathways. Make sure not to overlook the Mercado de San Telmo, a market brimming with antiques, street food, and local art. It's a place to soak up the ambiance and find one-of-a-kind mementos.*
- *The Palermo and La Boca neighborhoods are renowned for their murals and graffiti. Consider joining a guided street art tour to discover more about the artists and their creations. These tours often take you off the beaten path, offering a different perspective of Buenos Aires.*

- *Buenos Aires hosts a variety of events catering to a wide range of tastes. If you visit in February, don't miss the city's Carnival celebrations. The streets buzz with parades, music, and dancing. You'll see people in fantastical outfits, listen to the drum beats, and soak in the lively atmosphere of the crowds. It's a way to immerse yourself in the Buenos Aires vibe.*
- *Another notable event is the Buenos Aires Tango Festival, held annually in August. This festival is a must-visit for tango enthusiasts as it features performances, workshops, and competitions across the city. Even if you're new to tango, attending the festival promises an experience that will deepen your admiration for this dance form.*
- *Consider exploring the city's various parks and green areas for a peaceful outing. At Parque Tres de Febrero, or as more popularly known, Bosques de Palermo, you can rent paddle boats, take strolls, or unwind by the lake. Don't miss visiting Rosedal within the park - a rose garden perfect for a romantic walk - if you need a bit of charm.*
- *Do not overlook indulging in cuisine. Buenos Aires is renowned for its asados (barbecues) and empanadas (pastries), but sample some of the well-known dishes available. Experience an Argentine barbecue at a parrilla or indulge in a scoop of dulce de leche ice cream at a local heladería, a popular choice among residents. Exploring food tours can be a way to uncover dining spots while delving into the city's culinary heritage.*

Explore all of Buenos Aires as you continue reading. The Buenos Aires people are warm and welcoming. They'll embrace you with open arms and make you feel at home. Whether you get lost in conversation with a local at a hidden cafe or are swept away by the pass on of a tango performance, the spirit of Buenos Aires will leave a lasting impression.

CHAPTER

2 TO AND FROM THE AIRPORT

Buenos Aires has two main airports, like two open arms, welcoming travelers arriving from all over the world. The first is Ministro Pistarini International Airport, commonly known as Ezeiza Airport (EZE). It is Argentina's biggest and grandest entrance for international flights.

The second airport is Jorge Newbery Airfield, known as Aeroparque (AEP). This airport is closer to the city center of Buenos Aires, making it a convenient choice if you stay downtown. It mainly handles domestic flights and trips to nearby countries, perfect for shorter hops. No matter which airport you fly into, you'll find various ways to reach your destination in Buenos Aires. Ezeiza and Aeroparque offer several transportation options, like taxis, buses, and ride-sharing services. They have all the essential services, from currency exchange to places to grab a bite to eat or pick up travel essentials.

MINISTRO PISTARINI INTERNATIONAL AIRPORT (EZEIZA - EZE)

Ezeiza International Airport, also known as Ministro Pistarini International Airport, is the main airport serving Buenos Aires and all of Argentina. Unlike some cities with multiple airports serving different purposes, Ezeiza is the true international hub, the grand central station of air travel in Argentina. Ezeiza is the airport you'll likely fly into when arriving from further abroad. The airport is about 22 kilometers southwest of downtown Buenos Aires. The distance from the city center might seem like a drawback, but it allows more space for takeoffs and landings, which is especially important for larger international flights. Once you arrive, you'll find the airport consists of three terminals. These terminals are all within walking distance of each other, so you won't have to worry about catching an airport shuttle or train for a connecting flight.

Ezeiza International Airport, also known as Ministro Pistarini International Airport.[5]

The three terminals each have their own focus. Terminal A, built in 2000, is the oldest and handles most international traffic and where you'll arrive and depart if your flight is from or going to another country. Terminal B is a bit newer, opening its doors to passenger flights in 2013. This terminal handles domestic flights and some international arrivals and departures. Terminal C, known as the Mercedes Sosa Terminal, was built in 2011 and primarily deals with domestic flights to other parts of Argentina.

Upon arrival, travelers have various transportation options to reach the city center.

TRANSPORT OPTIONS

Taxi: Taxi are one of the most comfortable ways to travel from Ezeiza Airport to the city center. They line up outside the airport terminals. While convenient, they can be relatively expensive than other options, especially during peak hours when traffic congestion is high. Negotiating the fare with the driver beforehand or ensuring the meter is running to avoid overcharging is advisable.

- *Cost: approximately 40$ to 60$.*
- *Travel time: 35 minutes to 1 hour.*

Shuttle Service: Shuttle buses are a good choice for comfort and low cost. Several shuttle companies operate between Ezeiza Airport and downtown Buenos Aires. These services offer a cost-effective and stress-free way to reach the city center. You can buy tickets online or at the Airport ticket desk.

- *Cost: approximately 14$.*
- *Travel time: 50 minutes to 1 hour.*

Public Buses: While limited, public buses or urban colectivos are the cheapest way to travel around the city. They connect Ezeiza Airport to many parts of Buenos Aires. However, they can be crowded and less convenient for travelers with luggage. Checking the bus routes and schedules in advance is essential. You need a SUBE card to pay, which you can get at the airport for 1$. Be sure to load it as you can't pay for the bus with cash.

- *Cost: approximately 0.5$.*
- *Travel time: 75 minutes to 2 hours.*

Rental Cars: Several car rental companies operate within the airport terminal if you prefer flexibility and independent travel. Car rental is a good idea if you travel to surrounding areas because navigating Buenos Aires' busy streets and parking can be challenging for newcomers.

- *Cost: Depends on the car.*
- *Travel time: approximately 40 minutes.*

Ride-Sharing Services: Ride-sharing apps like Uber and Cabify are popular alternatives to taxis. They are a convenient and often cheaper transportation option, especially for solo travelers or small groups. However, availability may vary depending on the time of day.

- *Travel time: 40 minutes to 1 hour.*

PRACTICAL TIPS

- *Expect queues at immigration, especially during peak arrival times. Ensure you have all the necessary documents ready for inspection to facilitate the process.*

- *Taxi fares to downtown Buenos Aires depend on traffic conditions and your destination. Shuttle services may offer fixed rates or charge per person.*
- *Exercise caution when using taxis or ride-sharing services. Stick to authorized providers and avoid accepting rides from unregistered vehicles.*
- *Factor in travel time when planning your journey from Ezeiza Airport to the city center, especially during rush hours. Traffic congestion can significantly impact travel times.*

AIRPORT FACILITIES

Ezeiza Airport has many services and amenities to cater to passenger's needs. They include:

- *Information kiosks*
- *Banks / ATMs*
- *Currency exchange areas*
- *Lost and Found offices*
- *Lounges / Spa facilities*
- *Wi-Fi*
- *Pharmacies / Medical services*
- *Kids zone*
- *Many shopping options for souvenirs, travel essentials, and duty-free goods.*
- *Baggage wrapping / Luggage storage*
- *Special services and amenities for passengers with disabilities*
- *Restaurants / Bars*

JORGE NEWBERY AIRFIELD (AEROPARQUE - AEP)

Jorge Newbery Airfield, known as Aeroparque, is another major airport serving Buenos Aires. The airport is 2 kilometers northwest of downtown, on the La Plata River waterfront. It focuses on domestic flights, making it the most essential domestic airport in the country. It also handles flights to neighboring South American countries like Uruguay, Brazil, and Paraguay.

Aeroparque is a medium-sized airport that first began operations in 1948, and today, it handles over 15 million passengers yearly. Initially, it had a much shorter runway, but as years passed, it has been extended to accommodate larger airplanes. The airport used to have a small military base on its grounds.

TRANSPORT OPTIONS

Taxi: Consider taking a taxi for a more comfortable ride. They are readily available outside Aeroparque terminals. While more affordable, fares can vary depending on traffic conditions. Go to the Domestic Arrivals section, scan a QR code, and create your ticket from your cell phone to book a taxi. A fixed fare will appear. Show this to the cab driver when entering the taxi, and you'll be on your way to your destination.

- *Cost: approximately 10$*
- *Travel time: 10 minutes to 30 minutes (depending on the traffic)*

Ride-Sharing Services: Uber and Cabify operate at Aeroparque, providing travelers with a convenient and cost-effective transportation option. Open the Uber app and choose a ride option that suits you and your luggage.

- *Cost: 20$ to 30$*
- *Travel time: Depends on the traffic*

Public Buses: Aeroparque is well connected to Buenos Aires' public bus network, offering an economical but potentially crowded option for reaching the city center. They aren't the most comfortable choice, but they are the cheapest. Make sure you check bus routes and schedules in advance, and you need a SUBE card.

- *Cost: 1$*
- *Travel time: 30 minutes to 50 minutes*

Walking: If you stay in nearby neighborhoods, such as Palermo or Recoleta, walking may be a viable option, especially if you travel light. However, be mindful of your surroundings and pedestrian crossings.

- *Travel time: About 1 hour 30 minutes*

PRACTICAL TIPS

- *Aeroparque is close to downtown Buenos Aires, making it an ideal choice for domestic travelers.*
- *Taxi fares from Aeroparque to downtown Buenos Aires typically depend on the destination and traffic conditions. Ride-sharing services may offer similar or slightly lower fares.*
- *Be careful when using taxis or ride-sharing services, especially late at night. Stick to well-lit areas and avoid sharing personal information with drivers.*
- *The Aeroparque may be closer to downtown Buenos Aires, but you should still consider potential traffic*

delays, especially during peak hours. So, plan your journey accordingly to avoid missing flights or appointments.

AIRPORT FACILITIES

- *Wi-Fi*
- *Restaurant and bar*
- *ATMs*
- *Currency exchange areas*
- *Pharmacy*
- *Car rental services*
- *Duty-free shops that offer numerous travel essentials and souvenirs.*
- *Airport Hotel*
- *A chapel within the airport grounds is available for a moment of peace and reflection.*

Getting to and from the airports in Buenos Aires can give you the first impression of this exciting city. It can be like a walk in a park if you plan ahead. Prepare timeously. Consider how to get to your hotel or rental from the airport, how long it might take, and a few other handy tips. Whether on a business trip or a vacation, Buenos Aires is ready to welcome you and give you a trip you won't forget in a hurry.

CHAPTER

3 NORTHERN BUENOS AIRES

Buenos Aires' northern districts are one of the city's most visited. They have a rich history and blend of green spaces and urbanization perfectly. The northern part of Buenos Aires has been significant in the city's growth and development. The neighborhoods in this area provide a more 'peace and quiet' vibe than the ever-busy city center. The northern districts should be your next stop if you want a feel for Buenos Aires' refined side. You will discover what life at a steady pace could look like, enjoying the tranquility in the atmosphere and exploring the land's historical richness.

This chapter invites you to explore Buenos Aires' northern districts and neighborhoods from Belgrano to Palermo, Nuñez, and Vicente López (Part of Greater Buenos Aires).

BELGRANO DISTRICT

Belgrano is a leafy and charming neighborhood named after Manuel Belgrano, the esteemed politician and military leader who designed the Argentine flag. After Belgrano died in 1820, the Buenos Aires government paid homage to his legacy by decreeing that the next town established would bear his name. A new town was indeed established by the government and christened Belgrano. Soon enough, the town flourished until it became a full-blown city. Due to this massive growth, the city was considered and granted national capital status. However, this raised eyebrows and caused great offense, so after about two weeks and a lot of back and forth between the Buenos Aires province and the national government, Belgrano lost the national capital title, and it was given to Buenos Aires.

It was within Belgrano's walls that Buenos Aires was declared Argentina's federal capital during the brief time it was first made the capital. Although very short, Belgrano's national capital status cemented the city's place in Argentina's history. Today, it is one of Buenos Aires' most desirable neighborhoods. The city is known for its safety and affluence and exudes a tranquil and upscale atmosphere. Wide, tree-lined avenues are graced by grand architectural styles, reflecting the area's middle and upper-class character.

Did You Know?

The Rio de la Plata River used to reach the hills until the mid-1800s. When they built the Miter Railroad, a huge wall was constructed to hold back the water and dry the land, which is how the Barrancas de Belgrano Park came to be.

MAIN ATTRACTIONS

BARRIO CHINO

Don't miss out on exploring Barrio Chino, Buenos Aires' Chinatown. The neighborhood is dominated by immigrants from China, Japan, and Thailand. It's a lovely area with a giant archway marking the entrance, making it easy to find. Always buzzing with energy, there are no dull moments at the Barrio Chino, especially on Sundays when the rest of the city might be a little slower. It is a perfect spot to grab a bite if you're looking for something different. Are you a picky eater? Don't worry. You'll find tons of restaurants, mainly serving delicious Chinese and Japanese food.

Barrio Chino.[6]

As of the writing of this book, you can visit Barrio Chino at any time during your trip. However, please make sure to double-check the opening hours online should there be any slight changes to their schedule.

MUSEO DE ARTE ESPAÑOL ENRIQUE LARRETA

A hidden gem with stunning Spanish art and a beautiful Andalusian courtyard garden, perfect for art lovers and those seeking tranquility. It was the house of a famous Argentinian writer, but now it's open to everyone. This museum is packed with historic art from Spain, the Renaissance, and Baroque times. The house has a giant Spanish-style garden in the back. Imagine walking through a garden filled with fountains, statues, numerous plants, and some wild cats. The museum is interesting to visit, and you surely do not want to miss out.

Museo de Arte Español Enrique Larreta.[7]

As of the writing of this book, the museum is open Wednesday to Friday and Monday from 11 am to 7 pm, Saturday and Sunday from 11 am to 8 pm, and is closed on Tuesday. However, please make sure to double-check the opening hours online should there be any slight changes to their schedule.

Contact Details: +54 11 4783-2640

Address: Av. Juramento 2291, C1428DNK Cdad. Autónoma de Buenos Aires, Argentina

Barrancas de Belgrano: Plaza Barrancas de Belgrano, known as Barrancas de Belgrano, is a beautiful park with sloping hills in the Belgrano neighborhood. The famous French landscape architect Carlos Thays designed the park in 1892. He's also the designer behind Tres de Febrero Park and other squares in the city. Statues are throughout the park, many from the 19th century. An interesting one is a Statue of Liberty replica. It was sculpted by the same artist who designed the original in New York. On the higher part of the park, there's a little bandstand where, in the past, you might have heard orchestras playing. It's now a popular spot for people to gather and dance tango or folklore on Sundays.

Barrancas de Belgrano.[8]

As of the writing of this book, Barrancas de Belgrano is open 24 hours every day. However, please make sure to double-check the opening hours online should there be any slight changes to their schedule.

Address: Av. Juramento 1792, C1430 Cdad. Autónoma de Buenos Aires, Argentina

TRANSPORT OPTIONS

- *Buses*
- *Trains*
- *Subway*
- *Taxi*
- *Car*

EXPERIENCES

TIERRA SANTA AMUSEMENT PARK

Tierra Santa is a religious theme park in Argentina that serves as a cultural and historical bridge among Christianity, Judaism, and Islam. Officially recognized for its religious and educational significance, it has received blessings from Pope Francis and endorsements from various governmental authorities.

Address: Av. Costanera Rafael Obligado 5790, Buenos Aires C1425 Argentina

PARQUE DE LA MEMORIA

Park of Memory is a place for nostalgia, honor, witness, and contemplation. It is a public area designed as a memorial for the Victims of State Terrorism. It has the names of those who were not found or murdered during state repression. The project's purpose is to make people remember the damage that happened to prevent it from happening again in future generations.

Parque de la Memoria.[9]

Contact Details: +54 11 4780-5818.

Address: Av. Costanera Norte Rafael Obigado 6745 CP. 1428DAA, Buenos Aires, Argentina

WHERE TO EAT

GORDO VEGANO (VEGAN RESTAURANT).

Gordo Vegano restaurant offers flavorful and enjoyable dishes, making it a great choice even if you are not vegan. It has a welcoming atmosphere and friendly service, with great quality and flavor of the Asian-inspired menu, especially the remarkable Pad Thai. Guests leave impressed and eager to return.

Address: Echeverría 3078, C1428DSD Cdad. Autónoma de Buenos Aires, Argentina

SELQUET RESTAURANT + BAR

Selquet Restaurant + Bar offers a pleasant dining experience with options for breakfast, lunch, and dinner, making it perfect for any occasion. You can enjoy a relaxed meal while taking advantage of the free parking and a lovely atmosphere in the outdoor seating area. It is a great choice for celebrations and casual gatherings.

Address: Av. Pres. Figueroa Alcorta 6402, C1428 Cdad. Autónoma de Buenos Aires, Argentina

THE EMBERS BELGRANO

The Embers restaurant holds a high standard in both its food and ambiance. The grilled potatoes are highly recommended, and the ribs and burgers are tasty and delicious at a great price. It has options for indoor and outdoor seating, including a charming garden area, making it a great spot for a casual meal.

Address: Echeverría 3276, C1428 DTB, Cdad. Autónoma de Buenos Aires, Argentina

PLACES TO SHOP

GENERAL BELGRANO GALLERIES (SHOPPING MALL).

Galeria Belgrano is an active shopping place that features a diverse range of stores, including boutiques for men's and women's fashion like Fioretto and Pinel Urbano, jewelry stores like Milva, gift shops like Jazz, and bookshops like Rodriguez Bookstore.

Opening Hours: 09:00 am to 07:30 pm from Monday to Friday, 09:00 am to 02:00 pm on Saturday, and closed on Sunday.

Address: Av. Cabildo 1849, Vuelta de Obligado 1834 1850, C1426 Buenos Aires, Argentina

GALERÍA RÍO DE LA PLATA (SHOPPING MALL)

Galería Río de La Plata is one of Buenos Aires' premier shopping spots, with a dynamic mix of modern music and instrument stores, electronics, and tobacco shops. It is a must-visit for video games and vinyl records fans. This gallery offers a comprehensive shopping experience, from the latest gadgets to unique hobby items.

Opening Hours: 09:00 am to 08:00 pm from Monday to Saturday and closed on Sunday.

Address: Av. Cabildo 2280, C1428 Cdad. Autónoma de Buenos Aires, Argentina

GALERÍA RÍO DE JANEIRO (SHOPPING MALL)

Galería Río de Janeiro is an ideal shopping destination in Belgrano, Buenos Aires, if you are looking to shop for home décor, clothing, or jewelry. You can also enjoy quality hair care at Helena's salon and take Cuban dance classes. The gallery is well-maintained for both visitors and locals to enjoy.

Opening Hours: 12:00 pm to 07:00 pm on Monday and Tuesday, 10:00 am to 07:00 pm from Wednesday to Friday, 10:00 am to 05:00 pm on Saturday, and closed on Sunday.

Address: Galeria RIO DE JANEIRO, Av. Cabildo 2370 Local 39, C1428 Cdad. Autónoma de Buenos Aires, Argentina

GALERÍA LAS VEGAS (SHOPPING MALL)

Galería Las Vegas is a special shopping mall with over 80 stores. Visitors can enjoy a range of shops, from Gigi Store for beauty products and nail sets to Brumi Jewelry for elegant accessories. The gallery also has stores that sell sleepwear, mobile phone accessories, and beauty treatments.

Opening Hours: 09:00 am to 08:30 pm from Monday to Saturday and closed on Sunday.

Address: Av. Cabildo 2230, C1428 Cdad. Autónoma de Buenos Aires, Argentina

ACCOMMODATIONS

KER BELGRANO APART HOTEL & SPA

Ker Belgrano Apart Hotel & Spa is a chic accommodation in the Belgrano district, located just 20 minutes from the city center. Each room features a kitchenette, balcony, and air conditioning, along with complimentary Wi-Fi and cable TV. Guests appreciate the hotel's exceptional location, friendly, attentive staff, and the convenience of nearby public transport, shops, and dining options.

Contact Details: +54 11 5277-4600.

Address: Vuelta de Obligado 2727, C1428 Cdad. Autónoma de Buenos Aires, Argentina.

BABEL BELGRANO

Babel Belgrano presents its guests with a comfortable apartment complex featuring private parking, air-conditioning, a fully equipped kitchen, and a private balcony. Guests can enjoy free Wi-Fi, a sun terrace, and a hot tub. Babel Belgrano is located near attractions like Bosques del Palermo and River Plate Stadium. It is an ideal choice for couples and travelers seeking a home-like experience because of its cozy vibes and mindful host.

Contact Details: +54 11 6563-8854.

Address: Aguilar 2436, C1426 Cdad. Autónoma de Buenos Aires, Argentina.

MONROE SUITES

Monroe Suites is a great option for accommodation in Buenos Aires as it features air-conditioned apartments with city views, private balconies, a private bathroom with a hair dryer, and facilities for disabled guests. It has a fully equipped kitchen with a microwave, a kettle, and a fridge. It is located near River Plate Stadium, El Rosedal Park, and Bosques de Palermo, with Jorge Newbery Airfield Airport 5 km away. It is a top choice for couples looking for a comfortable stay.

Contact Details: +54 9 11 3677-7788.

Address: Av. Monroe 1555, C1428 Cdad. Autónoma de Buenos Aires, Argentina.

HOTEL BELGRANO

Hotel Belgrano is located in a nice neighborhood near small fabric shops in the Once district and the Art Deco Abasto shopping mall, top sights like Cementerio de la Recoleta, Teatro Colon, and El Ateneo Grand Splendid, making it a great place to stay for tourists. It is also within walking distance from public transport like Retiro-Mitre, Estacion Once, and Plaza Miserere. Aeroparque Internacional Jorge Newbery Airport is 27 minutes away by taxi, while Ezeiza International Airport is 40. You can go to close restaurants like El Espanol, Restaurant La Perlita, or La Gran Taberna.

Contact Details: +54 11 4951-0906.

Address: Av. Belgrano 2393, C1096AAA Cdad. Autónoma de Buenos Aires, Argentina.

PALERMO DISTRICT

Named after the "Saint Benedict of Palermo" abbey, possibly honoring him, Palermo was once the estate of Juan Manuel de Rosas before President Domingo Faustino Sarmiento transformed it in the late 19th century. Sarmiento's vision brought landmarks like the Buenos Aires Zoological Gardens and Parque Tres de Febrero, shaping Palermo's identity. Today, Palermo isn't only the city's largest neighborhood. It's a cultural hotspot with exclusive stores, cafes, and colorful street art.

MAIN ATTRACTIONS

Bosques de Palermo

The Bosques de Palermo, known as Parque Tres de Febrero, is like the green heart of Buenos Aires. It's the city's biggest park, making it a favorite spot for locals and visitors. It's a sprawling tree-filled park with lakes and walking paths, perfect for a refreshing nature walk or a relaxing picnic under the sunshine. Rent rollerblades and zip along the designated paths if you're feeling energetic, enjoying the breeze in your hair.

The Bosques de Palermo, known as Parque Tres de Febrero.[10]

As of the writing of this book, the Bosques de Palermo is open 24 hours every day. However, please make sure to double-check the opening hours online should there be any slight changes to their schedule.

Address: Av. Infanta Isabel 110, C1425 Cdad. Autónoma de Buenos Aires, Argentina

MALBA (Museo de Arte Latinoamericano de Buenos Aires): The Museo de Arte Latinoamericano de Buenos Aires, or MALBA for short, is a must-see for art lovers visiting Buenos Aires. This modern museum, with its shiny glass walls, is known for its impressive collection of Latin American art. The collection belongs to a wealthy art enthusiast, Eduardo Costantini, and features work by famous artists from all over Latin America. You'll find pieces by Argentine masters like Xul Solar and Antonio Berni alongside iconic Mexican artists like Diego Rivera and Frida Kahlo. The museum has a cinema for screening independent and art films.

The Museo de Arte Latinoamericano de Buenos Aires, or MALBA for short.[11]

As of the writing of this book, the opening hours are Thursday to Monday from 12 pm to 8 pm, Wednesday from 11 am to 8 pm, and is closed on Tuesday. However, please make sure to double-check the opening hours online should there be any slight changes to their schedule.

Address: Av. Pres. Figueroa Alcorta 3415, C1425CLA Cdad. Autónoma de Buenos Aires, Argentina

Jardín Botánico Carlos Thays: The Buenos Aires Botanical Garden is a giant park with over 6,000 plants and trees from all over the world, including Argentina. It's a great place to walk, relax, and learn about the various plants. The garden is enormous, covering about 17 acres. You'll find many garden styles, including Roman, French, and Eastern-inspired gardens, sections with plants grouped by origin, and an area showcasing plants native to Argentina. The gardens have a variety of sculptures placed throughout the gardens and much more.

The Buenos Aires Botanical Garden.[12]

As of the writing of this book, the opening hours are Monday to Friday from 8 am to 6:30 pm and Saturday and Sunday from 9:30 am to 6:30 pm. However, make sure to double-check the opening hours online should there be any slight changes to their schedule.

TRANSPORT OPTIONS

- *Subway*
- *Buses*
- *Train*
- *Taxi*

EXPERIENCES

TIGRE DELTA PREMIUM TOUR

If you are looking for a scenic getaway from the city, the Tigre Delta Premium Tour is the answer. You can enjoy a cruise through the picturesque Tigre River Delta. The tour offers a hotel pick-up and drop-off, a leisurely boat ride, and a chance to try delicious hand-made empanadas at Restaurante Vivanco. The tour also stops at the Puerto de Frutos fruit market and the Paseo Victorica coastal walk.

BUENOS AIRES FOOD TOUR

Secret Food Tours in Buenos Aires is a lovely culinary journey through the city's popular neighborhoods, including Palermo Soho and Old Palermo. You can savor authentic local dishes of Porteno cuisine while learning about Argentina's rich culinary heritage from knowledgeable guides. This carefully curated experience is perfect for food lovers who want to explore Buenos Aires' cultural legacy and traditions.

WHERE TO EAT

EL PREFERIDO DE PALERMO (RESTAURANT)

El Preferido de Palermo restaurant is a spacious and beautifully decorated restaurant famous for its tasty food and impeccable service. The menu has many delicious dishes, including vegetarian options. People who went there swear by their milanesas and potato pie. Reservations are recommended to avoid long waits, as the restaurant is often busy with families, couples, and friends.

Opening Hours: 11:00 am to 04:00 pm and 07:00 pm to 01:00 am daily.

Contact Details: +54 11 4774-6585.

Address: Jorge Luis Borges 2108, C1425 FFD, Cdad. Autónoma de Buenos Aires, Argentina

CALDEN DEL SOHO GRILL (ARGENTINIAN RESTAURANT)

Calden del Soho Grill is a steakhouse known for its delectable Argentinean cuisine. It has a warm, intimate atmosphere and great service. It is ideal for special occasions, romantic dinners, and gatherings with family or friends. The restaurant has outdoor seating and a bar, making it a great spot for lunch, dinner, or late-night drinks.

Opening Hours: 12:00 pm to 12:00 am every day.

Contact Details: +54 11 4833-2221.

Address: Honduras 4701, C1414BMK Cdad. Autónoma de Buenos Aires, Argentina

DON JULIO (GRILL)

Don Julio is a Michelin-star steakhouse in Buenos Aires owned by chef Pablo Rivero. The restaurant is popular for its Argentine grilling, which includes meticulously sourced Hereford and Angus meats. If you are looking for a fine dining experience with an open kitchen and rustic decor, look no further. Don Julio offers perfectly cooked steaks with a selection of fine local wines.

Opening Hours: 11:30 am to 04:00 pm and 07:00 pm to 01:00 am daily.

Contact Details: +54 11 4832-6058.

Address: Guatemala 4699, C1425 Cdad. Autónoma de Buenos Aires, Argentina

LA PESCADORITA (SEAFOOD RESTAURANT)

La Pescadorita is a seafood restaurant known for its cozy, marine-themed décor with fairy lights and calming music. It specializes in Mediterranean and Argentinean dishes, offering a variety of healthy options, including vegetarian and gluten-free meals. What guests love about it is its generous portions and the freshness of the seafood, with its reasonable prices as a bonus. The service is excellent as staff members often help with the dietary requirements of guests.

Opening Hours: 12:00 pm to 12:30 am every day.

Contact Details: +54 11 4773-0070.

Address: Humboldt 1905, C1414CTU Cdad. Autónoma de Buenos Aires, Argentina

PLACES TO SHOP

PORTAL PALERMO (SHOPPING MALL)

Portal Palermo is a shopping mall in Buenos Aires with a range of retail options, making it the perfect place for all your different shopping needs. Its stores include a large hypermarket for everyday essentials, local fashion stores like Akibara, and famous bakeries like Brioche

Doree. The mall is not overly luxurious, but it provides a practical, enjoyable shopping experience.

Opening Hours: 10:00 am to 09:30 pm every day.

Address: Av. Int. Bullrich 345, C1425 Cdad. Autónoma de Buenos Aires, Argentina

PANORAMA STORE (CLOTHING STORE)

Panorama Store is a cutting-edge boutique in Buenos Aires that presents a carefully curated selection of up-and-coming Argentine designers. It is run by three local creatives. The shop's interior has sleek white walls with neon elements that make a perfect backdrop for any piece. You can find leather bags, chunky knits, and stylish dresses from a range of different brands. If you consider yourself a fashionista, you can't miss visiting this store!

Opening Hours: 10:00 am to 08:00 pm from Monday to Saturday, and closed on Sunday.

Address: República de la India 2905, C1425 Cdad. Autónoma de Buenos Aires, Argentina

ALCORTA MALL (SHOPPING MALL)

Alcorta is a modern shopping mall located in Buenos Aires, with a variety of dining options, entertainment experiences, a supermarket, a food court, an outdoor playground for kids, and clothing and lifestyle shops. You can enjoy shopping in both local and international brands, then take a break in a café or restaurant to enjoy the comfortable atmosphere.

Opening Hours: 10:00 am to 09:00 pm every day.

Address: Jerónimo Salguero 3172, C1425 Cdad. Autónoma de Buenos Aires, Argentina

ALTO PALERMO (SHOPPING MALL)

Alto Palermo is one of the first shopping destinations in Argentina. Founded in 1990, Alto Palermo includes a mix of stores that cater to different styles and needs, from trendy fashion stores like Zara and H&M to luxury stores like Michael Kors and Swarovski to beauty and lifestyle options like Sephora and Nike. It has a parking lot, Wi-Fi, and bathrooms for the disabled.

Opening Hours: 10:00 am to 10:00 pm every day.

Address: Av. Sta. Fe 3253, 1091 Cdad. Autónoma de Buenos Aires, Argentina

DISTRITO ARCOS (OUTLET MALL)

Distrito Arcos is a lifestyle and shopping outlet known for its innovative design and outdoor shopping complex. It is a popular spot for locals and tourists to enjoy fashion, art, and food. Distrito Arcos differs from traditional shopping malls as it has plenty of green areas, a wine shop, and outdoor entertainment of Tango dancing and local music, making it a nice spot to go for a walk after work to unwind.

Opening Hours: 10:00 am to 10:00 pm every day.

Address: Báez 300, C1414 Cdad. Autónoma de Buenos Aires, Argentina

ENTERTAINMENT

BRUKBAR

BrukBar is a hidden gem in Palermo. It is a cozy open bar and is a perfect spot for pre-dinner drinks. The bartenders serve unique drinks, including a local favorite: Cynar. Visitors love its great vibes and music.

Address: Fray Justo Santa Maria de Oro 1801 Esquina Costa Rica, Buenos Aires 1414 Argentina

LA VIRTUA TANGO (DANCING SCHOOL)

La Virtua Tango is a dancing school located in the Armenian Cultural Center in Palermo, Buenos Aires. You can experience authentic Tango there, with live music and a spacious dance floor perfect for both beginners and experienced dancers. They have available classes in Tango, Milonga, Salsa, and Rock, so you can choose your favorite. It is a must-visit for anyone looking to learn about the culture of Tango.

Address: Calle Armenia 1366 1er. Subsuelo, Buenos Aires C1414DKD Argentina

SPORTS AND LEISURE

CAMPO MUNICIPAL DE GOLF JUAN BAUTISTA SEGURA

Campo Municipal de Golf Juan Bautista Segura offers an affordable and enjoyable golfing experience. It is well-kept, with a variety of fun holes with scenic views. Golfers of all skill levels are welcome.

Address: Av. Ernesto Tornquist 6397, C1426 Cdad. Autónoma de Buenos Aires, Argentina

BIKER STREET BUENOS AIRES BIKE TOURS

This Small Group Deluxe Bike Tour is held by Carlos, Julian, and Gilda. It is a well-crafted experience where you pedal through La Boca and Palermo neighborhoods as you learn about their rich culture and history. The tours are designed for small groups to ensure everyone receives equal attention and gets into engaging conversations. It is the perfect way to explore Buenos Aires through the eyes of true locals. You can book the tour online through their website or through their contact number.

Contact Details: +54 911 5634 5123, +54 911 6713 4438.

MEETING POINTS:

Palermo Area Meeting Point: 2269, Armenia St.

City Center Meeting Point: 762, Hipolito Yrigoyen St.

ACCOMMODATIONS

PALERMO SOHO HOSTEL

Palermo Soho Hostel is located only three blocks away from Serrano Square. It has a welcoming energy and cozy vibes. It offers comfortable rooms with heating, air-conditioning, and free Wi-Fi. Their rooms are categorized into family rooms, twin rooms, triple rooms, quadruple rooms, and bed-in 5-bed mixed dormitory rooms. Guests can enjoy a delicious American breakfast, relax on the patio, or unwind in the living room. You'll find designer shops, trendy cafes, and popular attractions like Buenos Aires Zoo and the Japanese Gardens within walking distance. It is highly rated for its great location.

Contact Details: +54 11 4833-0151.

Address: Nicaragua 4728, C1414 Cdad. Autónoma de Buenos Aires, Argentina.

BENS L'HOTEL PALERMO

BENS L'Hotel Palermo has great facilities like an outdoor swimming pool, non-smoking rooms, a 24-hour available front desk, and a delicious breakfast, along with facilities for disabled guests. It is a uniquely styled accommodation with vibrant yet cozy-colored decorations in the rooms. It is surrounded by top attractions like the Museum of Latin American Art of Buenos Aires MALBA, the Science Cultural Centre, and places with beautiful sceneries like the Palermo Lakes. It is a perfect stay for tourists because of its easy access to local attractions and public transport.

Contact Details: +54 11 4831-7198.

Address: Thames 1562, C1414 Cdad. Autónoma de Buenos Aires, Argentina.

BUE HOTEL

BUE Hotel is a modern hotel with great facilities like a cafeteria, fitness center, and a beautiful sun terrace, along with a good breakfast and free Wi-Fi. Each room comes with air-conditioning, a flat-screen TV, a minibar, and a safety deposit box, with private bathrooms that have free toiletries and a hairdryer. Located just 400 m away from the Carlos Thais Botanical Garden, it is a prime location for anyone who likes to go out and enjoy beautiful views. It is also very close to Jorge Newbery Airfield Airport.

Contact Details: +54 11 4789-9311.

Address: Thames 2446, C1425 FIJ, Cdad. Autónoma de Buenos Aires, Argentina.

SELINA PALERMO SOHO & COWORK

Selima Palermo is a stylish hotel with a colorful bohemian décor and vibrant energy. It has a shared lounge, terrace, and an on-site restaurant and bar. It offers a variety of food options, including a la carte, continental, and vegetarian choices to choose from, along with special diet menus on request. The hotel provides essential services such as luggage storage, air-conditioning, and airport transfers. It also offers wellness services like yoga classes and massages, entertainment services, board games and puzzles, and activities like happy hour, walking tours, movie nights, and live music or performances.

Contact Details: +54 11 4776-0307.

Address: Guatemala 4931, C1425BUQ Cdad. Autónoma de Buenos Aires, Argentina.

NUÑEZ DISTRICT

Núñez is a peaceful suburban area in Buenos Aires, Argentina, known for the famous Argentinian soccer team, River Plate's home ground. You can visit their museum to learn about the team's history. Nuñez is on the city's northern edge, next to the Rio de la Plata. The area was founded in 1873 and named after its founder, Don Florencio Emeterio Nuñez. Today, Núñez is popular with families and young professionals. It has a mix of modern apartment buildings, stores, and houses, creating a relaxed suburban vibe. Museo Sitio de Memoria ESMA is a must-visit museum nearby, which focuses on human rights.

MAIN ATTRACTIONS

ESTADIO MONUMENTAL

The home of River Plate, this stadium is a focal point for sports enthusiasts. The Estadio Monumental, nicknamec "El Monumental" or "River Plate Stadium," is a huge sports stadium. It's the home field for the famous Club Atlético River Plate soccer team and seats over 84,000 fans. Sometimes, Argentina's national soccer teams use this stadium for their games.

The Estadio Monumental, nicknamed "El Monumental" or "River Plate Stadium."[13]

As of the writing of this book, the opening hours are every day from 10 am to 7 pm except on match days. However, please make sure to double-check the opening hours online should there be any slight changes to their schedule.

Address: Av. Pres. Figueroa Alcorta 7597, C1428 Cdad. Autónoma de Buenos Aires, Argentina

PARQUE DE LOS NIÑOS

This park is one of the newest and largest in Buenos Aires, covering 32 hectares. It's a great place for nature lovers, especially birdwatchers, since it is home to indigenous species. like the benteveo, calandria, and chingolo. The park is near the northeast coast, so it's often windy and popular for flying kites. You can rent a kite if you don't have one, and there are fun playgrounds for kids.

As of the writing of this book, the opening hours are Tuesday to Sunday from 10 am to 7 pm and closed on Monday. However, please make sure to double-check the opening hours online should there be any slight changes to their schedule.

Address: Av. Int. Cantilo, Av. Gral. Paz &, Buenos Aires, Argentina

CIUDAD UNIVERSITARIA

Ciudad Universitaria is a giant university campus in the Núñez neighborhood and the country's biggest and most respected university. It sits on the edge of the Río de la Plata, a large river and estuary. Ciudad Universitaria is one of the largest green areas in Buenos Aires, and some parts are protected ecological reserve areas. Getting to the campus is easy because many buses and trains stop nearby.

Ciudad Universitaria.[14]

As of the writing of this book, you can visit Ciudad Universitaria at any time during your trip. However, please make sure to double-check the opening hours online should there be any slight changes to their schedule.

Address: Pabellón 3, Av. Int. Güiraldes, Buenos Aires, Argentina

TRANSPORT OPTIONS

- *Train*
- *Buses*
- *Car*
- *Subway*
- *Taxis*

FAMILY FUN

PLAZA BALCARCE

Balcarce Square is a public park in the heart of Buenos Aires that visitors consider a peaceful getaway from the city. The park has a lot of green areas and benches you can sit on and enjoy coffee with someone. It is family-friendly as it has a playground where children can play and enjoy themselves in the sun. You can also bring food and snacks and set up a nice picnic while enjoying the view.

Balcarce Square.[15]

Address: Gregorio Jaramillo 2321, C1425 Cdad. Autónoma de Buenos Aires, Argentina

WHERE TO EAT

ROJO Y NEGRO RESTAURANT

Rojo Y Negro Restaurant is the perfect balance between quality food, reasonable prices, and a great atmosphere. It is located across from Club Cuidad de Buenos Aires. Guests can enjoy watching sports on the TV screen while enjoying their meals, especially the delicious Milanesas they are famous for. The menu includes lunch, dinner, and late-night options. It accepts all forms of payment methods including credit cards. You can enjoy your food at the restaurant, takeaway, or have it delivered to where you are staying.

Opening Hours: 11:00 am to 12:00 am daily.

Contact Details: +54 11 4701-2661.

Address: Crisólogo Larralde 1520, C1429 Cdad. Autónoma de Buenos Aires, Argentina

TEMPERO (RESTAURANT)

Tempero is a restaurant in Buenos Aires known for its warm and inviting atmosphere that keeps guests coming back. It is located in a quiet, green neighborhood, making it a great place to enjoy a relaxing meal. It has a nice outdoor terrace where you can enjoy brunch, lunch, or dinner. Guests swear by their delicious pasta dishes and their exquisite desserts and cakes.

Opening Hours: 08:30 am to 12:00 am from Tuesday to Saturday and 08:30 am to 05:00 pm on Sunday and Monday.

Contact Details: +54 11 2059-0008.

Address: C1429CRH, Jaramillo 2274, C1429CRH Cdad. Autónoma de Buenos Aires, Argentina

NO TAN SANTOS NUÑEZ (RESTAURANT)

No Tan Santos Nunez is a grill house recognized for its exceptional Argentinean barbecue and steakhouse. It is a cozy restaurant with an outdoor patio with trees. It has great service and affordable prices. The portions are big and high-quality, especially the *entrana* and *bife de chorizo*, which is a must-order. Guests love its delicious *provoleta*, mojella, and sweet potatoes with honey appetizers. For dessert, don't miss their homemade flan and *chocotorta*!

Opening Hours: 10:00 am to 12:00 am every day.

Contact Details: +54 11 2065-4723.

Address: Nuñez 1650, C1429 Cdad. Autónoma de Buenos Aires, Argentina

PLACES TO SHOP

KIOSCO (GROCERY STORE)

Kiosco is a local grocery store in Buenos Aires where you can find everything you want easily without getting lost.

Opening Hours: 24 hours every day

Address: Av. del Libertador 7494. C1429 Cdad. Autónoma de Buenos Aires, Argentina

BRUNAPOINTT (CLOTHING STORE)

Brunapointt is a showroom that has a selection of different kinds of clothes, from trendy designs to capsule wardrobe items.

Opening Hours: 12:00 am to 07:30 pm from Wednesday to Saturday, 10:00 am to 07:30 pm on Monday, 07:00 am to 07:30 pm on Tuesday, and closed on Sunday.

Address: Arribeños 3600, C1429 Cdad. Autónoma de Buenos Aires, Argentina

MANYUS (SUPERMARKET)

Manyus supermarket provides good service and a variety of products at reasonable prices for your everyday needs.

Opening Hours: 08:30 am to 09:00 pm from Monday to Saturday, and 10:30 am to 02:00 pm / 05:30 pm to 09:30 pm on Sunday.

Address: 3 de Febrero 3552, C1429BFP Cdad. Autónoma de Buenos Aires, Argentina

ENTERTAINMENT

Laser Games

Laser Games is a thrilling and interactive experience perfect for kids' birthday parties or big group hangouts. The missions combine action, technology, and special effects that make an unforgettable memory. The challenges are guided by "Robot Pinky," who lets them engage in adventures like Space Battle and Tunnel Challenge, solving problems and working in teams along the way. At the end, there is a Trivia Match, where the teams recall details from their adventures to win prizes. If you are looking for a new way for your kids to have fun, Laser Games is the perfect place.

Contact Details: 54 11 4519-0103.

Address: Av. Comodoro Rivadavia 1420 Nunez, Buenos Aires 1429 Argentina

TREPARK

Trepark is Argentina's first indoor aerial park. It is an exhilarating adventure experience with six challenging circuits for maximum fun. It is suitable for children aged seven and up because of its 120 cm minimum height requirement. It has activities like trekking, tree climbing, mountaineering, bridge crossings, balance steps, rappelling, and climbing. The place ensures the safety of the children by a continuous lifeline system through each circuit. It is a great place to celebrate your kids' birthdays as they offer invitation cards, free snacks, pizzas, soft drinks, complete equipment, training and assistance, gifts for the birthday boy or girl, and souvenirs for the guests.

Contact Details: +540114703-5374, +54911 5051-0359.

Address: Miguel B. Sanchez 1041, Buenos Aires 1429 Argentina

SPORTS AND LEISURE

SENTITENIS (TENNIS LESSONS)

Sentitenis is the ideal destination for Tennis enthusiasts visiting Buenos Aires. It is an exciting way to release adrenaline, whether you love clay or hard courts. Sentitenis provides private and group classes from professional yet friendly coaches. Classes are easy to fit within your vacation schedule as you can book on the same day. Whether you are looking to improve your Tennis skills or simply enjoy a good game with friends, Sentitenis is the place for you.

Contact Details: +54 11 4422-4248.

Address: Av. del Libertador 7200, C1429 Cdad. Autónoma de Buenos Aires, Argentina

TRIANGULO ROJO KAYAK

Triangulo Rojo Kayak is a social ecotourism venture where they offer kayak and boat rentals and guided excursions in the Tigre Delta. The tour has a variety of activities, including visiting museums, exploring local island businesses, nature hikes, photo safaris, bird watching, workshops, and night trips with movies and live music. All necessary equipment is provided, from paddles to life jackets. They support sustainable tourism from a social and environmental point of view.

ACCOMMODATION

HOTEL PEDRAZA

Hotel Pedraza is a comfortable accommodation option in Buenos Aires, ensuring a pleasant stay for its guests. The rooms have a private bathroom, showers, free Wi-Fi, and cable channels. Breakfast is included, saving you the hassle of looking for a place to eat in the morning. It is located only 1 km away from the Congreso de Tucuman subway station and close to many attractions like Museo Nacional de Bellas Artes, Palacio Barolo, and the Buenos Aires Japanese Gardens.

Contact Details: +54 11 4703-4927.

Address: Manuela Pedraza 2189, C1429CCE Cdad. Autónoma de Buenos Aires, Argentina.

TOP RENTALS RESIDENCE NUÑEZ

Top Rentals Residence Nunez offers modern, well-equipped apartments to ensure guests have a comfortable stay in Buenos Aires. The apartments have a balcony, outdoor furniture, kitchenette, flat-screen TV, heating, air-conditioning, and free Wi-Fi. You can bring your pet with you as well as enjoy their outdoor swimming pool on the rooftop, beach chairs, and fitness center. To ensure the safety and security of the guests, the place has smoke alarms, 24-hour security, and a safety deposit box in every apartment. The location is great for couples as it is surrounded by beautiful places like Bosques de Palermo and El Rosedal Park, only 6 km away.

Contact Details: +54 9 11 6302-3094.

Address: Nuñez 2422, Cdad. Autónoma de Buenos Aires, Argentina.

HOTEL LAS FAMILIAS

Hotel Las Familias is a guest house in Nunez, Buenos Aires, offering a comfortable, family-friendly atmosphere for guests. It provides convenient services like a car hire and currency exchange. Your kids can enjoy organized children's activities while you enjoy access to a sauna, catering to the needs of the whole family. It is only a short distance from local attractions like El Viaje Argentino and Nunez Cerveza Local, and historical sites like Recoleta, Museo Nacional De Arte Decorativo, and Basilica de Nuestra Senora Del Pilar.

Contact Details: +54 11 4702-5687.

Address: Cuba 3146, C1429 AXH, Cdad. Autónoma de Buenos Aires, Argentina.

Sarum Hotel Design

Sarum Hotel Design, located in the heart of Buenos Aires, with guests rating it as an exceptional location, is a stylishly decorated hotel with a minimalistic theme, offering modern design and comfort. The rooms are furnished with sleek furniture and clean, linen bed sheets to guarantee the guests get a restful sleep. Each room has large windows that fill the room with warm sunlight, overlooking a nice view of the beautiful trees of the city. The staff are friendly and helpful, doing their best to satisfy all their guests' needs. The hotel is within walking distance from popular attractions like Paseo Renata and Plaza Arenales, local shops, and dining options like Burger King and Famenovo restaurant.

Contact Details: +54 11 4704-0039.

Address: Quesada 2370, C1429 COJ, Cdad. Autónoma de Buenos Aires, Argentina.

VICENTE LÓPEZ (PART OF GREATER BUENOS AIRES)

Vicente López, where old-fashioned charm meets modern life, is home to about 24,000 people. It is the first district north of Buenos Aires. The suburb is proud of its century-old history, yet it embraces contemporary living. Its location is beautiful, with peaceful Olivos to the north, lively Florida to the west, and the grand Río de la Plata to the east. It's close to the heart of Buenos Aires, making it easy to explore city life and nature. There are plenty of sights, from old streets to grand architectural mansions and a historic cinema studio. If you're into sports, nature, or culture, there's plenty here for you. The people are proud of their city, and it's easy to see why.

MAIN ATTRACTIONS

Paseo de la Costa

This waterfront area provides a leisurely setting for walks and cycling, highlighting the district's focus on quality of life and outdoor activities. It's the place to go to escape the urban jungle and find serenity. The park is along the banks of the Río de la Plata in Vicente López, and it offers a variety of activities to enjoy in the fresh air and stunning riverfront scenery. There is a dedicated wooden walkway for extended walks and a separate bike path for cyclists. The park has amenities like clean bathrooms and small bars offering drinks and burgers, adding to the park's convenience. Paseo de la Costa is a favorite among locals and tourists.

Paseo de la Costa.[16]

As of the writing of this book, you can visit Paseo de la Costa at any time during your trip. However, please make sure to double-check the opening hours online should there be any slight changes to their schedule.

Address: Gral. José de San Martín 201, B1638 Vicente López, Provincia de Buenos Aires, Argentina

Quinta de Olivos: This is the President's official residence and has been home to sixteen presidential families over the last 60 years. It was built in 1854 by Prilidiano Pueyrredón. It has an ancient look with touches of Neo-Gothic and Baroque styles, making it stand out. The house sits on a hill, so you can enjoy fantastic views of the Río de la Plata River from the area.

Address: Av. del Libertador 2200, B1636 Olivos, Provincia de Buenos Aires, Argentina

Museo de Arte de Tigre: By the banks of the Luján River in Tigre is the Tigre Art Museum (Museo de Arte Tigre). This museum was built in a fancy and ornate style and declared a National Historic Monument in 1979. The museum has a collection of amazing paintings by Argentinian artists, most created between 1800 and 1999. The artworks here are a must-see.

As of the writing of this book, the opening hours are Wednesday to Friday from 1 pm to 5:30 pm, Saturday and Sunday from 12 pm to 5:30 pm, and closed on Monday and Tuesday. However, please make sure to double-check the opening hours online should there be any slight changes to their schedule.

Address: Av. Victorica 972, B1648 Tigre, Provincia de Buenos Aires, Argentina

TRANSPORT OPTIONS

- *Train*
- *Buses*
- *Taxi*
- *Cars*

EXPERIENCES

HOP-ON HOP-OFF BUS TOUR

With the hop-on hop-off bus tour, you can enjoy Buenos Aires at your own pace with 20 different stops across the city. The buses have air-conditioning, a sunroof, and a multilingual audio guide, including English, German, Italian, French, Spanish, and Portuguese. You can enjoy the city views from the open-air upper deck or from the air-conditioned lower level, according to your preference. Food and drinks are not included, so make sure to get some snacks for the road!

SHERPA FOOD TOUR

Sherpa Food Tours take participants through an unforgettable culinary adventure by picking restaurants that make delectable food and wine, from local hidden gems to Michelin-star restaurants. You can choose from the different available tours like the Local Foodie Adventure, where you will try more than 14 dishes and drinks; the San Telmo Expedition, where you will try more than five dishes and drinks; or the Buenos Aires Private Experience, where you will try more than 10 dishes and drinks. Each tour takes an average of 3.5 hours, giving you the time you need to absorb the culinary heritage and stories behind each dish.

Contact Details: +541159842884.

ELECTRIC SCOOTERS TOUR

The E-scooter tour is a five-hour-long adventure through Buenos Aires' beautiful streets. It takes a maximum of 9 participants, aged 10 through 85, to make sure each one gets their fair share of attention. Along the way, you will stop and taste the *alfajor, mate, fernet,* and *chipa*, which are staples of Argentine cuisine. You will also stop at famous landmarks, including the Obelisco, Casa Rosada, and Recoleta Cemetery, where you will learn about the city's rich history and culture. This is a fun, exciting way to explore Buenos Aires you can't miss!

WHERE TO EAT

MÖOI VICENTE LÓPEZ

Möoi Vicente López is a unique restaurant owned by Jessica Lekerman, who makes sure to use high-quality ingredients in all her dishes. The menu is full of diverse Argentinean and South American dishes. It does not stick to a single trend or theme, making it easy to find something you like, no matter what your dietary preferences are. The space is decorated with beautiful colorful items like hanging lights that make the overall vibe warm and cozy, yet chic.

Opening Hours: 08:00 am to 01:00 am from Monday to Friday and 09:00 am to 01:00 am on Saturday and Sunday.

Contact Details: +54 9 11 5733-8074.

Address: Av. del Libertador 105, B1638 Vicente López, Provincia de Buenos Aires, Argentina

VIEJO NORTON RESTAURANTE

Viejo Norton Restaurante is a cozy, small hidden gem in the streets of Buenos Aires. The menu is extensive, with different Argentinean and South American dishes, guided by chef Juan Carlos. There is a different dish of the day every day, so make sure to ask about it! The food is served in generous portions with reasonable pricing, making it affordable for both tourists and residents. The restaurant serves alcohol which you can enjoy with your dinner. It also offers features like takeout, highchairs, free Wi-Fi, and wheelchairs, if needed.

Opening Hours: 12:00 pm to 03:00 pm and 08:00 pm to 11:00 pm every day.

Contact Details: +54 11 4797-9712.

Address: Miguel de Azcuénaga 900, B1638BBP Buenos Aires, Provincia de Buenos Aires, Argentina

RESTAURANTE VICENTE LÓPEZ

Restaurante Vicente López is a popular dining spot famous for its excellent fast service, inviting atmosphere, and a great selection of desserts, such as cakes, pastries, and traditional alfajores, which visitors highly recommend. It is a good place for a family breakfast, dinner, or an afternoon snack.

Opening Hours: 08:00 am to 12:00 am from Tuesday to Sunday, and closed on Monday.

Contact Details: +54 11 6205-2087.

Address: Av. Maipú 701, B1638 Vicente López, Provincia de Buenos Aires, Argentina

PLACES TO SHOP

CABAÑA DOÑA LOLA (MARKET)

Cabaña Doña Lola is a small local convenience store that sells everyday products. They include fresh bread, honey, nuts, cold cuts like pastrami, ham, salami, chorizo, olives, and all kinds of cheese from different brands. It is known for selling excellent quality, fresh ingredients, and good sale offers.

Opening Hours: 09:00 am to 08:00 pm from Monday to Friday, 10:00 am to 02:00 pm on Saturday, and closed on Sunday.

Contact Details: +54 11 7724-9632.

Address: Pres. Hipólito Yrigoyen 1484, B1602ABS Vicente López, Provincia de Buenos Aires, Argentina

Norcenter Lifestyle Mall (Shopping Mall)

Norcenter is a shopping center with various activity options such as shopping, dining, cinema and entertainment like an ice rink and bowling for both kids and grownups to enjoy themselves. It has convenient options like underground parking and a food court suitable for all food likings. The cinema is famous for its super comfortable seating and impressive sound quality, making it a great place to take your kids to see a new animated movie. It is popular for having multiple furniture and home décor stores.

Opening Hours: 12:00 pm to 08:00 pm every day.

Address: Esteban Echeverria 3750, B1605 Munro, Provincia de Buenos Aires, Argentina

SABE LA TIERRA (STREET MARKET)

Sabe la Tierra is an organic flea market that supports sustainability and direct trade between sellers and buyers. You can go each week and find a wide selection of fresh, seasonal fruits and vegetables. You can find whole-meal baked goods, cereal bars, local olive oil, vegan and vegetarian food options, plants and seedlings, and natural cosmetics. There are also healthy recipes on their website where you can use the fresh ingredients you bought. It also hosts special events like live music and cooking classes, where you can go to socialize and enjoy with friends or family.

Opening Hours: 10:00 am to 03:00 pm on Saturdays.

Address: Gral. José de San Martín 2400, B1602 Florida, Provincia de Buenos Aires, Argentina

SPORTS AND LEISURE

CAMPUS ESCALADA (ROCK CLIMBING GYM)

Campus Escalada is a gym that offers rock climbing lessons. It offers classes to different levels, from beginners to teach them the basics to experts to give them a new challenge. Students love the attention and care they get from the excellent instructors. The place has options to practice with rope, with many routes and boulders to climb. All the extensive details are on their Instagram page, including the timing of each course according to the skill level.

Contact Details: +54 9 11 5149-9757.

Address: Av. Libertador 981, B1638 BEI, Vicente Lopez, Buenos Aires, Argentina

MILITARY CIRCLE CLUB

The Military Circle Club offers a chance for relaxation and unwinding and a chance to enjoy playing sports. You can go with a friend to enjoy the views while sipping coffee or releasing some adrenaline with the sports facilities they provide. There is a swimming pool, eleven clay tennis courts, paddle tennis, basketball, volleyball, and a skating area. It is a good option for gatherings where you can enjoy the barbecue areas by the river.

Address: Libertador Avenue 2100, Vicente Lopez 1636, Buenos Aires, Argentina

BIBLIOTECA POPULAR SUDESTADA (PUBLIC LIBRARY)

Biblioteca Popular Sudestada is a public library that acts as a cultural hub in Buenos Aires. This beloved library is not just a place to borrow or read books, it is a gathering spot if what you are looking for is an authentic Argentine experience. It hosts events on the weekends, such as jazz cycles, author film screenings featuring discussions with filmmakers, and tango milongas with music from vinyl records. It also offers intellectual, artistic, and cultural workshops.

Contact Details: +54 11 7557-6648.

Address: EIC, Aristóbulo del Valle 1631, B1602 Vicente López, Provincia de Buenos Aires, Argentina

ACCOMMODATION

HOTEL VICENTE LÓPEZ

Hotel Vicente Lopez, located only 100 m away from the train station, which is convenient for travelers, offers comfortable rooms with free Wi-Fi, a flat-screen TV to unwind after a long day of exploring the city, free toiletries, a wardrobe, and a socket near the bed. They are also equipped with air-conditioning and heating to adjust the weather how you like. The hotel has a private parking area, elevator, laundry service, and wake-up service, so you don't miss your booked tours and daily housekeeping services.

Contact Details: +54 11 4797-3773.

Address: Av. del Libertador 902, B1638 Vicente López, Provincia de Buenos Aires, Argentina.

HOTEL MANZANARES PLAZA

Hotel Manzanares Plaza is a great place to stay if you are looking for both comfort and convenience. It is very close to Nunez train station, Congreso de Tucuman subway station, and Rivadavia train station. The rooms have satellite TV, cable channels, and a clothes rack, along with free toiletries, towels, and toilet paper in the bathrooms. Wi-Fi is available and free of charge in all hotel areas, including the guest rooms and common shared areas. The place also allows pets and has non-smoking room options.

Contact Details: +54 11 4702-6839.

Address: Manzanares 2339, C1429 Cdad. Autónoma de Buenos Aires, Argentina.

LO DE COSTA - BED & BREAKFAST

Lo De Costa is a beautiful bed and breakfast house with a serene garden and modern décor. It is located close to Dot Shopping Center, River Plate Stadium, and Jorge Newbery Airport, with restaurants and cafés like Pizza Strega, Adaluz, and Havanna nearby. Guests can enjoy a private bathroom, free internet, air-conditioning, and soundproof rooms. The rooms have a flat-screen TV with Netflix as a streaming option to relax at night, a minibar, wifi for your laptop, and a telephone. The host is very friendly and people leave very impressed.

Contact Details: +54 11 4795-1993.

Address: Gaspar Campos 1550, B1638ATD Vicente López, Provincia de Buenos Aires, Argentina.

LA CASONA DE GRACE

La Casona de Grace is a luxuricus bed and breakfast located in Vicente López, making you feel like you are in an old English movie. The rooms are soundproof with high-speed Wi-Fi, flat-screen TVs, desks, minibars, and kitchenettes with dishwashers, microwaves, and kitchenware. It is near top attractions like Concejo Deliberante and Quinta Trabucco, making it easy to explore the area. It is also within walking distance from local dining places like Confitera & Restaurant La Vicente López and Resto Centro Asturiano. Guests feel very welcome staying there because of the beautifully decorated rooms giving warm vibes.

Contact Details: +54 11 5512-4832.

Address: Gdor. Valentín Vergara 898 1638, B1638 Vicente López, Provincia de Buenos Aires, Argentina.

CHAPTER

4 SOUTHERN BUENOS AIRES

Buenos Aires changes as you travel south from the busy city center. The city slows down, with quieter streets and a more local feel. The southern neighborhoods, known as 'Sur' or "Barrio Sur,' blend old-fashioned charm with modern touches, creating an individual and intriguing atmosphere. Buenos Aires' southern part is home to some of the most laid-back places to visit, like La Boca. It is a must-see neighborhood famous for its colorful buildings, tango heritage, and the Caminito, a famous street museum. Barracas and Pompeya show their cultural diversity with architecture, food, and traditions, reflecting Italian, Spanish, and Eastern European influences.

Buenos Aires was a small town where ships could stop and re-stock because the Spanish rulers refused to allow trade with other places. The people in the South developed their way of life, based on agriculture and secret trade, without outside influences. Recently, the South has become a thriving center for creative expression. The proliferation of galleries, theaters, and cultural centers showcases local artists and performers. You can find everything from unusual art shows to passionate dancers' street performances. This chapter uncovers the districts that capture Buenos Aires's complex identity and must-see tourist attractions you shouldn't miss.

Did You Know?

Gabriela Sabatini, one of the top tennis players in the 1980s and 1990s, is from Buenos Aires. She won 41 tennis matches, including the US Open in 1990

BARRACAS DISTRICT

Barracas is the place to go if you want a peek into Buenos Aires' past. Its streets are lined with grand 19th-century mansions, a reminder of when Barracas housed the city's wealthy elite. As the city grew, the neighborhood became an industrial hub - factories were built, attracting immigrants and working-class families. This history is evident in the warehouses and workshops dotting the area, offering a glimpse into Barracas' industrial past.

Barracas' beauty lies in its originality, with hidden courtyards, tucked-away plazas, and local shops brimming with character. Barracas is a paradise for foodies seeking a taste of real Argentina. Abandoned factories have been transformed into art studios and galleries exhibiting the works of local talent. Visit Barracas if you are interested in venturing beyond the normal tourist path and discover a side of Buenos Aires brimming with local charm.

MAIN ATTRACTIONS

MERCADO DE LOS CARRUAJES

The Mercado de los Carruajes started as a busy market in 1900 and has been transformed into a lively cultural spot where people who love beautiful buildings and local art enjoy visiting. The market retains its old beauty with its colorful glass and wooden frames. The Mercado de los Carruajesis building has two levels. On the bottom level are many shops to browse. The top-level and outside areas have eateries and spaces for events. Several restaurants serve various cuisines, like Patagonia jams, gluten-free pasta, homemade beers, and delicious coffee. You can sample foods from other countries, such as Spanish desserts and Japanese cuisine. The building's original purpose was to house the president's horses and carriages.

As of the writing of this book, the opening hours are 08:30 am to 10:00 pm from Monday to Friday, 08:30 am to 12:00 pm on Thursday and Saturday, and 08:30 am to 08:00 pm on Sunday. However, please make sure to double-check the opening hours online should there be any slight changes to their schedule.

Address: Avenida Leandro Niceforo Alem 852, C1001AAQ, C1001 Cdad. Autónoma de Buenos Aires, Argentina

Calle Lanín

Lanín Street, sometimes called Lanín Passage, curves alongside railroad tracks, is lined with single-story houses and is paved with old cobblestones – a true piece of classic Buenos Aires. A local residential artist, Marino Santa Maria, added his unique touch in 2000. He renovated some of the building facades, then painted and decorated them with colorful mosaics - curvy shapes and creative patterns. His creativity sparked the inner artist in his neighbors, who joined the project. Their hard work resulted in over 40 building fronts covered in these amazing mosaics on Lanín Street, a true explosion of color and shapes, transforming the entire street into an open-air art gallery.

Calle Lanín.[17]

As of the writing of this book, you can visit Calle Lanín at any time during your trip. However, please make sure to double-check the opening hours online should there be any slight changes to their schedule.

Address: C1274 Buenos Aires, Argentina

MUSEO DE LA CARCOVA

This museum has copies of famous statues worldwide so that you can see these incredible artworks in one place. The museum's collection is massive, with over 4,000 tracings of masterpieces from all over the world. It's like a journey through time, with ancient art from the Renaissance and Gothic periods.

Museo de la Carcova.[18]

As of the writing of this book, the opening hours are 10:00 am to 05:00 pm from Tuesday to Sunday and closed on Monday. However, please make sure to double-check the opening hours online should there be any slight changes to their schedule.

Address: Av. España 1701, C1107CND Cdad. Autónoma de Buenos Aires, Argentina

TRANSPORT OPTIONS

- *Subway*
- *Taxi*
- *Buses*
- *Cars*
- *Train*

EXPERIENCES

SEÑOR TANGO

Señor Tango is a venue that presents live performance shows of skilled dancers, musicians, and singers like Fernando Soler, also known as Mr. Tango. You can book from different seating options, with VIP as the best one because it provides the clearest view. If you book the VIP ticket, you can choose from their fancy menu, including steak with fries, smoked salmon, fried shrimp, chicken, and tasty desserts like tiramisu or cheesecake. The show is highly recommended for couples to enjoy a glamorous night together. Another advantage is place is easily accessible with nearby parking.

Contact Details: +54 (11) 4303-0231 / 32 / 33 / 34.

Address: Barracas Calle Hipolito Vieytes 1655, Buenos Aires C1275AGQ, Argentina

CIRCUITO CULTURAL BARRACAS

Barracas Cultural Circuit is a community art project dedicated to promoting arts, culture, and community engagement. The centers offer many activities and events, including theatrical performances, workshops, art exhibitions, and musical concerts, regularly collaborating with local schools, organizations, and artists to host such events. It is a great place to go if you are an art enthusiast with a love for creative expression.

Contact Details: +54 9 11 4302-6825.

Address: Avenida Iriarte 2165 Barracas, Buenos Aires C1291ABQ, Argentina

PARROQUIA SAN ANTONIO MARÍA ZACCARIA (CHURCH)

The Parish of Saint Anthony Maria Zaccaria is one of the most modern churches in Barracas. It is simply and beautifully designed, with an inviting atmosphere for worshippers. Inside the parish, there is a striking mural of Jesus behind the illuminated altar, which makes visitors feel more spiritually connected to the place. The priest of the church is approachable and makes time for confessions before the evening service at 7 PM.

The Parish of Saint Anthony Maria Zaccaria.[19]

Contact Details: +54 11 7113-0122.

Address: Avenida Montes de Oca 1808, C1270 ABS, Cdad. Autónoma de Buenos Aires, Argentina

WHERE TO EAT

LA FLOR DE BARRACAS

La Flor de Barracas restaurant has a beautiful setting with an inviting atmosphere that keeps guests coming back. It serves authentic cuisine with vegetarian and gluten-free options to accommodate different dietary preferences. You can enjoy their specialties, like the gnocchi cooked in a smooth, tasty sauce, the lamb dish, and their exquisite ravioli.

Opening Hours: 07:30 am to 05:00 pm Monday to Thursday/ 07:30 am to 12:00 am on Friday/ 11:00 am to 12:00 am on Saturday/ closed on Sunday.

Contact Details: +54 11 4302-7924.

Address: Av. Suárez 2095, C1288 Cdad. Autónoma de Buenos Aires, Argentina

LA CABAÑA BARRACAS

La Cabaña Barracas is a German restaurant with cozy, welcoming vibes that offers a variety of dishes. Guests especially love their apple strudel. The restaurant is known for excellent service and polite, attentive staff. It offers affordable prices, which make it a good place to enjoy a casual meal or drinks in the afternoon.

Opening Hours: 09:00 am to 04:00 pm from Monday to Wednesday, 09:00 am to 12:00 am Thursday to Saturday, and closed on Sunday.

Contact Details: +54 11 4303-4897.

Address: Olavarría 1601, C1267 Cdad. Autónoma de Buenos Aires, Argentina

PIZZA-RESTO SAN MIGUEL BARRACAS

San Miguel is a classic neighborhood pizzeria located on Montes de Oca Avenue in Barracas. The interior resembles old Italian restaurants, with the tables lined with red sheets. The menu is full of delicious options for crispy pizzas topped with fresh mozzarella, making it a place both kids and adults will love. It also serves different dishes like Argentinean Italian-style Milanesa Napolitana, which is breaded, fried steak topped with a rich tomato sauce and cheese. You can also go enjoy breakfast there as it serves delicious warm croissants.

Opening Hours: 07:00 am to 11:00 pm every day.

Contact Details: +54 11 4303-7027.

Address: Av. Montes de Oca 1002, C1270 Cdad. Autónoma de Buenos Aires, Argentina

LA POSTA DE ANTONIO

La Posta de Antonio is a nice steakhouse in Barracas that has a relaxing atmosphere perfect for enjoying a hearty meal with friends and family. It is known for its parilla, which Is grilled meat, delicious empanadas, spinach fritters, and fresh salads. The restaurant offers a great price-per-value ratio, especially with its midweek discounts for cash payments. The staff is very friendly, and there is a good selection of wines you can choose from for afternoon drinks. After that, you can order their delicious Sabayon for dessert.

Opening Hours: 12:00 pm to 04:00 pm / 08:00 pm to 12:00 am from Monday to Saturday and 12:00 pm to 04:00 pm on Sunday.

Contact Details: +54 11 4302-8062.

Address: C. Gaspar M. de Jovellanos 919, C1269 Cdad. Autónoma de Buenos Aires, Argentina

PLACES TO SHOP

MULTI BAZAR BARRACAS (VARIETY STORE)

Multi Bazar is a spacious variety store that sells a range of products at competitive prices. Be sure to observe the items well while buying as some are less appealing than others. It is a solid choice for shoppers due to its variety and good prices. Customers appreciate the polite staff and convenient location near the bus stop.

Opening Hours: 09:00 am to 08:00 pm from Monday to Friday, 10:00 am to 08:00 pm on Saturday, and closed on Sunday.

Address: Av. Regimiento de Patricios 811, C1265AEB Cdad. Autónoma de Buenos Aires, Argentina

ENELDO - MERCADO NATURAL - BARRACAS (GROCERY STORE)

Eneldo Mercado Natural grocery store has a wonderful variety of quality products at affordable prices, which customers keep returning to. It is a place where you can discover new and unique items to incorporate into your dishes, like their exceptional smoked paprika. The store is owned by a friendly woman and her daughter, who create a welcoming environment for customers. While there may be cheaper options nearby, people come back for the comfort and special selection of goods.

Opening Hours: 09:30 am to 08:30 pm from Monday to Saturday, and closed Sunday.

Address: Av. Montes de Oca 962, C1270 Cdad. Autónoma de Buenos Aires, Argentina

ACCOMMODATIONS

L'ADRESSE HÔTEL

L'Adresse Hôtel is a charming boutique hotel with modern yet cozy interiors stylishly decorated. It is found in an excellent location near attractions like the Museum of Latin American Art of Buenos Aires, the Japanese Garden of Buenos Aires, Palermo Forests, and Plaza Serrano. There are multiple restaurants close by, like Babieca and Pizzeria SG. The rooms are fully equipped with household linen, a wardrobe, flat-screen TV, free internet, and air-conditioning. The bathrooms are provided with showers, towels, toilet paper, and a hairdryer, making everything you need easily accessible. The Hotel offers entertainment and family services like board games, as well as activities like cooking classes, game rooms, and bike and walking tours, all subject to extra charge.

Contact Details: +54 11 4307-2332.

Address: C1141AAE, Bolívar 1491, C1141AAE Cdad. Autónoma de Buenos Aires, Argentina.

HOSTEL CHE BUENOS AIRES

Hostel Che Buenos Aires, located only 300 m away from the Natural History Museum and 950 m away from Museo Penitenciario Antonio Ballve, is a great property perfect for travelers as it is just 8 km away from Jorge Newbery Airport. The Hostel is a good option for young travelers as it has a shared kitchen, bathroom, lounge area, and lockers. The kitchen is equipped with a coffee machine, toaster, kitchenware, microwave, and electric kettle, catering to everyday needs. There is a designated smoking area, as the rooms are generally non-smoking. There is no parking available, but there is an outdoor dining area and a terrace with furniture. There are restaurants and cafes nearby, like El Recreo, Pizzeria Bolivar, and On Tap.

Contact Details: +54 11 3366-1278.

Address: Dr. Enrique Finochietto 529, C1143ABC Cdad. Autónoma de Buenos Aires, Argentina.

COSME HOTEL

Cosme Hotel, located only 1 km away from the San Telmo district, offers rooms with cable channels, a flat-screen TV, and fire extinguishers. It offers good facilities such as daily housekeeping, concierge service, luggage storage, a 24-hour front desk, and currency exchange. All rooms have air-conditioning and heating. The hotel is located near beautiful attractions like Buenos Aires Japanese Gardens, Plaza Serrano Square, and Bosques de Palermo. There are options of close restaurants and cafes like El Encuento Resto Bar, 100 m away, Confitera de Antano, 250 m away, and La Esquina de Omar, 400 m away.

Contact Details: +54 11 4300-0445.

Address: Av. Brasil 921 - 923, C1154AAO Cdad. Autónoma de Buenos Aires, Argentina.

HOSTEL MEDIO MUNDO

Medio Mundo is a hostel near the Constitución train station in Buenos Aires. The area might raise safety concerns, and the rooms lack luxury, but it stands out for its cleanliness, friendly staff, and affordable rates. It has shared dorms, making it ideal for young travelers looking to socialize and make new friendships.

Contact Details: +54 11 3579-9182.

Address: Gral. Hornos 1054, C1288 C1272ACT, Cdad. Autónoma de Buenos Aires, Argentina.

LA BOCA DISTRICT

La Boca is a lively neighborhood where many European and Asian immigrants settled. It's famous for its colorful houses and a street museum called Caminito. You'll see tango dancers showing off their moves and buy souvenirs to remember the experience. There's a theater, La Ribera, many clubs playing tango music, and Italian restaurants for a bite to eat. However, the colorful area is quite small.

MAIN ATTRACTIONS

CAMINITO

Caminito.[20]

When you think of Caminito, imagine an outdoor museum. The street is primarily known for its brightly colored houses. These houses represent the culture of people who moved here from other countries in the late 1800s and early 1900s. The Caminito used to be where a small river joined the Riachuelo. However, a railway was built on it when the area became dryland. After the railway closed, nobody went to this street until the 1950s, when people living nearby revived the area. Benito Quinquela Martín painted the buildings, opening the door for artists from all over Argentina to showcase their artworks.

As of the writing of this book, you can visit Caminito at any time during your trip. However, please make sure to double-check the opening hours online should there be any slight changes to their schedule.

Address: Av. Don Pedro de Mendoza 1900, C1169 Cdad. Autónoma de Buenos Aires, Argentina

LA BOMBONERA

This stadium is a dream come true for football lovers. It's where fans cheer for their team, and the excitement is almost tangible. La Bombonera is the home stadium for the Boca Juniors football team and is known for its wild celebrations during games. The excitement starts on the streets before the match even begins. The stadium, officially called Alberto J. Armando, is shaped like a box of chocolates and has steep stands that put fans close to the action. It's an unforgettable experience to watch a game here. The stadium is decorated with artworks by famous Argentinian painters.

La Bombonera.[21]

As of the writing of this book, La Bombonera is open every day from 10 am to 6 pm. However, please make sure to double-check the opening hours online should there be any slight changes to their schedule.

Address: Brandsen 805, C1161AAQ Cdad. Autónoma de Buenos Aires, Argentina

FUNDACIÓN PROA

The Fundación Proa is a major arts center in Argentina. They focus on showing significant art from the 1900s and hold photographic exhibitions and concerts. They have special exhibits and host talks, classes, and other events. The multi-floor Proa Foundation building houses galleries, an area to watch movies and presentations, a bookstore, a restaurant with an outdoor area, and oversized windows to connect with the neighborhood.

The Fundación Proa.[22]

As of the writing of this book, the Fundación Proa is open Wednesday to Sunday from 12 pm to 7 pm and is closed on Monday and Tuesday. However, please make sure to double-check the opening hours online should there be any slight changes to their schedule.

Address: Av. Don Pedro de Mendoza 1929, C1169 Cdad. Autónoma de Buenos Aires, Argentina

Did You Know?

La Boca is known as the birthplace of the tango. Tango dancers perform on the famous Caminito Street.

TRANSPORT OPTIONS

- *Taxi*
- *Buses*
- *Subway*
- *Train*
- *Rideshares*

EXPERIENCES

MUSEO BENITO QUINQUELA MARTIN (MUSEUM)

The Benito Quinquela Martin Museum represents the life and work of one of Argentina's most iconic artists: Quinquela Martin. He is known as "The Painter of La Boca" as it is where he grew up, and many of his artworks were inspired by this area. The museum is in a school building with two floors as art galleries where you can enjoy a nice view of the La Boca port. It also has a section that shows the artist's room with old furniture from when he used to paint. The museum has a small but fascinating art collection of Quinquela's works.

The Benito Quinquela Martin Museum.[23]

Address: Av. Don Pedro de Mendoza 1835, C1169 Cdad. Autónoma de Buenos Aires, Argentina

EL GALPON DE CATALINAS (THEATER)

El Gapon de Catalinas is a one-of-a-kind experience you can have in Buenos Aires created by a group of locals. Most performances are musicals relating to the Murga tradition that mixes social criticism with original music. Their best play is El Fulgor Argentino, which translates to The Argentine Glow. It is a comedy that shows significant events in Argentina in the last century. It is a memorable experience and not your typical tourist attraction. Whether you want to learn more about Argentinean culture or have a night of entertainment, El Gapon de Catalinas is your go-to theater.

Address: Av. Benito Pérez Galdós 93, C1155 Cdad. Autónoma de Buenos Aires, Argentina

WHERE TO EAT

LA GRAN POCHA (PIZZA RESTAURANT)

La Gran Pocha restaurant is a great spot loved by locals for its delicious pizza and empanadas. It is a casual place where the food is homemade and authentic. You can grab a few slices of pizza, enjoy a cold beer, and sit outside to enjoy the open air. Keep in mind that there are no bathrooms, so make sure you go prepared.

Opening Hours: 12:00 pm to 08:00 pm every day.

Contact Details: +54 11 4301-9625.

Address: Olavarría 707, C1160 Cdad. Autónoma de Buenos Aires, Argentina

BRASSERIE PETANQUE (FRENCH RESTAURANT)

Petanque is a French restaurant where you can enjoy lunch, dinner, or a late-night outing. It is a great place, highly recommended by couples because the interior design is romantic and inviting. It is a blend of the South of France and the heart of Argentina. The service staff is professional and pleasant, and the owner treats guests like family. Guests love their lamb ravioli and risotto. For dessert, the crème brûlée is a lovely option.

Opening Hours: 08:00 am to 11:30 pm from Thursday to Saturday, 12:00 pm to 05:00 pm on Sunday, and closed from Monday to Wednesday.

Contact Details: +54 11 2551-8099.

Address: Defensa 596, C1065 Cdad. Autónoma de Buenos Aires, Argentina

EL CAMPEON DE LA BOCA (RESTAURANT)

El Campeon De La Boca is a cozy spot to eat homemade food at great prices in La Boca. It is like stepping into a classic, old-school Argentine restaurant. The menu includes dishes like Healthy Market Burger, flavorful Bandiola with fries, and classic Napolitana milanesa. It is a great place to relax and enjoy the friendly service and chill atmosphere.

Opening Hours: 07:30 am to 11:30 pm from Monday to Saturday and 10:00 am to 05:00 pm on Sunday.

Address: Av. Suárez 699, C1160 Cdad. Autónoma de Buenos Aires, Argentina

PLACES TO SHOP

PASEO DE COMPRAS CAMINITO SHOPPING (SHOPPING MALL)

Paseo de Compras Caminito is a colorful shopping mall that is excellent for tourists. There are antique shops, crafts shops, gift shops, and many places to eat. However, make sure you have enough money because some stores are expensive.

Opening Hours: 10:00 am to 08:00 pm every day.

Address: Magallanes 802, C1166ACA Cdad. Autónoma de Buenos Aires, Argentina

BRANDSEN PASION SOUVENIRS (SOUVENIR SHOP)

Brandsen Pasion Souvenirs is a small souvenir shop near Estadio Alberto José Armando, also known as The Bombonera Stadium. The shop has a collection of football-related souvenirs, such as footballs, flags, the World Cup, and Messi. It also sells miniatures of famous attractions in Argentina and Tango performers.

Opening Hours: 08:30 am to 06:30 pm every day.

Address: Brandsen 760, C1161AAP Cdad. Autónoma de Buenos Aires, Argentina

PASEO DE COMPRAS OLAVARRIA (GENERAL STORE)

Paseo de Compras Olavarria is a general store with a fine variety and affordable prices. It sells home goods such as standing fans, bathroom curtains, bed covers, and pillowcases.

Opening Hours: 10:00 am to 08:00 pm from Monday to Saturday and 10:00 am to 04:00 pm on Sunday.

Address: Olavarría 746, C1162 Cdad. Autónoma de Buenos Aires, Argentina

SUPERMERCADO LA AMISTAD (GROCERY STORE)

Supermercado La Amistad is a small grocery store with good service and prices. Customers like its high quality, cleanliness, and good organization of products.

Opening Hours: 09:00 am to 10:00 pm every day.

Address: Charrúa 3172, C1437AZF Cdad. Autónoma de Buenos Aires, Argentina

ACCOMMODATION

HOSTEL CASA & CAMPO

Hostel Casa & Campo is located 300 m from La Bombonera Stadium. It is also near top attractions like the Museum of Latin American Art of Buenos Aires MALBA, Plaza Serrano Square, and Bosques de Palermo. The host is nice and pleasant and makes guests feel at home. The hostel has a patio, garden, sun terrace, bar, shared kitchen, family rooms, and an outdoor swimming pool where all ages are welcome. The rooms have free Wi-Fi, a coffee maker, towels, and a clothes rack. You can enjoy a nice lunch in nearby restaurants like La Camorra, El Puerto de Ariel, and Café de los Artistas.

Contact Details: +54 11 4402-0801.

Address: Martín Rodríguez 724, C1159ADH Cdad. Autónoma de Buenos Aires, Argentina.

La Boca B&B Posada

La Boca Posada is a bed and breakfast with an exclusive area for guests to enjoy their breakfast. It has an exclusive restaurant for dinners but it requires a reservation in advance. It is within walking distance from La Bombonera Stadium and Caminitos. La Boca B&B Posada is near Plaza de Mayo Square, Bosques de Palermo, and Palermo Lakes. The facilities include dining and seating areas, heating, a fan, and a designated smoking area. This B&B only allows adults, so it is not a place to stay with your kids.

Contact Details: +54 11 5656-3738.

Address: Magallanes 1221, C1166 Cdad. Autónoma de Buenos Aires, Argentina.

Aristóbulo

Aristóbulo is a quiet, interesting bed and breakfast near Centro Cultural Kirchner and Plaza de Mayo Square. It has heating, air conditioning, and free Wi-Fi. The host serves a delicious breakfast and is very helpful and responsive. It is nicely decorated with paintings on the walls. The doors and windows are painted with vibrant colors: blue, green, and pink. The rooms have a flat-screen TV, cable channels, and a private bathroom with a shower, free toiletries, and towels. The restaurants nearby are Il Matterello, Café de los Artistas, and Menjunjes, and the nearby public transport options are Constitucion Subway Station, San Juan, and Hipolito Yrigoyen.

Contact Details: +54 9 11 5864-6200.

Address: Aristóbulo del Valle 543, C1161AEE, C1161 Cdad. Autónoma de Buenos Aires, Argentina.

PARQUE PATRICIOS DISTRICT

This neighborhood is known for its several public parks, making it a green oasis in the middle of the busy city. An added attraction was built in 2015 - a new government building designed by famous architect Norman Foster - brought new businesses and money into the neighborhood.

MAIN ATTRACTIONS

PARQUE DE LOS PATRICIOS

This is the neighborhood's big green heart. It's a peaceful spot to escape the city's rush and busy areas and enjoy fresh air. Parque Patricios is in the city's fourth district. It underwent significant change in the early 1900s when an old slaughterhouse and waste disposal facilities were removed. The neighborhood is now named after its main park, designed by well-known Argentinian landscape architect Carlos Thays, who planned many of Buenos Aires' green spaces. You might recognize it as the home of Club Atlético Huracán and their stadium if you're a sports fan.

Parque de los Patricios.[24]

As of the writing of this book, the opening hours are every day from 8 am to 8 pm. However, please make sure to double-check the opening hours online should there be any slight changes to their schedule.

Address: Av. Caseros 3021, C1437 Cdad. Autónoma de Buenos Aires, Argentina

DISTRITO TECNOLÓGICO

This part of the neighborhood has been converted into a center for all tech-related items. This southern area is perfectly situated for business thanks to its easy access. The subway line (H), the Metrobús bus system, and direct access from a major highway connect it to the port and Ezeiza International Airport. The district has clear boundaries, marked by avenues and streets. Parque de los Patricios has entirely transformed since its establishment. Today, over 450 companies call it home, employing more than 23,000 people (including many who work remotely or combine home and office). This tech hub is a business activity hive, bringing new energy to the neighborhood.

As of the writing of this book, you can visit Distrito Tecnológico at any time during your trip. However, please make sure to double-check the opening hours online should there be any slight changes to their schedule.

TEATRO COLÓN'S PRODUCTION WORKSHOPS

The amazing costumes and sets for the opera house are made here. The Teatro Colón is a self-contained production studio thanks to its creative workshops. These workshops are vital as they make everything for the theater put on a show, from curtains to set designs. The workshops are dedicated areas for set-painting, creating special effects, and recording and video production facilities. All this hard work by skilled craftspeople helps create Teatro Colón's famous acoustic quality.

As of the writing of this book, the opening hours are Friday to Sunday from 12 pm to 6 pm, and is closed from Monday to Thursday. However, please make sure to double-check the opening hours online should there be any slight changes to their schedule.

Address: Av. Don Pedro de Mendoza 2163, C1169AAF Cdad. Autónoma de Buenos Aires, Argentina

TRANSPORT OPTIONS

- *Buses*
- *Taxi*
- *Subway*
- *Bikes*
- *Walking*

EXPERIENCES

Explore Tecnópolis, enjoy cultural events, taste traditional Argentine cuisine, and join local festivals celebrating culture, music, and food.

Tecnópolis

Tecnópolis is a giant, family-friendly, interactive theme park with exhibitions on science, math, history, art, and technology. You can explore displays about dinosaurs, cows, and famous artists such as Leonardo Da Vinci and watch 180-degree films of several genres. You can also watch musical performances, kids' shows, and a lot of other fun activities. Tecnópolis is open from May to November, so it is worth a visit if you are in Buenos Aires during that time. The place is safe for children, has free parking, and is free to enter with affordable food options.

Tecnópolis.[25]

Address: B1603 Villa Martelli, Buenos Aires Province, Argentina

CASA DE GOBIERNO

Also known as Casa Rosada or the Presidential Palace, Casa De Gobierno is a historic building in Buenos Aires famous for its bright pink color. The vivid pink color is a symbol of the efforts to unite opposing political groups. Some say the color came from combining white paint with cow blood. The president's offices are located there, although that is not where they currently live. There are free guided tours to the place on weekends, but they must be booked online in advance.

Casa De Gobierno.[26]

Address: Balcarce 78, C1064 Cdad. Autónoma de Buenos Aires, Argentina

WHERE TO EAT

LAS FAMILIAS (BAR AND GRILL)

Las Familias is a family-friendly bar and grill in Buenos Aires, Argentina. It is known for offering generous portions and delicious food. The restaurant is air-conditioned and super clean, from the toilets to the dining room. People go to try their tasty sandwiches. The best one is the Milanese sandwich on gourmet bread with potato wedges. It also has good coffee that you can enjoy after your meal.

Opening Hours: 07:00 am to 10:00 pm every day.

Contact Details: +54 11 4911-9224.

Address: AAV, Av. Caseros 2802, C1264 Buenos Aires, Argentina

PIZZERÍA EL GLOBITO (PIZZA RESTAURANT)

Pizzería El Globito is located near the Park of the Patricios, the Sanctuary of Saint Anthony of Padua, and the Office Museum of Dr. Genaro Giacobini. You can enjoy a pizza there after a day full of tours. Apart from pizza, they also serve calzones, focaccia, cakes, and all kinds of flatbreads. The place is clean and has friendly and pleasant service. It is a great place to enjoy lunch and cold beer with friends.

Opening Hours: 08:00 am to 12:00 am every day.

Contact Details: +54 11 4943-3680.

Address: Av. Caseros 3015, C1264 AAK, Cdad. Autónoma de Buenos Aires, Argentina

LAS MELLIS (RESTAURANT)

Las Mellis is a small place that serves homemade Argentinean food. They offer daily lunch specials that are always delicious and affordable. This is the place to go if you are craving an authentic Argentine food experience without the typical tourist vibe. Football fans will especially love this place as there are two signed Messi t-shirts from when he visited the place.

Opening Hours: 08:00 am to 10:00 pm from Monday to Saturday and 10:00 am to 03:00 pm on Sunday.

Address: La Rioja 1928, C1244ABP, C1244 ABP, Cdad. Autónoma de Buenos Aires, Argentina

PLACES TO SHOP

FERIA PARQUE PATRICIOS (HANDICRAFT FAIR)

Feria Parque Patricios is a lively market in Buenos Aires. Many stalls sell everything from clothes to toys to crafts, home décor, and cosmetics. It is a great place to wander around and discover unique finds to buy. You will find new and second-hand items, including some cool vintage jewelry. It is a family-friendly place; there is food, cafés, and games for kids. The only downside is that prices may be a bit high, and some stalls don't let you try on clothes or accept debit cards. However, overall, it is a fun place to explore and spend your day in.

Opening Hours: 10:00 am to 08:00 pm on Saturday and Sunday.

Address: Av. Caseros 3063, C1437 Cdad. Autónoma de Buenos Aires, Argentina

PATRICIOS INDUMENTARIA (CLOTHING SHOP)

Patricios Indumentaria is a clothing store in Buenos Aires known for its great quality, customer service, and friendly staff. They have a wide selection of high-quality, comfortable clothes for both men and women. You will find trendy outfits as well as classic pieces. The store is well-organized with everything in good condition. If you are looking to shop for clothes at affordable prices, Patricios Indumentaria is a place you can't miss going to.

Opening Hours: 10:00 am to 08:00 pm from Monday to Saturday and closed on Sunday.

Address: La Rioja 2185 La Rioja 2154, La Rioja 2111, 1437 Buenos Aires, Argentina

NUEVA CASA JAPONESA (JAPANESE GROCERY STORE)

Nueva Casa Japonesa is a grocery store and restaurant with a Japanese menu. Whether you are craving authentic Japanese food like ramen, sushi, udon, or teriyaki chicken or looking for fresh Japanese ingredients from the attached supermarket to cook with at home, kitchen gadgets, or home goods, this is the place for you. The place has a great vibe, tasty food, and delicious portions. The dining area is spacious and relaxed. The staff is friendly and helpful, but there is a self-service option if you are in a rush.

Opening Hours: 10:00 am to 07:00 pm from Tuesday to Sunday and closed on Monday.

Address: Humberto 1º 2357, C1229 Cdad. Autónoma de Buenos Aires, Argentina

HERBALIFE PARQUE PATRICIOS

Herbalife Parque Patricios is a health and wellness-focused store in Buenos Aires. They offer a variety of products to help you sustain a healthier lifestyle. There is a range of nutritional supplements, protein shakes, and energy drinks. The staff is friendly and knowledgeable and can help recommend the right products based on your needs, whether maintaining or losing weight or improving your fitness and overall health.

Opening Hours: 8:00 am to 7:00 pm from Monday to Saturday and closed on Sunday.

Address: Av. Entre Ríos 2183, C1133 Cdad. Autónoma de Buenos Aires, Argentina

ACCOMMODATIONS

POSADA GOTAN

Posada Gotan is a small hostel managed by the family of the original homeowners, Thibaud and Gabriela. The house is a bed and breakfast built in the 1890s. It is near Plaza Martin Fierro Square, The Obelisk of Buenos Aires, and one of Buenos Aires' top attractions: Bosques de Palermo. The accommodation has free Wi-Fi, a parking garage, a coffee house, and air conditioning. It is a great place to stay with kids because it has an indoor play area, board games and puzzles, and babysitting services for an extra charge. To have a nice dinner at the end of the day, you can go to the restaurants close by, such as San Miguel, El Motivo, and Bier Welt. Guests love the hosts' kindness and attention and the overall cleanliness of the place.

Contact Details: +54 11 6356-3346.

Address: Sánchez de Loria 1618, C1241 Cdad. Autónoma de Buenos Aires, Argentina.

CASA BOEDO

Casa Boedo is a bed and breakfast homestay in a convenient location near Palacio Barolo, General Urquiza, Boedo metro stations, and Once Railway train station. Top attractions like Centro Cultural Kirchner, Plaza de Mayo Square, and Flores y Plantas Loft are nearby. The rooms have a CD player, DVD player, cable channels, and Netflix streaming service. The rooms are non-smoking with free Wi-Fi and air-conditioning, but there is a designated smoking area. For safety and security, the place is equipped with fire extinguishers, smoke alarms, and security alarms. If you need help with transportation, ask the staff. They are helpful and will tell you how to get to places and teach you how to use the bus and subway. The place is adult-only, so don't book it if your kids are with you.

Contact Details: +54 11 2480-0801.

Address: Virrey Liniers 1043, C1220AAK Cdad. Autónoma de Buenos Aires, Argentina.

ANDIAMO GUEST HOUSE

Andiamo Guest House has beautiful garden views, a fitness center, an open-air bath, barbecue facilities, and a shared lounge. It is near Palermo Woods, Buenos Aires Japanese Gardens, and the National Museum of Fine Arts. The shared kitchen has a coffee machine, cleaning products, a microwave, and a fridge. The interior décor has stylish details like house plants and colorful paintings. The walls are painted with vibrant colors like purple and orange. To enjoy a delicious lunch or dinner, you can go to nearby restaurants like Pizzeria Los Patricios, Honest Food, and Los Corrales.

Contact Details: +54 11 2765-0007.

Address: Arriola 268, C1437FAF Cdad. Autónoma de Buenos Aires, Argentina.

HOTEL GUADALUPE

Hotel Guadalupe is a well-maintained, clean, and affordable option to stay in when you are visiting Buenos Aires. It has private rooms with a TV in each one. If you have a car, there is a paid garage nearby.

Contact Details: +54 11 4306-9773.

Address: Av. Entre Ríos 2083, C1133 Cdad. Autónoma de Buenos Aires, Argentina.

NUEVA POMPEYA DISTRICT

Nueva Pompeya, often nicknamed Pompeya, is a working-class neighborhood in southern Buenos Aires, bubbling with tango history. While historians debate the founding location of Buenos Aires, some believe it might have been near the Penna and Churruca Hospitals, across the bridge from modern-day Pompeya. Back then, the land where Pompeya sits now was flood-prone and remained under government control for a long time. Eventually, the land was acquired by Bartolomé Burgos, who gave his name to a crucial crossing point over the Riachuelo River. This crossing became essential because it was one of the few easy ways to cross the river. Populated with only a few houses, Pompeya rose in importance due to the crossing, making it a key spot for people and goods traveling from the south.

PARROQUIA NUESTRA SENORA DE POMPEYA

The Parroquia Nuestra Senora de Pompeya is a place of worship dedicated to the Virgin Mary, where people pray and connect with their faith. It was founded by Italian priest Darío Broggi, who placed it under the patronage of Our Lady of the Rosary. The church was later blessed by the Archbishop of Buenos Aires, Monsignor Uladislao Castellano.

The Parroquia Nuestra Senora de Pompeya.[27]

As of the writing of this book, the opening hours are every day from 7:30 am to 11:45 am and from 3 pm to 7 pm. However, please make sure to double-check the opening hours online should there be any slight changes to their schedule.

Address: 974, JPB, Esquiú, C1437 Cdad. Autónoma de Buenos Aires, Argentina

EL PUENTE ALSINA

The Alsina Bridge is one way to get from one place to another in Buenos Aires. Originally called the Uriburu Bridge and built in 1938, it stretches across the Riachuelo River. It connects the Nueva Pompeya neighborhood with the Valentín Alsina city. The Alsina Bridge is a significant landmark for residents and visitors with its neo-colonial architecture. It's seen Buenos Aires change over time and is still a strong passageway for countless people every day. Everyone who crosses it carries their stories, both old and new.

El Puente Alsina.[28]

As of the writing of this book, you can visit El Puente Alsina at any time during your trip. However, please make sure to double-check the opening hours online should there be any slight changes to their schedule.

Address: Av. Sáenz, C1437 Cdad. Autónoma de Buenos Aires, Argentina

TRANSPORT OPTIONS

- *Taxi*
- *Subway*
- *Bikes*
- *Buses*

EXPERIENCES

Visit cultural centers, workshops, tango shows, outdoor activities like picnics, walking tours, and local festivals.

MUSEO PORTEÑO LO DE GUSTAVO

Museo Porteño Lo de Gustavo is a unique place to visit in Buenos Aires, especially if you love nostalgia. Lo de Gustavo is not your typical museum, it is packed with a rare collection of items from the past that take you back in time, reflecting Buenos Aires' life and culture. You will find old pieces like vintage cars and toys to cigarette boxes from different eras. It is a two-story house, with objects filling every corner. Gustavo, the guide, adds a personal touch to guests by sharing interesting anecdotes and stories of his collections. If you are in the area, Museo Porteño Lo de Gustavo is definitely worth a visit.

Address: Corrales 1862, C1437GLP Cdad. Autónoma de Buenos Aires, Argentina

WHERE TO EAT

ESQUINA POMPEYA RESTAURANT BAR

Esquina Pompeya Restaurant Bar is a comfortable, clean place to eat impeccable food at affordable prices. It is known for having the freshest ingredients and fast service. If you are planning to go, you have to try their gnocchi and Neapolitan with fries.

Opening Hours: 06:00 am to 05:00 pm from Monday to Saturday and closed on Sunday.

Contact Details: +54 11 2857-9746.

Address: Av. Gral. Francisco Fernández de la Cruz 1100, C1437 Cdad. Autónoma de Buenos Aires, Argentina

MANCORA RESTAURANT

Mancora is a Peruvian restaurant in Buenos Aires that serves hearty and delicious meals. It is a family-friendly place where you can enjoy generous portions and fast and attentive service. They serve many traditional Peruvian dishes, such as chaufa (fried rice), Milanesa de Mancora (meat, eggs, and breadcrumbs), and their popular conga trembles. The good thing is their prices are good for the amount of food you get. The restaurant might be a bit old, and the bathrooms need a little work, but the excellent food and service make up for it.

Opening Hours: 12:00 pm to 12:00 am from Monday to Saturday, 12:00 pm to 11:00 pm on Sunday, and closed on Tuesday.

Contact Details: +54 11 2108-3204.

Address: Av. Sáenz 611, C1437 Cdad. Autónoma de Buenos Aires, Argentina

EL RINCÓN DE MORENA (FAST FOOD RESTAURANT)

El Rincón de Morena is a fast-food restaurant where you can enjoy a casual meal with friends. It is a cozy place with purple-painted walls that give an edgy vibe. The prices are good, and the service is excellent. Customers particularly love the attention given to them by the staff.

Opening Hours: 11:00 am to 10:00 pm from Monday to Saturday and 08:00 pm to 10:30 pm on Sunday.

Contact Details: +54 11 4919-4648.

Address: Abraham J. Luppi 941, C1437 FRA, Cdad. Autónoma de Buenos Aires, Argentina

PLACES TO SHOP

PASEO DE COMPRAS SAENZ (SHOPPING MALL).

Paseo de Compras Saenz, also known as Paseo Gran Pompeya, is a shopping mall in Buenos Aires with plenty of stores. You will find the latest fashion trends in shoes and clothes, such as jeans, hoodies, skirts, pants, and dresses. You will also find places to buy small gifts like caps or jewelry for your friends and family. There are also nail salons to pamper yourself, watch stores, and swimwear shops.

Opening Hours: 10:00 am to 08:00 pm from Monday to Saturday and 10:00 am to 2:00 pm on Sunday.

Address: C1437 Buenos Aires, Argentina

GALERIA GUARANI (SHOPPING MALL)

Galeria Guarani is a shopping mall in Buenos Aires with multiple shops you can explore and wander around while enjoying your evening. You will find everything you need, from men's to women's to babies' clothes, jewelry stores, and beauty salons at reasonable prices. Customers like its convenient, commercial location near the Bompie sports venue and the Nuestra Senora de Pompeya church.

Opening Hours: 10:00 am to 07:00 pm from Monday to Saturday and closed on Sunday.

Address: Av. Sáenz 1075, C1437 DOC, Cdad. Autónoma de Buenos Aires, Argentina

ROLLER CLUB DE NUEVA POMPEYA (GROCERY STORE)

Roller Club de Nueva Pompeya is a small supermarket that sells everyday products. It is convenient for grocery shopping because of its affordable prices and good selection of fresh produce. The store is known for its friendly staff and welcoming atmosphere.

Opening Hours: 09:00 am to 12:30 pm every day.

Address: FLA, C. Carlos M. Ramirez 815, C1437 C1437FLA, Cdad. Autónoma de Buenos Aires, Argentina

BAYRESSHOP (CLOTHING STORE)

Bayersshop is a popular clothing store in Buenos Aires known for its affordable prices. It has a rare same-day delivery service that most stores in Argentina don't offer. The clothes aren't high-end or luxurious, but they are comfortable and ideal for running errands or casual outings. They have everything from jackets to t-shirts, swimsuits, and even slippers. Customers go for the good prices, quality, and vibes. They also love the service as the staff is friendly and helpful.

Opening Hours: 10:00 am to 07:00 pm from Monday to Saturday and closed on Sunday.

Address: Av. Sáenz 1168, C1437 Cdad. Autónoma de Buenos Aires, Argentina

ACCOMMODATIONS

HOTEL SAN CARLOS

Hotel San Carlos is a great accommodation in Buenos Aires located near Miserere Square, the Museum of Latin American Art of Buenos Aires (MALBA), and the Obelisk of Buenos Aires. The hotel's services include but are not limited to a 24-hour front desk service, concierge service, laundry service, wake-up service, and tourist information service. The rooms have free Wi-Fi, a flat-screen TV, cable channels, showers, a clothes rack, and a plug near the bed for convenience. Outside, there is a patio, dining area, and a yard. Smoking is not allowed anywhere in the hotel, but the place is pet-friendly, so you can bring your cat or dog if you have one.

Contact Details: +54 11 4049-8345.

Address: Moreno 3054, C1209ABF Cdad. Autónoma de Buenos Aires, Argentina.

HOTEL MINERVA

Hotel Minerva in Buenos Aires is near Tortoni Café, Flores y Plantas Loft, and Plaza de Mayo Square. It has family rooms, daily housekeeping, a security alarm, smoke alarms, and a designated smoking area. Outdoor, there is furniture, a sun terrace, and a garden to enjoy the breeze of air and the view. The hotel is surrounded by Rissollo, La Tranquera, and Momentos de Azúcar restaurants, where you can enjoy lunch or dinner. Many public transport options are nearby, such as San José and Independencia (E) metro stations, Constitución Railway, and Once train stations.

Contact Details: +54 11 4305-0682.

Address: Carlos Calvo 1434 1102, C1102ABD Cdad. Autónoma de Buenos Aires, Argentina.

HOTEL JARDIN DE BUENOS AIRES

Hotel Jardin de Buenos Aires is where you need to stay if you are looking for a comfortable and quiet place. The entrance and decorations are pleasant and welcoming. It is located in a great area, a few blocks away from shopping and clothing stores. The rooms are spacious and clean. The staff is friendly and responds to the guests' needs. The hotel has made several improvements over the years, and the price is reasonable for the quality of service guests receive.

Contact Details: +54 11 4931-7530

Address: Catamarca 985, C1231 AAI, Cdad. Autónoma de Buenos Aires, Argentina.

CHAPTER

5 EASTERN BUENOS AIRES

Are you up for epic waterfront views? Then, book a ticket to the eastern part of Buenos Aires. Like the northern and southern parts, the districts in this part of the city combine liveliness and coziness, providing a place to relax and breathe. It's where you can lose yourself for hours, wandering down tree-lined streets and soaking in the atmosphere. You'll come across Recoleta, an elegant neighborhood with Paris-style houses traveling further east. The district features grand old buildings side by side with great boutiques and upscale restaurants. Recoleta Cemetery is one reason the eastern axes are famous, where visitors from across the nation and outside pay their respects to some of Argentina's most influential figures.

These eastern districts are some of the best for tourists and business travelers, with a range of restaurants scattered across the district, sleek skyscrapers with international tenants and expensive apartments, fascinating museums, and antique stores. This chapter explores life in Buenos Aires' eastern districts: Puerto Madero, Retiro, Recoleta, and San Telmo.

PUERTO MADERO DISTRICT

Puerto Madero, a neighborhood in Buenos Aires' Central Business District, is called the Puerto Madero Waterfront by those in the urban planning sector. The district, which takes up a large area of the Río de la Plata riverside, is home to several tall skyscrapers and opulent hotels featuring the newest architectural styles. It is the barrio with the highest property prices. However, before the city became popular, it was a port initially. Puerto Madero is one of the few cities that went through a successful reinvention. Argentina's government entrusted businessman Eduardo Madero with building a new, modern port to address the limitations of the existing one in 1882. After his efforts, several plans were proposed throughout the 20th century to demolish or refurbish it through urbanization. Today, the neighborhood is one of the most visited tourist centers in Buenos Aires.

Did You Know?

The Puerto Madero streets are named after women paying homage to the women who planted their footprints in the sands of time throughout Argentina's history.

MAIN ATTRACTIONS

PUENTE DE LA MUJER

The Puente de la Mujer, Spanish for "Woman's Bridge," was designed by architect Santiago Calatrava. It is mainly constructed of steel and reinforced concrete. It is a rotating footbridge, making this bridge a feature that stands out. The bridge's design is a testament to how Buenos Aires embraces modern and innovative architecture alongside its historic masterpieces. The bridge has one tall pole and cables holding up part of it that opens to let boats pass underneath. When it swings open, the end of the bridge rests on a support to hold it steady, so it also functions as a swing bridge.

Puente de la Mujer.[29]

As of the writing of this book, you can visit Puente de la Mujer at any time during your trip. However, please double-check the opening hours online should there be any slight changes to their schedule.

Address: GORRITI JUANA MANUELA 900, C1107 Cdad. Autónoma de Buenos Aires, Argentina

RESERVA ECOLÓGICA COSTANERA SUR

The Reserva Ecológica Costanera Sur is one area nature lovers can visit for the love of green spaces and nature walks. You could spend hours here relaxing with your loved ones. The Costanera Sur is the most extensive biodiverse area in which to appreciate nature and walk along paths to the river. Although close to the busy city, the area epitomizes calm and peace. You'll love this place if you love nature and animals, as there are over 2,000 plant and animal species.

The Reserva Ecológica Costanera Sur.[30]

As of the writing of this book, the opening hours are Tuesday to Sunday from 8 am to 5:30 pm and closed on Monday. However, please make sure to double-check the opening hours online should there be any slight changes to their schedule.

Address: Av. Dr. Tristán Achával Rodríguez 1550, C1768 Cdad. Autónoma de Buenos Aires, Argentina

MUSEO FRAGATA SARMIENTO

What used to be a training ship for the Argentine Navy centuries ago is now a museum ship. The frigate was first launched in 1897 and named in honor of President Domino Faustino Sarmiento, who founded the Argentine Navy Academy. For decades, the ship carried out over 30 trips outside of Argentina. During the late 1900s, it became a historic monument.

Museo Fragata Sarmiento.[31]

As of the writing of this book, the opening hours are as follows:

- *Thursday and Friday from 1 pm to 7 pm*
- *Saturday and Sunday from 10 am to 7 pm*
- *Closed from Monday to Wednesday*

However, please make sure to double-check the opening hours online should there be any slight changes to their schedule.

Address: Darsena 3, Av. Alicia Moreau de Justo 900, C1107AAT Cdad. Autónoma de Buenos Aires, Argentina

TRANSPORT OPTIONS

- *Buses*
- *Taxi*
- *Cabs*

EXPERIENCES

Visit the bridge by a guided tour, explore the environs, the sea, the ports, etc.

FUENTE DE LAS NEREIDAS (FOUNTAIN)

Fuente de Las Nereidas is a huge marble fountain at the end of Costanera Sur, near Rio de la Plata in Buenos Aires. The fountain was created in 1903 by an Argentine female sculptor, Dolores Mora de Hernández, famous by Lola Mora. It portrays a scene from Greek Mythology where the sea goddess Venus sits on a seashell surrounded by nymphs, tritons, and horses. Nymphs are the nature goddesses, and tritons are half-human, half-fish male sea creatures that look like mermaids. If you are a fan of Greek mythology and sculptures, you will love to marvel at this captivating piece of art.

Fuente de Las Nereidas.[32]

Address: Av. Dr. Tristán Achával Rodríguez 1401, C1107 Cdad. Autónoma de Buenos Aires, Argentina

COLECCIÓN DE ARTE AMALIA LACROZE DE FORTABAT (MUSEUM)

Amalia Lacroze from Fortabat Art Collection is a private art collection in Puerto Madero that is considered a hidden gem. It has a mixture of Argentine and international art. You will find works by top artists like Andy Warhol, Marc Chagall, Rodin, and many other renowned artists. The museum is in a modern building and the collection takes up several floors. If you are an art lover, you will love this place, especially since it is not as touristy as other similar places.

Colección de Arte Amalia Lacroze de Fortabat.[33]

Opening Hours: 12:00 pm to 8:00 pm from Thursday to Sunday.

Address: Olga Cossettini 141, C1107 Autonomous City of Buenos Aires, Argentina

MICAELA BASTIDAS PARK

Micaela Bastidas is a lovely outdoor space where you can relax with friends or family. It is a spacious, open space, modern, with lots of greenery and red flowers. It is a great place for walking, jogging, or just winding down. The park is pet-friendly, and you will find several food trucks around to grab a snack or drink. Kids can enjoy biking, rollerblading, or taking photos of the beautiful surroundings.

Address: Julieta Lanteri 1506, C1106 Puerto Madero, Autonomous City of Buenos Aires, Argentina

WHERE TO EAT

PUERTO CRISTAL (FINE DINING RESTAURANT)

Puerto Cristal is a top fine dining restaurant in Buenos Aires. It is popular for its delicious food, Mediterranean dishes, and classic Argentine cuts of meat. The menu offers gluten-free and vegetarian options to suit all kinds of dietary preferences. Their dishes include steak or fish with potatoes, octopus, smoked salmon, clams, and pasta. For dessert, they have a chocolate brownie topped with vanilla ice cream and strawberries to die for. Their menu is available in English, Spanish, Portuguese, and Braille. They have an impressive wine list and excellent service. The interior is fancy and romantic, with glass windows overlooking the beautiful view of the city.

Opening Hours: 12:30 pm to 12:00 am every day.

Contact Details: +34 648 12 03 24.

Address: Av. Alicia Moreau de Justo 1082, C1107AAV Cdad. Autónoma de Buenos Aires, Argentina

RODIZIO PUERTO MADERO (RESTAURANT)

Rodizio Puerto Madero is a steakhouse that serves barbecue and Argentinean cuisine. It has a salad bar that contains smoked salmon and Salad Rousse, starters such as empanadas, several cuts of meats for the main course, and dessert. They also have a selection of fine wines to go with the meat. The interior is fancy yet cozy, with outdoor or indoor seating options. It is the perfect place for a date. Parking and valet services are available, and a wheelchair is accessible if needed.

Opening Hours: 12:00 pm to 01:00 am from Sunday to Thursday and 12:00 pm to 02:00 am on Friday and Saturday.

Contact Details: +54 11 4334-3638.

Address: Av. Alicia Moreau de Justo 838, C1107 Cdad. Autónoma de Buenos Aires, Argentina

LA PAROLACCIA TRATTORIA (ITALIAN RESTAURANT)

La Parolaccia Trattoria is the perfect Italian restaurant for anyone craving authentic pasta. The ambiance is warm and intimate, with soft lighting giving a romantic atmosphere to the place. It is the perfect spot for a special date night with your partner. The tables are covered with a white tablecloth with a single red flower in the center. The menu includes shrimp avocado salad, red sauce pasta with clams or meatballs, fried clams, Tortellini pasta with a white, creamy, rich sauce, and homemade lasagna. Their top dessert is the flan, garnished with fruits like blackberries and strawberries.

Opening Hours: 12:00 pm to 12:00 am from Sunday to Thursday and 12:00 pm to 01:00 am on Friday and Saturday.

Contact Details: +54 11 4343-1679.

Address: Av. Alicia Moreau de Justo 1052, C1107AAV Cdad. Autónoma de Buenos Aires, Argentina

GIUSEPPE RESTAURANTE (ITALIAN RESTAURANT)

Giuseppe Restaurante is an Italian restaurant that serves amazing food at affordable prices. Their pizza is delicious; some even say it is the best pizza they've tried in Buenos Aires! Guests describe the waiters as passionate, attentive, and always happy to help. The place is chic, with outdoor and indoor seating options with outdoor tables viewing the river.

Opening Hours: 12:00 pm to 01:00 am from Monday to Thursday and 12:00 pm to 02:00 am from Friday to Sunday.

Contact Details: +54 11 4313-7023.

Address: Olga Cossettini 1011, C1107 Cdad. Autónoma de Buenos Aires, Argentina

PLACES TO SHOP

I LOVE GIFTS

I Love Gifts is a gift shop with plenty of items to choose from as Argentine souvenirs for your friends or family back home. It has magnets, pins, postcards, and keychains.

Opening Hours: 10:00 am to 09:00 pm every day.

Address: Av. Corrientes 1444, C1043 Cdad. Autónoma de Buenos Aires, Argentina

R & B MAXI STORE

R & B Maxi Store is a beverage distributor in the heart of Puerto Madero. They have a wide variety of beverages, and they offer customized drinks based on your needs and preferences. Don't hesitate to ask the staff for help because they value customer satisfaction and will assist in the best way they can.

Opening Hours: 09:00 am to 12:00 am from Monday to Thursday and 09:00 am to 06:00 am from Friday to Sunday.

Address: Juana Manso 1133, C1107 Cdad. Autónoma de Buenos Aires, Argentina

LAURENTTINO

Laurentino is a clothing store that sells men's casual wear, such as everyday T-shirts, jeans, sweatpants, and hoodies. You will also find accessories like caps and belts.

Opening Hours: 09:30 am to 07:30 pm from Monday to Saturday and closed on Sunday.

Address: Av. Alicia Moreau de Justo 1150, C1107AAX, C1107 AAX, Cdad. Autónoma de Buenos Aires, Argentina

BLISTER PACK

Blister Pack is a shopping mall in Buenos Aires with an impressive selection of stores where you can spend your day browsing and shopping for all kinds of products. It has stylish, up to date options at competitive prices with good deals. They also have excellent customer service with responsive staff.

Opening Hours: 10:00 am to 05:00 pm from Monday to Friday and closed on Saturday and Sunday.

Address: Juana Manso 1746, C1107 Cdad. Autónoma de Buenos Aires, Argentina

ACCOMMODATIONS

BELIEVE MADERO HOTEL

Believe Madero Hotel is a modern and luxurious hotel in Buenos Aires, near La Manzana de Las Luces, Fragata Presidente Sarmiento Museum Ship, and Museo de Arte Moderno de Buenos Aires. The hotel has a 24-hour reception service, concierge service, wake-up service, and shuttle service with an additional charge. The rooms have amazing panoramic views of the city and the waterfront. They are provided with a flat-screen TV, cable channels, a minibar, air conditioning, and a private bathroom with towels, free toiletries, and a hairdryer. The breakfast buffet opens from 7:00 am to 11:00 am. They have coffee, fresh juices, cold cuts such as roast beef and salami, scrambled eggs, multiple types of bread, cereal, and seasonal fruits.

Contact Details: +54 11 7090-2584.

Address: Chile 80, C1011 Cdad. Autónoma de Buenos Aires, Argentina.

MODERN APARTMENTS IN PUERTO MADERO

If you are looking for a comfortable and chic stay in Buenos Aires, Modern Apartments in Puerto Madero is the place to go. The apartments have stunning views, featuring an outdoor swimming pool and a beautiful garden full of colorful flowers. It is only a short distance from Museo Penitenciario Antonio Ballve, Fragata Presidente Sarmiento Museum, and ARA Presidente Sarmiento Museum Ship. Each apartment has air conditioning, free Wi-Fi, a cozy seating area, a drying rack for clothing, a flat-screen TV with streaming services like Netflix, a mosquito net, and a socket near the bed for convenience. The kitchen has a stovetop, oven, toaster, coffee machine, microwave, and cleaning products. The rooms are soundproof and non-smoking. The restaurants nearby are Red Resto & Lounge, Stud Emma B, and Starbucks Café.

Contact Details: +54 11 3683-5472.

Address: Aimé Painé 1635, C1107 Cdad. Autónoma de Buenos Aires, Argentina.

HOTEL MADERO

Hotel Madero is the place to receive world-class service in Buenos Aires. The rooms are bright, spacious, clean, elegant, and chic. They have a minibar, snack bar, heating, and air conditioning. The hotel thought about everything: allergy-free rooms for affected people. A breakfast buffet with pastries, cereals, fresh fruits, and healthy options is available every morning. For entertainment, The White Bar serves customized cocktails based on your preferences, a billiards table to compete with your friends or partner, and meals you can eat on the terrace. There is a spa on the rooftop where you can see panoramic city views and enjoy a sauna or a hot tub. You can also treat yourself to a massage for an additional charge. Hotel Madero is near Plaza de los Trabajadores, Costanera Sur Ecological Reserve, and Buenos Aires Japanese Gardens. Although restaurants nearby are Olga Bar and Steakhouse, and Starbucks, you won't need them because the food at the hotel is excellent and prepared by professional Chef Alejandro Bontempo.

Contact Details: +54 11 5776-7777.

Address: Dique 2, Rosario Vera Peñaloza 360, C1107CLA Cdad. Autónoma de Buenos Aires, Argentina.

RIBERA SUR HOTEL

Ribera Sur Hotel is a warm and charming place to stay in Buenos Aires, where the staff is friendly and works hard to make guests feel at home. The rooms, furnished with stylish furniture, have either twin or king-sized beds. They are equipped with air-conditioning, free internet, a minibar, a flat-screen TV with cable and pay-per-view channels, and a private bathroom with towels, a bidet, and slippers. They also offer wine and champagne at an additional charge. The rooms are non-smoking, but there is a designated smoking area. The restaurants and cafés nearby are Ninas, Café Bar, and Starbucks. The hotel is near top attractions like Museo de Arte Moderno de Buenos Aires, Plaza de los Trabajadores, Plaza de los Trabajadores, and Buenos Aires Japanese Gardens.

Contact Details: +54 11 5031-4516.

Address: Av. Paseo Colón 1145, C1063ACL Cdad. Autónoma de Buenos Aires, Argentina.

RECOLETA DISTRICT

The district derives its name from the Recollect Convent dedicated to Nuestra Señora del Pilar, established in the early 18th century, which included a church and cemetery. The Recoleta pathway in the center of the neighborhood attracted wealthy families escaping the yellow fever outbreak in the late 19th century, leading to its reputation as one of Buenos Aires' most affluent areas. After the Church of Nuestra Señora del Pilar's completion in 1732, it became a historical focal point, sometimes referred to as El Pilar. This transformation in the neighborhood led to the rise of private mansions, embassies, and luxury hotels, like the Alvear Palace Hotel.

CEMENTERIO DE LA RECOLETA

The Recoleta cemetery is considered one of the most unusual cemeteries in the world, making it a tourist attraction for visitors from within and outside the country. The cemetery covers about 14 acres, and over 4,600 vaults and mausoleums are built above ground, which are no ordinary burial plots. The architectural designs of the mausoleums are extraordinary. Egyptian pyramids stand shoulder-to-shoulder with Gothic cathedrals, and you can see each family's wealth and social standing by looking at their tombs. Over 90 remarkable structures are considered National Historical Monuments, ensuring their preservation for generations. This cemetery is the final resting place of some of Argentina's notable figures. The most visited tomb is undoubtedly Eva Perón's, one of Argentina's first ladies whose life and legacy continue to captivate the nation.

As of the writing of this book, the opening hours are every day from 9 am to 5 pm. However, please make sure to double-check the opening hours online should there be any slight changes to their schedule.

Address: Junín 1760, C1113 Cdad. Autónoma de Buenos Aires, Argentina

MUSEO NACIONAL DE BELLAS ARTES

The museum houses an impressive Argentine and international art collection, showcasing the country's artistic strength and role in the global art scene. The National Museum of Fine Arts has moved a few times since it opened in 1895. Now it's in a building previously a water station. You can find famous works by Argentine artists alongside pieces by artists like Picasso and Van Gogh. Entrance to the museum is free, so it's a great place to visit for art lovers in Buenos Aires.

Museo Nacional de Bellas Artes.[34]

As of the writing of this book, the opening hours are as follows:

- *Tuesday to Friday from 11 am to 7:30 pm*
- *Saturday and Sunday from 10 am to 7:30 pm*
- *Closed on Monday*

However, please make sure to double-check the opening hours online should there be any slight changes to their schedule.

Address: Av. del Libertador 1473, C1425 Cdad. Autónoma de Buenos Aires, Argentina

FLORALIS GENÉRICA

A massive metallic sculpture of a giant moving metal flower that blooms daily. Argentine architect Eduardo Catalano gifted it to the city in 2002. The flower opens its petals around eight in the morning and closes them at sunset, like a real flower. The flower, over 100 feet wide when open, is made of shiny aluminum and reflects the city around it. The flower stays open all night on special dates like May 25 (May Day Revolution), December 24, September 21 (Spring Day), and December 31.

Floralis Genérica.[35]

Address: Av. Pres. Figueroa Alcorta 2301, C1425 Cdad. Autónoma de Buenos Aires, Argentina

TRANSPORT OPTIONS

- *Buses*
- *Subway*
- *Taxis*
- *Walking*

EXPERIENCES

The elegant cemetery with great architectural designs, museums, upscale shopping, and café culture.

BASILICA DE NUESTRA SENORA DEL PILAR (CHURCH)

Basilica of our Lady of the Pillar is a beautiful church right next to the Recoleta Cemetery in Buenos Aires. It has a bright white exterior and a tall tower that catches the eye. Although it might be smaller than other churches, its interior is impressive and has intricate details and unique side altars. It displays historical artifacts, some of which are more than one hundred years old. The church is surrounded by a nice park and cafés where you can stop for coffee and a warm pastry along the way. If you are a fan of history and architecture, this basilica is worth a visit if you are in Recoleta.

Basilica de Nuestra Senora Del Pilar.[36]

Opening Hours: 7:30 am to 10:00 pm Monday to Friday, 8:00 am to 10 pm Saturday to Sunday.

Contact Details: +54 11 4803-6793

Address: C1113AAV, Junín 1898, C1113 Autonomous City of Buenos Aires, Argentina

GOMERO DE LA RECOLETA

Gomero de la Recoleta is considered a historical landmark. It is a giant tree found outside the Recoleta Cemetery in Buenos Aires. The tree is over two centuries old. It has massive branches that stretch out wide. They are so heavy to the point where they are supported by iron and wooden jack posts, with one branch held up by a sculpture of Atlas, the Greek titan. It is a lovely spot to relax with surrounding cafés to take a break.

Address: C1112 Buenos Aires, Argentina

WHERE TO EAT

OVIEDO RESTAURANTE

Oviedo Restaurante is a Spanish restaurant that offers Mediterranean, European, and seafood dishes with vegan and gluten-free options to suit everyone's needs and preferences. Customers especially love their lamb, ceviche, strip loin steak, and Merluza Negra (hake fish). The interior decorations are classic, with leather sofas, wooden chairs, and white tablecloths on every table. Their top dessert is the dulce de leche pancakes. The service is excellent, and the staff is friendly and professional.

Opening Hours: 12:00 pm to 04:00 pm / 07:00 pm to 12:30 am from Tuesday to Sunday, closed on Monday.

Contact Details: +54 11 4822-5415.

Address: Beruti 2602, C1425BBD Cdad. Autónoma de Buenos Aires, Argentina

EL BURLADERO

El Burladero is a standout Spanish restaurant that offers Mediterranean, Basque, and Catalan dishes with vegetarian-friendly and gluten-free options to cater to everyone's needs. From the moment you arrive, every guest gets treated like a special VIP guest. The service is excellent; helpful, patient, and friendly. The restaurant has a warm, welcoming atmosphere that makes guests want to come back every time they are in the area. Customers love the tapas plate appetizer. If you are a fan of seafood, you can't miss the fried calamari and white anchovies. For a classic Spanish dish, the shellfish paella is a must-try with the pisco sour and reasonably priced wines.

Opening Hours: 12:00 pm to 04:00 pm / 07:30 pm to 12:00 am daily.

Contact Details: +54 11 3691-2717.

Address: Pres. José Evaristo Uriburu 1488, C1425AAN Cdad. Autónoma de Buenos Aires, Argentina

LA PAROLACCIA RECOLETA

La Parolaccia Recoleta is an Italian restaurant with casual yet classic vibes. The interior is classic, decorated with red leather chairs and white tablecloths on every table. The outdoor seating area has more casual furniture with chair cushions, throw pillows, and wide white umbrellas as a shade. Their best dishes are the red sauce pasta with clams, homemade lasagna, red sauce pasta with meatballs, pasta with shrimp, and shrimp avocado salad. Appetizers include the fresh pears with camembert and the burrata with prosciutto, two dishes you won't want to miss.

Opening Hours: 12:00 pm to 12:00 am from Sunday to Thursday and 12:00 pm to 01:00 am on Friday and Saturday.

Contact Details: +54 11 4804-0016.

Address: Pres. Roberto M. Ortiz 1865, C1113 Cdad. Autónoma de Buenos Aires, Argentina

RESTAURANTE MARCELO COCINA ITALIANA INTERSUR

Marcelo Italian Cuisine Intersur Recoleta is an authentic Italian restaurant inside the Intersur Recoleta Hotel. It serves delicious pizza bread, seafood dishes such as the Oysters Parmigiana or Black Cod with fish smoke and tomato grilled trout, tasty pasta dishes with shrimp, white clams, or baked zucchini, and creamy risottos with mushroom, chicken and leeks, or Jerez and ham. There are vegetarian and vegan options if needed. For dessert, the filled chocolate bomb is a treat you can't miss. Customers describe the service as efficient, friendly, and professional. The atmosphere of the restaurant is elegant and warm. Want to have a fancy date night at reasonable prices? Marcelo Italian Cuisine Intersur Recoleta is your go-to place. Don't forget to make a reservation before you go!

Opening Hours: 12:00 pm to 03:00 pm / 07:00 pm to 12:00 am daily.

Contact Details: +54 11 4804-0016.

Address: Av. Callao 1764, C1024 Cdad. Autónoma de Buenos Aires, Argentina

PLACES TO SHOP

RECOLETA URBAN MALL

Recoleta Urban Mall is a small shopping center located in a safe area across the street from the Loi Suites Recoleta Hotel and Recoleta Cemetery. There are multiple stores where you will find all kinds of things you need. The staff will help you with anything you ask, from directions to product prices. There are many restaurants and cafés nearby, like Starbucks.

Opening Hours: 10:00 am to 09:00 pm every day.

Address: Vicente López 2050, C1128 Cdad. Autónoma de Buenos Aires, Argentina

ROUSACCEL

Rousaccel in Buenos Aires is worth a visit if you are looking for a variety of things to do in the same place. It is well-organized with a good atmosphere and is ideal for a casual stroll and a little shopping. There are plenty of different venues to explore where you will find items on sale. There is a place that sells Venezuelan food that customers particularly like, where the owners are friendly and welcoming.

Opening Hours: 11:00 am to 07:30 pm from Monday to Saturday and closed on Sunday.

Address: Av. Sta. Fe 1714 LOCAL 10, C1060 Cdad. Autónoma de Buenos Aires, Argentina

GALERIAS SANTA FE

Open since 1953, Santa Fe Gallery is a shopping mall in Buenos Aires. It was a bustling spot with chic boutiques and art galleries, but now only a few businesses remain open. Despite this, Galerias Santa Fe still has an artistic appeal, with its highlight as the mural in the center of the gallery, including artworks by famous artists like Raúl Soldi. The place is worth a visit for its historical significance, but not too much for shopping. Don't miss El Ateneo Bookstore if you are in the area. It is just around the corner and is worth a visit to check out.

Opening Hours: 09:00 am to 08:00 pm from Monday to Saturday and closed on Sunday.

Address: Av. Sta. Fe 1660, C1021ABP Cdad. Autónoma de Buenos Aires, Argentina

GALLERY CONCORDE

Gallery Concorde is a shopping mall where you can have a nice walk and explore several stores at affordable prices. The place is neat and clean, as it is managed by owners who take good care of it and provide excellent service to customers. Despite the many closed stores, you will still find everything you are looking for.

Opening Hours: 10:00 am to 08:30 pm from Monday to Friday, 10:00 am to 03:00 pm on Saturday, and closed on Sunday.

Address: Av. Sta. Fe 1480, C1060 ABN, Cdad. Autónoma de Buenos Aires, Argentina

SPORTS AND LEISURE

GUIDED BIKE TOUR TO RECOLETA AND PALERMO

This bike tour is a 3.5-hour bike ride that starts in San Telmo, pedaling through Puerto Madero and then heading to Recoleta. You will pass by Barrio Parque, the Buenos Aires Zoo, the Polo Fields, The Galileo Galilei Planetarium, and the Botanical Garden. The tour guides are friendly and share stories of the city's history and architecture along the way. It is a fun way to explore the different districts of Buenos Aires while burning some calories! You will get a bike, helmet, and an optional chair for kids if you need one. For your safety, they provide you with water and medical support. However, hotel pickups or drop-offs, food, and drinks are not included in the tour. Participants must be at least 150 cm or 4'9" tall.

STAND UP CLUB

Stand Up Club is a comedy club that presents several comedy shows. Owned by comedian Kristof and actress Marina, this comedy club has an intimate atmosphere and international standards. It is a small yet comfortable place that will give you a little break from the hustle and bustle of the city. People who watched their shows say they didn't stop laughing from beginning to end! Looking for a good laugh and jokes to tell your friends back home? This club is your go-to.

Opening Hours: 9:00 pm to 12:00 am from Wednesday to Saturday.

Contact Details: +54 11 2394-7857

Address: Paraná 1021, C1018 Cdad. Autónoma de Buenos Aires, Argentina

ACCOMMODATIONS

UP RECOLETA HOTEL

Up Recoleta Hotel is a luxurious accommodation in Buenos Aires, located only 100 m from Libertador Avenue, 700 m from Plaza Francia Square, and 1.4 km from Buenos Aires Japanese Gardens. The hotel is very well-maintained by excellent room and concierge services. All the rooms have a private bath or shower, free toiletries, and a hairdryer. They also have a flat-screen TV with Netflix streaming service and satellite channels, a telephone, a clothes rack, and a socket near the bed. There is air conditioning, heating, and fire extinguishers in case of emergencies. The hotel's cleanliness and professionalism exceed guests' expectations. The place is non-smoking throughout and has allergy-free rooms available upon request. Restaurants and cafes nearby include Síntesis Tapas Asiáticas, Ferminao, and Starbucks.

Contact Details: +54 9 11 4495-2233.

Address: José León Pagano 2684, C1425 Cdad. Autónoma de Buenos Aires, Argentina.

SUMA RECOLETA HOTEL

SuMa Recoleta is a luxurious hotel in Buenos Aires with modern rooms. It is in the heart of Recoleta District, only 950 m away from the Recoleta Cemetery, 350 m away from Plazoleta Isidoro Ruiz Moreno, and 2.4 km away from the Museum of Latin American Art of Buenos Aires (MALBA). The rooms provide guests with a safety deposit box, free toiletries in the bathroom, a flat-screen TV with cable channels, a telephone, a minibar, and a closet. Guests love the hotel's breakfast as they serve fresh juices, several cereals and breads, scrambled eggs, and fresh fruits. The hotel also provides wake-up, concierge, and daily housekeeping services. Restaurants nearby include Clarisimo and Convite.

Contact Details: +54 11 2078-5170.

Address: Parera 183, C1014 Cdad. Autónoma de Buenos Aires, Argentina.

URBAN SUITES RECOLETA

Urban Suites Recoleta is a luxurious hotel in Buenos Aires located near Plazoleta Isidoro Ruiz Moreno, Museum of Latin American Art of Buenos Aires MALBA, and Museo Participativo de Ciencias. The hotel includes a fitness center, sauna, and gym facilities. The rooms have a flat-screen TV with cable channels, heating, a snack bar, a minibar, and free Wi-Fi. They are beautifully designed with wooden parquet floors, warm-colored fabrics, and comfortable throw pillows. Some rooms even have a private balcony. The hotel offers a breakfast buffet every morning with baked goods like croissants and fresh fruits. The hotel has facilities for disabled guests, such as a lower bathroom sink, taller toilets, wheelchairs, and visual aids (Braille). Restaurants and cafés nearby include Epa Beer House, Sahara Continent, and Distal Café.

Contact Details: +54 11 4803-2300.

Address: Junín 1727, C1113 Cdad. Autónoma de Buenos Aires, Argentina.

MELIÁ RECOLETA PLAZA

Meliá Recoleta Plaza is a small boutique hotel located near top attractions like Buenos Aires Japanese Gardens, The Obelisk of Buenos Aires, and Museo Nacional de Bellas Artes. The hotel provides facilities such as an outdoor swimming pool, a fitness center, spa and wellness center, and packed lunches. The rooms are styled with hardwood floors, floor-to-ceiling curtains, wood furniture, and a smart 55-inch TV with streaming services and cable channels. There is also high-speed internet and a safety box for your valuable belongings. They have air conditioning, a private bathroom with a bathrobe and a hairdryer, a minibar, and a snack bar. The hotel offers breakfast in the room and special diet menus upon request. Restaurants nearby include Bistró Recoleta, Jazz Voyeur, and Terraza Jardín Mallorca, all 4 m away. Public transportation nearby includes Facultad de Derecho - Julieta Lanteri and Las Heras metro stations and Retiro and Retito San Martín train stations.

Contact Details: +54 11 5353-4000.

Address: Posadas 1557, C1112ADA Cdad. Autónoma de Buenos Aires, Argentina.

SAN TELMO DISTRICT

If you walk the streets of San Telmo, vibrant street murals, trendy pop-up art galleries, and late-night bars with pulsating music will greet you. The neighborhood is lined with antique shops packed with treasures. Some areas that should be on your itinerary include Defensa Street, a paradise for those seeking one-of-a-kind souvenirs, and Plaza Dorrego, the district's central square. British troops invaded Buenos Aires in 1806, hoping to take advantage of the people, but were met by fierce resistance from a local militia on Defensa Street. Four years later, Buenos Aires became one of the first Latin American cities to declare independence. The 19th century unfolded with a wealthy and flourishing San Telmo. The district became one of the must-visit areas for fun or to feed the historian in you.

MAIN ATTRACTIONS

MERCADO DE SAN TELMO

The Mercado de San Telmo is a lively market opened in 1897 to initially cater to the needs of immigrants in the district. Today, the market is where you can get a feel for how people in the San Telmo district live. It is a big fair with plenty of attractions to see and buy. The corners are lined with booths selling antiques, hand-crafted goods, and delicious traditional foods. The market reflects the free-spirited vibe of the San Telmo neighborhood.

Mercado de San Telmo.[37]

As of the writing of this book, the opening hours are every day from 9 am to 8 pm. However, please make sure to double-check the opening hours online should there be any slight changes to their schedule.

Address: Defensa 963, C1066AAQ C1066AAQ, Cdad. Autónoma de Buenos Aires, Argentina

PLAZA DORREGO

Plaza Dorrego is a square in the center of San Telmo. San Telmo was the primary residential district of Buenos Aires in the 19th century, and Plaza Dorrego was the most important. The heart of San Telmo is known for the flea market and outdoor tango performances, capturing the essence of Buenos Aires' cultural traditions.

As of the writing of this book, the opening hours are 24 hours every day. However, please make sure to double-check the opening hours online should there be any slight changes to their schedule.

Plaza Dorrego.[38]

Address: Humberto 1º 400, C1103 Cdad. Autónoma de Buenos Aires, Argentina

MUSEO DE ARTE MODERNO DE BUENOS AIRES (MAMBA)

The Museum showcases contemporary Argentine and Latin American art, emphasizing San Telmo's role as a cultural hub and influence on modern artistic movements.

As of the writing of this book, the opening hours are Wednesday to Monday from 12 pm to 7 pm and closed on Tuesday. However, please make sure to double-check the opening hours online should there be any slight changes to their schedule.

Address: Av. Caseros 828, C1152 Cdad. Autónoma de Buenos Aires, Argentina

TRANSPORT OPTIONS

- *Walking*
- *Buses*
- *Taxis*

EXPERIENCES

Bohemian atmosphere, antique markets, tango performances, street art.

GALERIA DEL ASOMBRO (GALLERY OF WONDER)

If you love mystery, suspense, fun, and adventure, you can't miss going to Galería del Asombro in Buenos Aires. It is a one-of-a-kind experience created by Arteo Gerbernstein. The gallery has fictional characters, animals, and an eerie, intense setting that makes you intrigued the whole time. The lighting and sound effects are professionally designed to scare you and keep you on edge. It is a fun yet smoky adventure to experience with your family or friends. The place is usually busy, so you may wait some time to enter and get out. However, the adrenaline is worth the wait.

Opening Hours: 12:00 pm to 6:00 pm from Friday to Sunday.

Address: Defensa 1295, C1143 Cdad. Autónoma de Buenos Aires, Argentina

FUNDACIÓN MERCEDES SOSA

Mercedes Sosa Foundation is a non-profit cultural organization in Buenos Aires. The purpose of this cultural center is to preserve the legacy of Mercedes Sosa, the Argentine singer, and honor her. The foundation promotes Latin American culture through different activities and events to keep her music alive for future generations. The foundation does an exhibition called The Voice of Latin America, demonstrating her music, photos, and personal items. It is also a place where artists, volunteers, and supporters come together to celebrate. If you are a music and culture fan, this is a place you cannot miss.

Opening Hours: 11:00 am to 7:00 pm from Tuesday to Sunday.

Address: Humberto 1o 378, C1103ACH Cdad. Autónoma de Buenos Aires, Argentina

WHERE TO EAT

EL FEDERAL BAR

El Federal Bar is an old-school restaurant and bar in the heart of San Telmo, Buenos Aires. It is known for its historic vibe because of the antique bottles and beautiful wooden bars. They serve a mix of Spanish, Portuguese, and Argentine dishes. The best dishes on the menu are the steaks, fresh picadas (meat and cheese plates), and the tortilla de papas. You can also enjoy a wide range of wines and artisanal beer. The atmosphere is friendly and relaxed, and the staff are welcoming and provide excellent service. Whether you are craving a delicious meal or having a drink, El Federal is the perfect spot for you.

Opening Hours: 08:00 am to 02:00 am every day.

Contact Details: +54 11 4361-7328.

Address: Carlos Calvo 599, C1068 Cdad. Autónoma de Buenos Aires, Argentina

CAFÉ SAN JUAN

Café San Juan is a small, cozy restaurant in Buenos Aires located just a short walk from Plaza Dorrego in San Telmo. The restaurant offers Italian and Spanish-inspired dishes with an Argentine twist. Guests love the high quality and flavorful taste of the food, especially the burrata cheese with tomato pesto, short rib ravioli, smoked pork chops, and chocolate terrine. The staff is friendly and professional, with waiters who genuinely want you to have a great experience. The restaurant has an open kitchen, which shows how confident they are in the quality of the food they serve. If you are in the mood for pasta, seafood, or chocolate, Café San Juan is a place you can't miss.

Opening Hours: 12:00 pm to 04:00 pm / 07:30 pm to 12:00 am from Tuesday to Sunday, and closed on Monday.

Contact Details: +54 11 6295-3349.

Address: Av. San Juan 450, C1147 Cdad. Autónoma de Buenos Aires, Argentina

CARACOL

Caracol is an Argentine restaurant with a warm atmosphere and friendly staff. It serves hearty, delicious dishes at reasonable prices. Their top dishes are the Venetian liver eggplant tart, and rump steak with green onions.

Opening Hours: 07:00 am to 11:00 pm from Sunday to Friday and 07:00 am to 12:00 am on Saturday.

Contact Details: +54 11 4361-6497.

Address: Bolívar 1101, C1066AAW Cdad. Autónoma de Buenos Aires, Argentina

BABIECA

Babieca is an Argentine steakhouse with a full bar, free Wi-Fi, and good service. Their top dishes are the spinach fritters, potatoes, and risotto with sweetbreads, as well as the passion fruit cheesecake and brownies with berries for dessert.

Opening Hours: 12:00 pm to 04:00 pm / 08:00 pm to 12:00 am every day.

Contact Details: +54 11 4300-0237.

Address: Bolívar 1520, C1141 Cdad. Autónoma de Buenos Aires, Argentina

PLACES TO SHOP

GALERÍA DE LA INMACULADA CONCEPCIÓN

This gallery combines shopping, food, and history in one place. It has several antique shops that sell collectibles and leather jackets, along with other items that might surprise you. There are also cozy cafés and bars where you can stop for a dessert like Alfajores. The place is clean, organized, and has an old-school vibe.

Opening Hours: 10:00 am to 06:45 pm from Tuesday to Friday, 10:00 am to 07:00 pm on Saturday, 09:30 am to 07:30 pm on Sunday, and closed on Monday.

Address: Defensa 845, C1065 Cdad. Autónoma de Buenos Aires, Argentina

GALERÍA SOLAR DE FRENCH

Galería Solar de French is a small shopping mall only a short walk from the central food market in Buenos Aires. It is a lovely place with cobbled streets and colorful umbrellas hanging overhead. The stores include unique boutiques selling antiques, handmade jewelry, custom shoes, and local crafts.

Opening Hours: 10:00 am to 08:00 pm every day.

Address: Defensa 1066, C1065 AAT, Cdad. Autónoma de Buenos Aires, Argentina

SAN TELMO ANTIQUES FAIR

San Telmo Antiques Fair is a must-visit on Sundays in Buenos Aires! This huge market is full of special finds, from antiques to vintage items to local handmade crafts, paintings, clothes, and more. It is a great experience, especially with tango dancers performing around the area.

Opening Hours: 10:00 am to 05:00 pm on Sunday.

Address: Humberto 1º 401, C1103 Cdad. Autónoma de Buenos Aires, Argentina

PASEO DEL ANTICUARIO

This hidden gem is a small gallery just a short walk from Defensa Street and San Telmo Market. The area has an old-world feel and a lot of greenery. The place has a great antiques selection to browse.

Opening Hours: 11:00 am to 06:00 pm from Monday to Saturday and 11:00 am to 07:00 pm on Sunday.

Address: Carlos Calvo 421, C1102AAI Cdad. Autónoma de Buenos Aires, Argentina

ACCOMMODATIONS

PATIOS DE SAN TELMO

Patios de San Telmo is a stylish boutique hotel in the heart of Buenos Aires. It has a relaxing rooftop swimming pool, solarium, and free Wi-Fi. The hotel is a short walk from Plaza de Mayo and San Telmo Market. It is in a restored 19th-century building. Rooms are equipped with flat-screen TVs, laptop safes, minibars, and cozy, elegant decor. For extra relaxation, book one of the upgraded rooms, which feature a hydro-massage tub.

Contact Details: +54 9 11 3084-2917.

Address: Chacabuco 752, C1070AAP Cdad. Autónoma de Buenos Aires, Argentina.

VIA VIA BUENOS AIRES, SAN TELMO

Via Via Buenos Aires is a bed and breakfast guest house in a great location in San Telmo near Centro Cultural Kirchner and Antonio Ballve Penitentiary Museum. It has air-conditioned rooms with a patio, free Wi-Fi, and private bathrooms. The place also has attentive and friendly staff. The guesthouse has a lovely terrace with barbecue facilities, where you can enjoy an American breakfast each morning.

Contact Details: +54 11 3186-0441.

Address: Chile 324, C1098 AAH, Cdad. Autónoma de Buenos Aires, Argentina.

TELMHO HOTEL BOUTIQUE

Telmho Hotel Boutique, located in the heart of Sam Telmo, just a few steps away from Dorrego Square, offers rooms with clean bedding and private bathrooms. The rooms also have flat-screen TVs, free Wi-Fi, and wireless phones. In the bathrooms, there are luxurious toiletries and hairdryers for added comfort. The hotel's restaurant serves a continental breakfast every morning, with relaxed music playing and drinks available 24/7.

Contact Details: +54 11 5898-7984.

Address: Defensa 1086, C1065AAT Cdad. Autónoma de Buenos Aires, Argentina.

HOTEL CHIPRE, SAN TELMO

Located in a great location near many restaurants, shops, and local attractions, Hotel Chipre is a budget-friendly accommodation option in San Telmo, Buenos Aires. The hotel has simple but clean rooms with air conditioning and a private bathroom. It can get a bit noisy, especially with lots of people around, but it is perfect for backpackers and younger travelers looking for an affordable place to stay. The staff is friendly, and the owner is helpful.

Contact Details: +54 11 4362-5665.

Address: Perú 1053, C1068 Cdad. Autónoma de Buenos Aires, Argentina.

RETIRO DISTRICT

Retiro is a neighborhood with quiet streets known for its art galleries and trendy cafes dotted along the route to the busy Retiro railway station. Overlooking Plaza San Martín is the Art Deco tower, Edificio Kavanagh. The area became significant in history for the battles between Liniers' troops and the British army during the 1806 and 1807 invasions. Fascinating modern attractions like leather boutiques, souvenir shops, and tango performances are on the pedestrianized Florida Street.

MAIN ATTRACTIONS

PLAZA SAN MARTÍN

A historic square surrounded by architectural landmarks. The massive park in the Retiro neighborhood is saturated with lush greenery. The park is decorated with impressive statues and artwork. Its beautiful design is thanks to landscape architect Carlos Thays. It is a perfect place for a leisurely stroll and picnic.

Plaza San Martín.[39]

As of the writing of this book, you can visit Plaza San Martín at any time during your trip. However, please make sure to double-check the opening hours should there be any slight changes to their schedule.

Address: B1650 Buenos Aires, Buenos Aires Province, Argentina

TORRE MONUMENTAL

Formerly known as Torre de los Ingleses ("the Tower of the English"), this clock tower stands as a symbol of the city's European influences and the ties between Argentina and the UK. They built it to celebrate 100 years since Argentina's May Revolution. The name was changed after the war between Argentina and the UK. The tower has a lookout spot from where you can see incredible city views.

Torre Monumental.[40]

As of the writing of this book, the opening hours are Wednesday to Monday from 11 am to 5:40 pm and closed on Tuesday. However, please make sure to double-check the opening hours online should there be any slight changes to their schedule.

Address: Av. Dr. José María Ramos Mejía 1315, C1104 Cdad. Autónoma de Buenos Aires, Argentina

Edificio Kavanagh

Once the tallest building in South America, its sleek design and history make it a prime example of Buenos Aires' unique architectural taste. The skyscraper was built in 1936 and is an impressive 120 meters tall. When it was first completed, it held the title of the tallest building in South America. The design is modern, with clean lines and minimal exterior embellishments. The building is named after Corina Kavanagh, who paid for its construction. Only residents and their guests are able to go inside.

Edificio Kavanagh.[41]

Address: Florida 1065, C1005 Cdad. Autónoma de Buenos Aires, Argentina

TRANSPORT OPTIONS

- *Buses*
- *Walking*
- *Taxis*

Green spaces to walk and enjoy nature, historic train station, Plaza San Martín, and upscale dining.

CROQUE MADAME - PALAZIO PAZ

Palazio Paz is a historic building with French-style rooms. The place is only accessible through guided tours that take you through lavish rooms with gold gilding, stained glass windows, chandeliers, and marble floors. The building is near Plaza San Martin, a short walk from the Florida shopping area.

Palazio Paz.[42]

Address: Av. Sta. Fe 750, C1006 Cdad. Autónoma de Buenos Aires, Argentina

WHERE TO EAT

DADA BISTRÓ

Dada Bistró is a small local bar and restaurant that serves Argentinean food. Their signature dish is the Lomo Dada. The restaurant has a cool, laid-back vibe where customers enjoy lunch, dinner, and drinks.

Opening Hours: 12:00 pm to 03:00 am from Tuesday to Saturday, and closed on Sunday and Monday.

Contact Details: +54 11 4314-4787.

Address: San Martín 941, C1004 Cdad. Autónoma de Buenos Aires, Argentina

SANTOS MANJARES

Santos Manjares is a casual and cozy steakhouse that has excellent service and good value for money. The place is loved by tourists and locals. The menu includes juicy ribeye steaks, Provoleta, chorizo sausage, French fries, mashed pumpkin, and mashed potatoes. The prices are affordable, and the quality is high.

Opening Hours: 11:30 am to 12:00 am from Monday to Saturday, and closed on Sunday.

Contact Details: +54 9 11 6050-2225.

Address: Paraguay 938, C1057 AAN, Cdad. Autónoma de Buenos Aires, Argentina

TANCAT

Tancat is a cozy Spanish restaurant that offers generous portions and top-quality food. The menu includes paella, shrimp, octopus, salmon, and fried calamari. Their top dish is the *jamón crudo a la manera Tancat*, which tastes great when paired with a glass of Malbec. The staff is friendly and helpful. The food is reasonably priced compared to similar quality restaurants.

Opening Hours: 12:00 pm to 04:00 pm on Monday and Tuesday, 12:00 pm to 04:00 pm / 07:00 pm to 11:30 pm from Wednesday to Friday, 07:00 pm to 11:30 pm on Saturday, and closed on Sunday.

Contact Details: +54 11 6221-9721.

Address: Paraguay 645, C1057AAG Cdad. Autónoma de Buenos Aires, Argentina

RESTAURANTE DORA

Dora is a traditional restaurant ideal for those craving fish and classic Argentine dishes. The place is warm and welcoming, with top-notch service. The menu includes grilled or fried prawns, crispy Provoleta, Milanesa, punto (Spanish tortilla), and black hake crepe. It also has Malbec ice cream for dessert.

Opening Hours: 12:00 pm to 06:00 pm from Monday to Saturday, and closed on Sunday.

Contact Details: +54 11 4311-2891.

Address: Avenida Leandro Niceforo Alem 1016, C1001AAS Cdad. Autónoma de Buenos Aires, Argentina

PLACES TO SHOP

PASEO DE COMPRAS RETIRO

Paseo de Compras Retiro is a great spot for affordable shopping in Buenos Aires. It has a variety of stores, including clothes, sportswear, and accessories for men and women. The place is clean and organized, and the staff is helpful and offers advice when you are unsure what to get. There are also budget-friendly food stalls where you can grab a bite when hungry.

Opening Hours: 10:00 am to 08:00 pm from Monday to Saturday, and closed on Sunday.

Address: C1106AAA, Av. Dr. José María Ramos Mejía 1415, 1104 Buenos Aires, Argentina

MAXI PLAZA

Maxi Plaza is a small shopping center in Buenos Aires where you can find gifts for friends and family, such as colorful sunglasses and chocolates.

Opening Hours: 08:30 am to 08:00 pm from Monday to Friday, 09:00 am to 08:30 pm on Saturday, and closed on Sunday.

Address: Esmeralda 1077, C1007ABM Cdad. Autónoma de Buenos Aires, Argentina

TUYUNTI ARTESANIAS

Tutunti Artesanias is a souvenir shop where you can find artwork, flags, paintings, statues, and picture frames perfect for decorating your office or home. It also has earrings and other accessories to buy as gifts.

Opening Hours: 10:30 am to 06:00 pm from Monday to Friday, and closed on Saturday and Sunday.

Address: Florida 971, C1005 Cdad. Autónoma de Buenos Aires, Argentina

ACCOMMODATIONS

WALDORF HOTEL BUENOS AIRES

Hotel Waldorf is a comfortable place to stay in Buenos Aires, only a short walk from Florida Street and Centro Cultural Borges. It is a great accommodation choice when you are looking to explore the city as it is close to many pubs, restaurants, and shops. The rooms are modern and have air conditioning, cable TV, a minibar, and digital safes. They offer free daily housekeeping, plus ironing and dry-cleaning services for an extra charge.

Contact Details: +54 11 4312-2070.

Address: Paraguay 450, C1057 AAD, Cdad. Autónoma de Buenos Aires, Argentina.

EMBAJADOR HOTEL

Embajador Hotel is in a convenient location in Buenos Aires a short distance from the Torre Monumental. It has a 24-hour reception, wake-up service, and vending machines for drinks and snacks. It also serves a daily continental breakfast in a spacious dining area. The rooms have an air conditioner, TV, a work desk, and a private bathroom with a shower and towels. There are plenty of restaurants nearby, like Natacha Café and Huacho.

Contact Details: +54 11 5254-6835.

Address: Carlos Pellegrini 1185, C1009ABW Cdad. Autónoma de Buenos Aires, Argentina.

BISONTE LIBERTAD

Bisonte Libertad is a cozy hotel in Buenos Aires, just a short walk from Teatro Colon and Avenida Corrientes. It's in a safe area with plenty of restaurants and attractions nearby, including the famous pizzeria around the corner. The rooms are not modern but comfortable and clean, with a great shower and heating. The staff are top-notch and give guests an unforgettable stay.

Contact Details: +54 11 3723-2500.

Address: Libertad 902, C1012 Cdad. Autónoma de Buenos Aires, Argentina.

UP RETIRO

Up Retiro is a 3-star hotel in the heart of Buenos Aires, just a short walk from Plazoleta Isidoro Ruiz Moreno, Reserva Ecológica Costanera Sur, and Plaza San Martin Square. The rooms have a desk, TV, safety deposit box, a telephone, and a private bathroom with free toiletries and a bidet. The hotel offers a concierge service, currency exchange, and free Wi-Fi. Up Retito is surrounded by plenty of restaurants, including Doble Q, Bread, and Pekin.

Contact Details: +54 11 4312-5681.

Address: Marcelo Torcuato de Alvear 444, C1058 Cdad. Autónoma de Buenos Aires, Argentina.

CHAPTER

6 WESTERN BUENOS AIRES

Welcome to the western neighborhoods of Buenos Aires. These districts are well known for their cultural significance, art galleries, stylish restaurants, and numerous shopping options. Buenos Aires's west side mixes old and new with beautiful streets and historic buildings. Every corner has something to tell - stories of the city's past, creativity, and its never-ending charm. You've learned about the city's northern, southern, and eastern parts. Now, it's time to discover what attracts tourists and visitors to the city's western part. Who wouldn't want to experience friendly Argentinian hospitality? You can get a feel of their hospitality by exploring these neighborhoods. Are you ready to explore the western parts of Buenos Aires, where the past meets the present in a mix of culture, community, and nature? This chapter will guide you through the western districts from Caballito to Floresta, Villa Luro, and Liniers.

CABALLITO DISTRICT

Caballito neighborhood is the best place to experience Buenos Aires' local culture. Although this neighborhood is at the heart of Buenos Aires, it maintains a low profile. The city is named after a horse-shaped weather vane that adorns a landmark local store opened by Nicolás Vila in 1821. Rich people from Buenos Aires would come to Caballito on leisure weekends in the past. Some of the large houses can be seen on Avenida Rivadavia, like the home of Ambrosio Lezica, known for his wine business. Nowadays, Caballito is a part of the University of Buenos Aires campus. Students from the Faculty of Philosophy give the area a more relaxed and less formal vibe.

Did You Know?

The day after Valentine's Day, February 15, was declared Caballito Day in 2002. It is a day when the entire neighborhood comes together to celebrate their community and cultural pride. The day is so meaningful to the people they host special events, and restaurants offer discounts on some traditional dishes.

MAIN ATTRACTIONS

Parque Centenario

This is a popular park in the Caballito district and a meeting place for locals in neighborhoods like the Almargo and Batucada. The park is a venue for outdoor sports, training sessions, and fun and cultural activities. It is home to museums and provides plenty of space to relax and play - no wonder it is a popular spot for locals. The park is known for its beautiful gardens, a lake with ducks and geese, and a big amphitheater where live performances are held.

Parque Centenario.[43]

As of the writing of this book, the opening hours are every day from 8 am to 8 pm. However, please make sure to double-check the opening hours online should there be any slight changes to their schedule.

Address: Av. Díaz Vélez 4859, C1405DCD Cdad. Autónoma de Buenos Aires, Argentina

MUSEO ARGENTINO DE CIENCIAS NATURALES BERNARDINO RIVADAVIA

The Museo Argentino de Ciencias is a public natural science museum. It's an enormous museum named after Bernardino Rivadavia, where you can learn about animals and local geology. The museum is well-known for its impressive displays of dinosaurs and skeletons that were only found in Argentina. You might want to make a stop here for an afternoon visit.

Museo Argentino de Ciencias Naturales Bernardino Rivadavia.[44]

As of the writing of this book, the opening hours are every day from 2 pm to 7 pm. However, please make sure to double-check the opening hours online should there be any slight changes to their schedule.

Address: Av. Patricias Argentinas 480, C1405 Cdad. Autónoma de Buenos Aires, Argentina

MERCADO DEL PROGRESO

Mercado del Progreso is an old market filled with ancient history where you can enjoy traditional food and crafts. It opened in 1889 and is one of the city's oldest markets. You'll find several shops, including bars, pizzerias, wine shops, meat sellers, bakeries, and fish sellers. The market has kept its traditional feel, with stalls run by the grandchildren of the original owners. The Mercado del

Progreso is a key part of Caballito's history and a busy place where locals shop for fresh food and goods.

Mercado del Progreso.[45]

As of the writing of this book, Mercado del Progreso is open every day from 8 am to 1 pm and from 5 pm to 8 pm. However, please make sure to double-check the opening hours online should there be any slight changes to their schedule.

Address: Av. Rivadavia 5430, C1424 CEW, Cdad. Autónoma de Buenos Aires, Argentina

TRANSPORT OPTIONS

- *Subway*
- *Buses*
- *Trains*
- *Taxis*
- *Bikes*
- *Car*

EXPERIENCES

Taste Argentinian street food, join a guided tour of historical sites, attend a local festival, visit the museum, and stroll along the Parque Centenario.

MUSEO DE ESCULTURAS LUIS PERLOTTI

This museum presents the works of the famous Argentine sculptor Luis Perlotti. His works include sculptures, reliefs, and busts made from Carrara marble, bronze, and cement. If you are in the area, The Luis Perlotti Sculpture Museum is worth a visit if you are looking for a quick and affordable cultural tour.

Address: Pujol 644, C1405ALD Autonomous City of Buenos Aires, Argentina

WHERE TO EAT

ROSÉ RESTAURANT BAR

From the moment you arrive at ROSÉ Restaurant Bar, you will notice the beautiful décor and warm atmosphere. The staff is always ready to assist. The drinks are superb, and the quality of the food keeps people coming back. Many customers highly recommend this place.

Opening Hours: 12:00 pm to 01:00 am from Monday to Saturday, and closed on Sunday.

Contact Details: +54 11 4903-2857.

Address: Guayaquil 556, C1424 Cdad. Autónoma de Buenos Aires, Argentina

BOCA DE LOBO CABALLITO

Boca De Lobo is a hamburger restaurant that serves massive, tasty burgers with a generous portion of fries. Some of the customers' favorites include rustic potatoes, Roquefort burgers, and Choripans. The staff is friendly and quick to serve. Customers love the outdoor seating area. The restaurant offers wheelchairs to make it accessible for everyone to enjoy a meal there.

Opening Hours: 10:00 am to 04:00 pm / 06:00 pm to 12:00 am from Monday to Saturday, and closed on Sunday.

Contact Details: +54 11 3983-8676.

Address: Yerbal 1100, C1406 Cdad. Autónoma de Buenos Aires, Argentina

PIZZA-CAFÉ EL CABALLITO

Pizza-Café El Caballito is a cozy and friendly Argentinian restaurant perfect for a casual meal or coffee.

The menu includes tasty, homemade dishes like pizzas, empanadas, and croissants. The restaurant has friendly staff who make sure you feel welcome and taken care of.

Opening Hours: 08:00 am to 12:00 am from Monday to Saturday and 09:00 am to 05:00 pm on Sunday.

Contact Details: +54 11 4432-2782.

Address: Av. Rivadavia 5452, C1424 Cdad. Autónoma de Buenos Aires, Argentina

PROSCIUTTO RESTOBAR

Proscuitto Restobar is perfect for enjoying a quick snack, lunch, or dinner. The portions are generous and have great value for money. It is known for always having fresh food with great flavors. The place is spacious, with indoor and outdoor seating areas. The menu includes pasta, steaks, seafood, and sandwiches. You can reserve rooms in Proscuitto for events such as conventions, anniversaries, private meetings, or groups.

Opening Hours: 09:00 am to 12:00 am every day.

Contact Details: +54 11 3242-4560.

Address: Av. José María Moreno 318, C1424 Cdad. Autónoma de Buenos Aires, Argentina

PLACES TO SHOP

CABALLITO SHOPPING CENTER

Caballito Shopping Center is a mini shopping mall in Buenos Aires. It is not overly luxurious, but it is clean and safe. There are good stores and dining options, like Mercat Caballito on the third floor, which sells a delicious Nordica sandwich. The mall also includes a cinema, food court, game center, clothes shops, and a library.

Opening Hours: 10:00 am to 09:00 pm every day.

Address: Av. Rivadavia 5108, C1424 Cdad. Autónoma de Buenos Aires, Argentina

GALERÍA PARÍS

Galería París is a shopping mall in Buenos Aires that is considered a local gem. It has a mix of stores and products for every taste. The place is well-lit and air-conditioned, making it ideal for shopping or browsing. It has a variety of stores, including clothing, perfumes, accessories, and food and drinks. It also has tattoo shops and stores that sell party clothing and Argentinean leather goods.

Opening Hours: 10:00 am to 08:00 pm from Monday to Saturday, and closed on Sunday.

Address: Av. Rivadavia 4975, C1424 Cdad. Autónoma de Buenos Aires, Argentina

SI SUPIERAS CABALLITO

Si Supieras Caballito is a clothing store that sells high-quality clothes at great prices. The staff is attentive and helps you find your size. You will find casual T-shirts, sundresses, blazers, leather jackets, hoodies, and pants.

Opening Hours: 11:00 am to 08:00 pm from Monday to Saturday, and closed on Sunday.

Address: Av. Acoyte 85 Local 40, C1424 Cdad. Autónoma de Buenos Aires, Argentina

SPORTS AND LEISURE

Jog or relax in the parks or visit the skate park for breathtaking fun.

CLUB ITALIANO

Club Italiano is a social, sports, and cultural club where you can enjoy many activities like volleyball, swimming, basketball, soccer, rugby, tennis, hockey, and yoga. You can also find places to relax, like barbecue areas, quinchos, and play zones for kids. There is a theatre room for live performances and a large hall for presentations. It is also a place for personal development as there are courses and workshops in arts and other areas.

Address: Avenida Rivadavia 4731, Buenos Aires C1424CEC Argentina

ACCOMMODATIONS

MITRE SUITES HOTEL

Mitre Suites is a budget-friendly hostel in Caballito, Buenos Aires. It offers rooms with cable TV, heating, a ceiling fan, and free Wi-Fi. The place is clean, and the staff is kind and helpful. Many entertainment options surround the hostel, including bars, cinemas, and top attractions such as The Obelisk of Buenos Aires and Honorio de Pueyrredon. Restaurants nearby include Ugis, Parrilla 83, and El Vasquito.

Contact Details: +54 11 4978-0803.

Address: C1201ABE, Bartolomé Mitre 4315, C1201ABE Cdad. Autónoma de Buenos Aires, Argentina.

HOTEL BOUTIQUE RACÓ DE BUENOS AIRES

Hotel Boutique Racó has spacious rooms and is just a short walk to the subway. The rooms have air conditioning, free Wi-Fi, a safe, a flat-screen TV, and a hairdryer. The staff is friendly and recommends local trips that suit your preferences. The hotel also offers room service and luggage storage. It is close to popular areas like Palermo Soho and Plaza Serrano.

Contact Details: +54 11 3471-3312.

Address: C1202ACE, Yapeyú 271, C1202ACE Buenos Aires, Argentina.

SAN CARLOS HOTEL

San Carlos Hotel is an excellent accommodation in Buenos Aires if you are looking for a modern place to stay. The rooms have a minimalistic style with pops of color. You will find a clothes rack, cable channels on the TV, and a socket near the bed. The place is near Centenario Park, Abril Plantas, and Castro Barros Subway Station. The hotel has top-notch service and staff; a guest even rated the hotel 11 out of 10!

Contact Details: +54 11 4981-5542.

Address: Av. Hipólito Yrigoyen 4080, C1208 Cdad. Autónoma de Buenos Aires, Argentina.

KONKE BUENOS AIRES HOTEL

Konke Buenos Aires is a hotel with luggage storage, a heated indoor swimming pool open all year, an outdoor terrace with furniture to relax on, a garden, and wellness activities such as yoga classes, full body massages, a steam room, and a sauna. It also offers business facilities, such as fax or photocopying, and meeting rooms for an additional charge. The rooms have a private bathroom with a hairdryer, towels, and an emergency cord. They are also soundproof, carpeted, and air-conditioned. The place is near top attractions like Buenos Aires Japanese Gardens and restaurants like Los Floristas and del Norte.

Contact Details: +54 11 5284-8300.

Address: Av. Corrientes 4320, C1195AAP, C1195 Cdad. Autónoma de Buenos Aires, Argentina.

FLORESTA DISTRICT

Floresta is a lovely area in the western part of Buenos Aires. It grew around the city's first railway station, La Floresta, in 1857 and was named after it. The neighborhood was originally a garden area. The name in English is "the forest." As a result of urbanization, it slowly became part of the city, filled with family homes. However, it is a countryside retreat for those in the city center and beyond. The beautiful tree-lined streets of Floresta are a distinctive characteristic of this peaceful, green neighborhood. Several squares are scattered across the district for people to stroll, relax, and enjoy fresh air. The local cultural and historical society keeps a library with the neighborhood's history. Floresta is a place where you can enjoy quiet parks, beautiful buildings, and cultural events.

Did You Know?

Floresta's Avellaneda Park was constructed on land previously occupied by a monastery.

MAIN ATTRACTIONS

PLAZA VELEZ SARSFIELD

Plaza Velez Sarsfield is a historic square in Floresta where tourists can relax and enjoy watching the world go by. The park has trees, benches, and a big fountain in the middle. People often come here to walk their dogs, have a picnic, or take a break from the city's busy life. There are playgrounds for kids and, sometimes, you might catch local musicians busking. It's a peaceful spot where you can soak up the local atmosphere and enjoy nature.

As of the writing of this book, you can visit Plaza Velez Sarsfield at any time during your trip. However, please make sure to double-check the opening hours online should there be any changes to their schedule.

Address: Av. Avellaneda 3800, C1407EJR Cdad. Autónoma de Buenos Aires, Argentina

AVENIDA AVELLANEDA

A long street famous for its lively atmosphere and colorful shops. Walking along this avenue, you'll find many stores selling clothes, shoes, and accessories. The street is always busy with people coming and going, browsing through the many shops. There are cafes and restaurants where you can stop for a bite to eat or a cup of coffee. Avenida Avellaneda is a fun place that will infect you with the unmistakable vibe of Buenos Aires. You can pick up unusual souvenirs, and it is a good place for a fashionista with all the fashion shops. The street is a road artery to many other streets and is known as a place to get new clothes without spending much.

As of the writing of this book, you can visit Avenida Avellaneda at any time during your trip.

Address: Buenos Aires, Argentina

TEATRO GRAN RIVADAVIA

An old theatre in Floresta that hosts performances, including plays, musicals, concerts, and dance shows. The theater's grand architecture and elegant interior will leave you awestruck. It's a popular venue for locals and tourists who want to experience Buenos Aires' art scene. Don't miss a visit to the neighborhood for a fun time if you're a theater, music, or dance fan.

As of the writing of this book, the opening hours are Monday to Friday from 12 pm to 7 pm and closed on Saturday and Sunday. However, please make sure to double-check the opening hours online should there be any slight changes to their schedule.

Address: Av. Rivadavia 8636, C1407 Cdad. Autónoma de Buenos Aires, Argentina

TRANSPORT OPTIONS

- *Train*
- *Subway*
- *Bus*
- *Taxis*
- *Rental Car*

EXPERIENCE

Catch a show at the theatre, take a scenic bike ride, stroll along the Avenida Avellaneda, and explore the neighborhood's historic architectural design.

EL TEATRO FLORES

The Flores Theater is a concert hall in Buenos Aires where live music shows performances. The acoustics are amazing, and the setup makes it perfect to enjoy live bands while having close contact with the artists. Multiple seating options are available, including a ground floor and an upper level. There is a bar on-site where they sell drinks. The place is easy to get to, with transport options nearby. There are also many restaurants and cafés if you want to grab a bite before or after the show.

Contact Details: +54 11 4555-1145

Address: Av. Rivadavia 7806, C1407 Autonomous City of Buenos Aires, Argentina

FAMILY FUN

Visit Parque Avellaneda - a lovely park perfect for you and yours. It's a great spot for family and friends to walk and play outside. It's open every day.

PLAZA DE LA MISERICORDIA

Plaza de la Misericordia is a beautiful, peaceful garden. It is full of birds, flowers, and statues. It is a place where your kids can run and play while you relax and enjoy the views of nature. It is a safe, pet-friendly place, so you can bring your cat or dog if you have one. There is a crafts fair on Thursdays and Saturdays where you can buy soaps and many other on-sale products.

Opening Hours: 8:00 am to 10:30 pm daily.

Contact Details: +54 9 922 301-1147

Address: Av. Directorio 2000, C1406 Cdad. Autónoma de Buenos Aires, Argentina

WHERE TO EAT

CHE MIRANDA SALÓN DE PIZZAS

Che Miranda Salón De Pizzas is a cozy pizza restaurant in Buenos Aires with good vibes and friendly service. Customers love the pizza dough with several toppings, including provolone cheese. The calzones and the knife-style meat empanadas are worth a try. Customers recommend pairing your meal with their selection of Patagonia beers. The prices are reasonable, and they offer delivery if you are craving pizza but not feeling like going out.

Opening Hours: 09:00 am to 1:00 am from Sunday to Thursday and 09:00 am to 01:00 am on Friday and Saturday.

Contact Details: +54 11 4671-8718.

Address: Av. Avellaneda 4199, C1407 Cdad. Autónoma de Buenos Aires, Argentina

BUFFET "LA FLORESTA"

La Floresta is a dining spot inside a community club. It is not a touristy place like other similar pizza restaurants. You will feel like you belong to the neighborhood when you step inside. Their top dish is the asado, a feast of grilled meats. Orders are customizable according to your preference and are great to pair with a bottle of wine from Mendoza. For dessert, don't miss the dulce de leche!

Opening Hours: from 09:00 am to 12:00 am from Tuesday to Sunday, and closed on Monday.

Contact Details: +54 11 7364-1782.

Address: Av. Avellaneda 3899, C1407 Cdad. Autónoma de Buenos Aires, Argentina

LA ESTACION - FLORES - PIZZA, BIRRA & BURGER

La Estacion - Flores is a lovely restaurant in Buenos Aires where you can enjoy tasty pizzas, burgers, and empanadas. The perk of this restaurant is the large drinks, almost the size of big bottles of beer, ideal for a group outing. The prices are affordable, and you get decent value for money. The only downside is that you may experience inconsistency in the quality of service based on the time or day of your visit.

Opening Hours: 11:00 am to 11:30 pm from Sunday to Thursday and 11:00 am to 02:00 am on Friday and Saturday.

Contact Details: +54 11 4612-9118.

Address: Av. Rivadavia 8100, C1407 Cdad. Autónoma de Buenos Aires, Argentina

PLACES TO SHOP

FLORES MALL

Flores Mall is a great place to shop at a variety of stores at reasonable prices. It is perfect for shopping in bulk; they have deals on clothes, accessories, home décor, and furniture. Customers love that most stores have all sizes of clothes. The mall is popular, so it gets crowded on weekends, and you might find it a little hard to park near the entrance.

Opening Hours: 08:00 am to 04:00 pm from Monday to Friday, 07:30 am to 02:00 pm on Saturday, and closed on Sunday.

Address: Bogotá 3172, C1406 GCH, Cdad. Autónoma de Buenos Aires, Argentina

GALERÍA VÍA FLORES

Galería Vía Flores is a busy shopping mall with various clothing stores for the whole family. It has everything from affordable fashion to wholesale deals, making it a place for bargain hunters. Some stores require bulk purchasing for discounts. The prices are generally good, but the quality may vary.

Opening Hours: 08:30 am to 06:00 pm from Monday to Friday, 08:30 am to 02:30 pm on Saturday, and closed on Sunday.

Address: Bacacay 3231, C1406GEG Cdad. Autónoma de Buenos Aires, Argentina

FASHION WALK

Fashion Walk is a clothing store in Buenos Aires that sells clothes for men, women, and children. It has all kinds of clothes, from T-shirts to pants, and running shoes in different colors. It is a place where you can find unique items at reasonable prices.

Opening Hours: 08:00 am to 05:00 pm from Monday to Friday, 08:00 am to 02:00 pm on Saturday, and closed on Sunday.

Address: Bogotá 3375, C1407 ESA, Cdad. Autónoma de Buenos Aires, Argentina

ACCOMMODATIONS

REAL SPLENDID HOTEL

The rooms in Real Splendid Hotel have heating, air conditioning, and fire extinguishers. The hotel offers concierge service, daily housekeeping, and a shared lounge with a TV to unwind. It's also close to San Pedrito Subway Station and only a 15-minute drive from Jorge Newbery Airport. Nearby, you'll find parks, restaurants, and cafés like Grill and Seventh Art, and it's easy to get to popular spots like Flag Square, Avellaneda Sports Center, and Palermo Woods by public transport.

Contact Details: +54 11 4611-4610.

Address: Cnel. Ramón L. Falcón 2799, C1406GOC Cdad. Autónoma de Buenos Aires, Argentina.

HOSPEDAJE LA RANA

Hospedaje La Rana is a hostel in Buenos Aires that you can easily spot from a distance because it is in a purple-painted building. Services include concierge and luggage storage and grocery delivery at an additional charge. The rooms have heating, a safety deposit box, and a shower. The interiors are super colorful, with closets and walls painted vibrant colors like orange, blue, and lime green. A designated smoking area and entertainment options like puzzles and board games are available. The hostel is close to Flores and San Pedrito stations and top attractions such as Plaza Arenales and Palacio Barolo. Restaurants nearby include Pizza Show and Snack al Paso.

Contact Details: +54 9 11 6018-3002.

Address: Bogotá 2785, C1406GBY Cdad. Autónoma de Buenos Aires, Argentina.

HOTEL SANTA CRUZ

Hotel Santa Cruz is near San Pedrito and Flores stations. It is also close to Parque Avellaneda, Plaza de la Bandera, and Honorio de Pueyrredon. The rooms have a flat-screen TV, shower, and socket near the bed. There is also air conditioning and free Wi-Fi. There is a shared lounge with a TV and a 24-hour front desk service. Parking on-site is available and costs $20 per day.

Contact Details: +54 11 4611-2133.

Address: GCB, Bogotá 2858, C1406 Cdad. Autónoma de Buenos Aires, Argentina.

HOTEL YERBAL

Hotel Yerbal in Buenos Aires is just a short walk from San José de Flores and Floresta stations. Nearby, you will find top attractions like Paque GG, Okidoki Kids Café Premium, and Plaza Arenales. Restaurants nearby include Costumbres Argentinas and Pollos Broaster y al Spiedo. The rooms have a closet, a private bathroom with a shower and toilet paper, and a flat-screen TV. There is a kitchen with a dining table and a microwave. The hotel outdoors includes a terrace and a garden.

Contact Details: +54 11 4611-6558.

Address: Yerbal 2854, C1406 GKL, Cdad. Autónoma de Buenos Aires, Argentina.

VILLA LURO DISTRICT

Villa Luro is a western district known for its good weather and peaceful streets full of trees. The neighborhood is named after Dr. Pedro Luro, a well-known doctor who sold most of his properties in the 1870s to help people get shelter, making Villa Luro the welcoming place it is today. The streets in Villa Luro are named after well-known poets, giving it a poetic atmosphere. The neighborhood is more residential than commercial, with more individual homes than tall apartment buildings, creating a warm and friendly environment. One tourist attraction in the district is the Plaza Ejército de los Andes, a square offering a quiet spot for people to relax. Places like the Church and Institute of Our Lady of Perpetual Help and the Villa Luro Association of Plastic Arts are great places for visitors to explore more of western Buenos Aires.

MAIN ATTRACTIONS

BOULEVARD RAMÓN FALCÓN

Boulevard Ramón Falcón is a beautiful tree-lined street. Instead of busy traffic and tall buildings, you'll find elegant houses. It's a peaceful place to walk and enjoy a slower pace of life while watching the locals interact and admire nature.

As of the writing of this book, you can visit Boulevard Ramón Falcón at any time during your trip. However, please make sure to double-check the opening hours online should there be any slight changes to their schedule.

PLAZA EJÉRCITO DE LOS ANDES

A communal green space for relaxation and events named after the Army of the Andes, a military force that played a significant role in South American history. In Plaza Ejército de los Andes, you'll find green spaces, benches, and pathways perfect for a leisurely stroll. The square is surrounded by trees, providing shade, making it a perfect spot to sit and chat with friends or enjoy a picnic on a sunny day.

As of the writing of this book, you can visit Plaza Ejército de los Andes at any time during your trip. However, please make sure to double-check the opening hours online should there be any slight changes to their schedule,

Address: Av. Rivadavia 10300, C1408AAP Cdad. Autónoma de Buenos Aires, Argentina

HISTORIC DISTRICT

Villa Luro is a historic district with many interesting buildings. These buildings are a mix of old-fashioned low-rise and new low-rise houses. The change in the architectural design of the structures in the neighborhood over the years tells much about the district's history and advancement and how proud the locals are of their homes.

TRANSPORT OPTIONS

- *Train*
- *Bus*
- *Bicycle*
- *Cars*
- *Walking*

EXPERIENCES

Join a guided tour, visit Villa Luro Park, walk along Avenida Rivadavia, and explore cultural centers.

WHERE TO EAT

ALMA Y FUEGO

Alma y Fuego means Soul and Fire. The restaurant offers excellent service with a cozy yet modern vibe. It is a great place to go with family and friends for a casual meal or to celebrate a rare occasion. Customers recommend starters like Papas Rotas, main dishes like the Bife de Chorizo and Provoleta, and desserts like Torta and Postre. Guests appreciate the staff's detailed explanations about the dishes and wines. There might be occasional delays due to the number of waitstaff, but overall, people leave happy with the experience.

Opening Hours: 09:00 am to 12:00 am from Tuesday to Sunday, and closed on Mondays.

Contact Details: +54 11 6646-8506.

Address: Av. Rivadavia 10399, C1408 Cdad. Autónoma de Buenos Aires, Argentina

EL TRÉBOL RESTO BAR

This place is a local gem with strong word-of-mouth recommendations for its fresh, homemade, hearty food and great vibes. Guests love their Milaneses, sandwiches, and Neapolitan Supermas dish. The restaurant has reasonable prices and a good value for money. It offers delivery services, but the food often comes cold, so it is better to enjoy it in-house.

Opening Hours: 10:00 am to 10:00 pm from Monday to Saturday, and closed on Sunday.

Contact Details: +54 11 4635-9472.

Address: Av. Lope de Vega 14, C1407BMN Cdad. Autónoma de Buenos Aires, Argentina

BURGER UP VILLA LURO

If you are a burger lover, Burger Up Villa Luro is the place to go. It is known for its juicy, tasty burgers like the Crispy Bacon and Caramel Bacon. They also have vegan options. It always impresses its customers with high-quality ingredients and creative, surprisingly delicious combinations. The fried are always crispy and golden. The in-house service and delivery are quick. There is no indoor seating as it is more of a grab-and-go place.

Opening Hours: 11:30 am to 11:30 pm from Sunday to Thursday and 11:30 am to 12:30 am on Friday and Saturday.

Contact Details: +54 11 6570-3950.

Address: Av. Rivadavia 9377, C1407 Cdad. Autónoma de Buenos Aires, Argentina

LA CANTINA STENTORIANA

La Cantina Stentoriana is an ideal restaurant for a casual meal. The menu includes burgers, pizzas, fresh arugula and parmesan salad, and banana pudding with chocolate for dessert. The food is high-quality, and you won't wait long to receive your order. A lot of families eat inside so it might get a bit noisy. For a calmer environment, the outdoor tables might suit you better.

Opening Hours: 10:00 am to 12:00 am every day.

Contact Details: +54 11 4823-4198.

Address: Saráchaga 5634, C1407 Cdad. Autónoma de Buenos Aires, Argentina

PLACES TO SHOP

LURO SHOPPING TRIP

Luro Shopping Trip is a small shopping mall with many shops, including hairdressers and nail salons. The place could use some improvements regarding appearance and variety in stores. However, it is the place to go if you are looking for talented nail artists and barbers.

Opening Hours: 09:30 am to 08:30 pm from Monday to Saturday, and closed on Sunday.

Address: Av. Rivadavia 9545, C1407 DZE, Cdad. Autónoma de Buenos Aires, Argentina

KIOSKO VILLA LURO NORTE

Villa Luro North Kiosk has many drink options, such as Fanta, Sprite, and Coca-Cola. It also has cigarettes and chocolates like Cofler Blanco, Leche, Relleno Bon O Bon, and Milka. It is situated next to a school, making it the perfect spot for an after-school snack for students.

Opening Hours: 09:00 am to 08:30 pm from Monday to Saturday, and closed on Sunday.

Address: C1407 Buenos Aires, Argentina

LA HUERTA DE VILLA LURO

The Orchard of Villa Luro is a greengrocery shop that sells all kinds of fruits and vegetables, including tomatoes, cucumbers, corn, grapes, strawberries, and avocados. The staff is helpful, and the prices are affordable.

Opening Hours: 08:00 am to 12:00 am from Monday to Thursday, 08:00 am to 04:00 am on Friday and Saturday, and closed on Sunday.

Address: Av. Rivadavia 9786, C1407 DZT, Cdad. Autónoma de Buenos Aires, Argentina

TIENDA DE ROPA ZINGARA

Tienda de Ropa Zingara is a small dress shop in Buenos Aires. They have many fabrics in different colors. If you are looking for something special, they can make custom dresses just for you. It is nice to get something tailored to your taste instead of shopping at popular malls and looking like everybody else.

Opening Hours: 10:00 am to 08:30 pm from Monday to Friday, 10:00 am to 01:00 pm on Saturday, and closed on Sunday.

Address: Av. Rivadavia 9661, C1407 DZF, Cdad. Autónoma de Buenos Aires, Argentina

ACCOMMODATIONS

HOTEL PIZARRO

Hotel Pizarro offers a basic, no-frills stay in a quiet area in Buenos Aires. While it is not a luxury spot, it is decent for short stays. The rooms have a private bathroom with hot water. There are a couple of shared areas, such as patio and kitchen. The location is convenient, with easy access to transportation, cafés, and restaurants nearby.

Contact Details: +54 11 4683-5973.

Address: Pizarro 5367, C1440BZC Cdad. Autónoma de Buenos Aires, Argentina.

BAHÍA DEL SOL HOTEL

Bahía del Sol Hotel is a decent spot to stay if you are looking for affordable prices and a quiet atmosphere. It has private parking and is convenient for short stays. Guests enjoy the spacious rooms with jacuzzis. It is not luxurious; some rooms might need maintenance, like an occasional issue with hot water in the bathrooms.

Contact Details: +54 9 11 5229-2852.

Address: Bahía Blanca 1137, C1407 ABU, Cdad. Autónoma de Buenos Aires, Argentina.

LINIERS DISTRICT

Liniers is a lively and exciting part of Buenos Aires' west side. The neighborhood is a friendly place where you can feel the history just by being there. Liniers is known for its efficient transport options, with a huge train station and a main bus area connecting to the city's underground trains and the larger region. Liniers is a key spot for working or visiting people. The main road is Rivadavia Avenue, packed with shops and places to eat, showing off the area's mix of cultures. You can find the Vélez Sársfield football stadium and the San Cayetano Church, which many people visit to pray for work or to give thanks. Liniers is always busy with people buying and selling, especially famous for its markets and street sellers. It's a place you wouldn't want to miss visiting.

Did You Know?

Liniers was named after a French nobleman, Santiago de Liniers, who defended the city when the British invaded it in the early 19th century. He was born in France but his legacy lives on in the hearts of the Liniers neighborhood.

SANCTUARY OF SAN CAYETANO

The holy sanctuary is a beautiful church dedicated to San Cayetano, the patron saint of work and bread. Thousands of visitors come here every year to pray for work, employment, and financial blessings. The church has a peaceful atmosphere, perfect for quiet reflection and prayer. The Sanctuary of San Cayetano symbolizes hope and faith for many in the community. The Sanctuary of San Cayetano is known for hosting one of the biggest events in the neighborhood on the 7th of August every year.

Sanctuary of San Cayetano.[46]

As of the writing of this book, the Sanctuary of San Cayetano is open Monday to Saturday from 6:30 am to 7 pm and Sunday from 7:30 am to 7 pm. However, please make sure to double-check the opening hours online should there be any slight changes to their schedule.

Address: Cuzco 150, C1408BLD Cdad. Autónoma de Buenos Aires, Argentina

AVENIDA RIVADAVIA

This Avenida Rivadavia is a big street lined with shops, cafes, and old buildings. As you walk along Avenida Rivadavia, you'll encounter a variety of stores selling everything from clothing and shoes to electronics and household goods. This is where most locals and visitors like to shop and run errands. The street is always busy with people going about their day, giving it a lively energy. Alongside the shops, you'll find cafes, restaurants, and street vendors offering tasty snacks and refreshments.

As of the writing of this book, you can visit Avenida Rivadavia at any time during your trip. However, please make sure to double-check the opening hours online should there be any slight changes to their schedule.

TRANSPORT OPTIONS

- *Train*
- *Bus*
- *Cars*
- *Taxis*
- *Uber*

Food tour, relax in Plaza Ejército de los Andes, shop at Avenida Rivadavia, and taste the neighborhood's local cuisine.

NUESTRA SEÑORA DE LAS NIEVES

Nuestra Señora de las Nieves is a Catholic church in Buenos Aires. The church welcomes people of all ages and backgrounds. Visitors love the peaceful atmosphere and spiritual support they receive. It has regular services, including the Eucharistic Exposition, and is known for having kind and friendly priests.

Nuestra Señora de las Nieves.[47]

Address: Ventura Bosch 6656, C1408 Cdad. Autónoma de Buenos Aires, Argentina

Take your family to the Estadio Jose Amalfitani, a huge stadium where you can watch exciting games like football and rugby.

ESTADIO JOSE AMALFITANI

Also known as El Fortín, Estadio Jose Amalfitani is one the most iconic stadiums in Argentina. The stadium is massive, and you can have a great view from almost any seat. It was one of the venues for the 1978 FIFA World Cup. Whether attending a show or a match, it will be an experience you will never forget.

Estadio Jose Amalfitani.[48]

Address: Av. Juan Bautista Justo 9200, C1408AKU Cdad. Autónoma de Buenos Aires, Argentina

WHERE TO EAT

CASTRO GRILL

Castro Grill is a restaurant in Buenos Aires that serves Argentinean and South American food. It offers meats like chorizo steak and seafood with generous portions. The prices might be a little high, but worth it. The place is cozy and nicely decorated, and the staff is attentive and helpful. It is perfect for family outings, dining with friends, or a special celebration. If you are spending your birthday in Buenos Aires, this is a great place to go as they bring a toast and mini cake to celebrate.

Opening Hours: 08:00 am to 12:00 am from Sunday to Thursday, 08:00 am to 12:30 am on Friday, and 08:00 am to 01:00 am on Saturday.

Contact Details: +54 11 4644-2003

Address: Av. Emilio Castro 7603, C1408IHA Cdad. Autónoma de Buenos Aires, Argentina

TACO BOX MATADEROS

Taco Box Mataderos is a Mexican restaurant in Buenos Aires, ideal for a hangout with your partner or your friends, but not so much for a family gathering with kids. Their popular dishes include the Botana Mexican snack platter, tacos, and quesadillas. The drinks are a hit, especially the Mexican Bulldog, tequila, beer, and margarita. The place is mostly quiet on weekdays and busy on weekends.

Opening Hours: 08:00 pm to 12:00 am from Monday to Thursday, 08:00 pm to 1:30 am on Friday, 1 pm - 4 pm and 8 pm to 1:30 am on Saturday, 1 pm to 4:30 pm and 8 pm to 12 am on Sunday.

Contact Details: +54 9 11 5602-4684.

Address: Av. Emilio Castro 7483, C1408IGL C1408IGL, Cdad. Autónoma de Buenos Aires, Argentina

LO DE SILVIA

Lo de Silvia is perfect for a quick bite or casual meal. The place is well-known for its homemade dishes like Milanesa sandwiches and fries. The portions are generous, the prices are low, and the service is friendly, which makes people come back. Silicia's is open 24/7, so whenever you are feeling like having a late-night snack, you know where to go!

Opening Hours: 24 hours every day.

Contact Details: +54 46426809.

Address: FED, Acassuso 6484, C1408 C1408FED, Cdad. Autónoma de Buenos Aires, Argentina

PLACES TO SHOP

LINIERS PLAZA SHOPPING

Liniers Plaza Shopping is a small, convenient mall in Liniers District located next to the train and bus stations. You will find a mix of stores, kids' clothes, books, and men's and women's fashion. The mall is safe with security guards on-site and gets busy on weekends. It is a great spot for a quick shopping trip if you are in the area.

Opening Hours: 10:00 am to 09:00 pm every day.

Address: Cnel. Ramón L. Falcón 7145, C1408 Cdad. Autónoma de Buenos Aires, Argentina

MERCADO ANDINO DE LINIERS

Mercado Andino de Liniers, or Andean Market or Liniers, is a busy shopping mall where you can find a range of products from South American countries like Peru and Bolivia. It has a variety of grains, nuts, spices, dried fruits, and traditional Andean foods. It has something for everyone. Prices are generally affordable but can vary from one store to another. So, it is better to look around before buying. You will also find Bolivian and Peruvian snacks like empanadas, chicha morada, and salchipapas.

Opening Hours: 08:00 am to 08:00 pm from Monday to Saturday and 08:00 am to 06:00 pm on Sunday.

Address: José León Suárez 200, C1408 FND, Cdad. Autónoma de Buenos Aires, Argentina

La Feliz de Liniers

La Feliz de Liniers, also known as The Happy One of Liniers, is a shopping center in Buenos Aires that sells clothes, tech gadgets, and toys for kids. It is a great place for bargain hunting, and music plays everywhere as you walk around. Whether you need a new outfit, phone accessory, or a gift for your kids, you will find it here.

Opening Hours: 10:00 am to 08:00 pm from Monday to Friday, 10:00 am to 02:00 pm / 04:00 pm to 08:00 pm on Saturday, and closed on Sunday.

Address: José León Suárez 89, C1408FNA C1408FNA, Cdad. Autónoma de Buenos Aires, Argentina

PASEO COMERCIAL LINIERS

Paseo Comercial Liniers is a shopping mall in Buenos Aires with various stores to shop, including clothing, accessories, hair salons, and collectibles. Some areas are clean, while others have declined over time and could use some attention and improvement. It is not a super fancy place, but it has affordable prices and many products to choose from.

Opening Hours: 09:00 am to 08:00 pm from Monday to Saturday, and closed on Sunday.

Address: José León Suárez 44, C1408FNB C1408FNB, Cdad. Autónoma de Buenos Aires, Argentina

ENTERTAINMENT

Visit the zoo, the beautiful church of Parroquia y Santuario San Cayetano, and the Estadio José Amalfitani stadium.

PARROQUIA Y SANTUARIO SAN CAYETANO

The parish and sanctuary of San Cayetano was founded in 1875. It is simple in design and has spiritual significance, especially for those seeking or giving thanks for work. It is most famous for its feast day on August 7th, when thousands of pilgrims gather to pray for jobs and express gratitude for the work they found. Inside, you will find an altar with a large wooden cross and a statue of San Cayetano holding baby Jesus. The church is not luxurious but has a calm and peaceful atmosphere. Regardless of the reason for your visit, the church is a meaningful place with a lot of history.

Parroquia y Santuario San Cayetano.[49]

Address: Cuzco 150, C1408BLD Cdad. Autónoma de Buenos Aires, Argentina

ACCOMMODATIONS

HOTEL VIEDMA

Hotel Viedma is a budget-friendly accommodation option in Buenos Aires, especially if you plan to attend events at the Vélez Sarsfield stadium just a short walk away. Liniers Train Station is also close by. The rooms are simple but clean, with everything you need for a comfortable stay. They have a TV, a private bathroom, and air conditioning. Guests love the service and attentive reception staff. The hotel doesn't serve breakfast, but there are many cafés nearby you can go to in the morning.

Contact Details: +54 11 6763-6150.

Address: Bueras 123, C1408 Cdad. Autónoma de Buenos Aires, Argentina.

HOTEL ARIEL

Hotel Ariel is a contemporary hotel with cozy interiors in a strategic location near Plaza Liniers Shopping and the top city attractions. The rooms are clean and comfortable, with daily housekeeping. All the essentials are there to ensure a comfortable stay. Free Wi-Fi and a continental breakfast are included. The staff is friendly and always ready to assist with any needs.

Contact Details: +54 11 4644-4987

Address: José León Suárez 41, C1408 FNA, Cdad. Autónoma de Buenos Aires, Argentina

HOTEL SOLANGE

Hotel Solange is an affordable yet comfortable accommodation in Buenos Aires. The location is convenient, in front of the Liniers bus terminal and near a shopping center. The rooms are good for a short stay and ideal for sleeping and showering. Previous guests recommended bringing your own toiletries, such as towels, shampoo, and toothbrush. The staff is friendly and helpful and takes good care of the guests.

Contact Details: +54 11 4641-4911

Address: Ibarrola 7217, C1408 Cdad. Autónoma de Buenos Aires, Argentina

CHAPTER

7 Central Buenos Aires

It is time to explore Buenos Aires city center, where grand European architecture brushes shoulder the vibrant Latin American spirit. History whispers from every corner in the central districts. You can spend hours browsing streets in neighborhoods that are the city's lifeblood. Plaza de Mayo, Argentina's political scene's epicenter, welcomes you with open arms. Get ready to feel the weight of history as you stand in this iconic square, a stage for countless revolutions and celebrations. Around the corner, you'll find Corrientes Avenue dancing with endless energy. This is the city's cultural heart, where theaters pump out passionate tango shows, cafes spill onto the sidewalks filled with lively conversation, and elegant buildings stand proudly next to modern skyscrapers as proof of Buenos Aires' constant evolution.

SAN NICOLÁS (OFTEN REFERRED TO AS EL CENTRO)

San Nicolas is a neighborhood in Buenos Aires' center. Whenever you hear the porteños talk about "Microcentro," know they refer to this neighborhood. It's the heart of the city's business district. One of the widest streets in the world, Avenida 9 de Julio, cuts through San Nicolas. This avenue is home to the famous Obelisk, a tall, pointed monument popular for photos. Art lovers will appreciate the beautiful Teatro Colon, a renowned opera house known for its superb acoustics. You can take a behind-the-scenes tour. Avenida Corrientes is a lively avenue lined with art deco theaters, casual pizza places, and bookstores that stay open late at night. San Nicolas boasts a rich history and architecture. The neighborhood has many historic buildings dating back to the founding of Buenos Aires.

MAIN ATTRACTIONS

TEATRO COLÓN

The Teatro Colón in Buenos Aires is a world-class opera house famous for its acoustics and beautiful design. Singers and dancers from all over the world come here to perform. Recently, it was named the best opera house in the world. The Teatro Colón offers a variety of shows, from operas and ballets to concerts and special events for families and kids. There's something for everyone. Head over to their website to see what's playing, grab your tickets, and get ready to be mesmerized.

Teatro Colón.[50]

As of the writing of this book, Teatro Colón's ticket office is open Monday to Saturday from 9 am to 8 pm and Sunday from 9 am to 5 pm. However, please make sure to double-check the opening hours online should there be any slight changes to their schedule.

Address: Tucumán 1171, C1049 Cdad. Autónoma de Buenos Aires, Argentina

OBELISCO DE BUENOS AIRES

The monument was built in 1936 and stands 68 meters (almost 223 feet) tall. The Obelisk's location is particularly significant. It was built on the exact spot where the Argentine flag was first raised, making it a place steeped in national pride. The Obelisk occupies the former location of a chapel dedicated to Saint Nicholas - hence the neighborhood's name, San Nicolas. Visiting the Obelisk is a must when visiting Buenos Aires.

Obelisco de Buenos Aires.[51]

As of the writing of this book, you can visit Obelisco de Buenos Aires at any time during your trip. However, please make sure to double-check the opening hours online should there be any slight changes to their schedule.

Address: Av. 9 de Julio s/n, C1043 Cdad. Autónoma de Buenos Aires, Argentina

AVENIDA CORRIENTES

Corrientes Street, known as "the street that never sleeps," is a must-visit in Buenos Aires. This lively avenue lives up to its nickname, humming with activities day and night. Corrientes Street is a cultural hub. You can get lost in the numerous bookstores, browsing and souvenir hunting. If you love theaters, you have a wide range of productions, from classic plays to contemporary shows.

Avenida Corrientes.[52]

As of the writing of this book, you can visit Avenida Corrientes at any time during your trip. However, please make sure to double-check the opening hours online should there be any slight changes to their schedule.

Address: Av. Corrientes 3247-3299, C1193AAE Cdad. Autónoma de Buenos Aires, Argentina

TRANSPORT OPTIONS

- *Buses*
- *Subway*
- *Cars*
- *Taxi*
- *Walking*

EXPERIENCES

Guided tour of the Teatro Colon, visit the Cathedral Primada, and join a bus tour to explore the entire city at your own pace.

CATHEDRAL PRIMADA

If you love architecture, culture, and history, Cathedral Primada is a must-see in San Nicolas, Buenos Aires. The exterior does not stand out as much, but the interior is beautiful and represents a rich history. One of its highlights is the marble mausoleum, where the remains of General José de San Martín are kept. The cathedral is free to enter, and taking pictures without a flash is allowed.

Opening Hours: 7:30 am to 6:30 pm from Monday to Friday, 9:00 am to 6:45 pm on Saturday and Sunday.

Address: San Martín 27, C1004 Cdad. Autónoma de Buenos Aires, Argentina

WHERE TO EAT

LA SUSANA BISTRÓ

La Susana Bistró has an old-school atmosphere ideal for a relaxed lunch with friends. The menu includes gourmet dishes, such as risotto and salads. The location is convenient, as it is close to Florida Street Shopping, so it is a great place to stop for lunch or dinner after a long day of shopping.

Opening Hours: 11:00 am to 10:30 pm from Monday to Friday, 12:00 pm to 10:00 pm on Saturday and Sunday.

Contact Details: +54 11 7139-7068.

Address: Reconquista 687, C1003 San Nicolas, Cdad. Autónoma de Buenos Aires, Argentina

LOS INMORTALES

Los Inmortales is a classic, authentic pizza restaurant in Buenos Aires that has been around for years. They serve pizzas and empanadas with vegetarian options, and they also serve salads. The pizzas are different than you might find in Italy, with less tomato sauce and more dough and cheese. Their top pizza is the Fugazzetta, an onion and cheese pizza you will never forget the taste of. They also serve drinks, including cocktails and wines. The restaurant has indoor and outdoor seating options and a kids' menu.

Opening Hours: 07:00 am to 01:30 am from Monday to Friday, 07:00 am to 02:00 am on Saturday and Sunday.

Contact Details: +54 11 4322-5493.

Address: Av. Corrientes 1369, C1043 Cdad. Autónoma de Buenos Aires, Argentina

EL CONJURO PIZZA BAR

El Conjuro Pizza Bar is a casual, fun place with good food and great service. The upstairs space is better for larger groups as it is more laid-back and relaxed. Unlike other similar restaurants, they do themed nights and karaoke, which is perfect for a night out with friends.

Opening Hours: 09:00 am to 04:00 pm every day.

Contact Details: 54 9 11 5327-9907.

Address: Bartolomé Mitre 838, C1036 San Nicolas, Cdad. Autónoma de Buenos Aires, Argentina

LD WINERY

LD Winery, located in Edificio Plaza De La Republica, is the perfect place for drinks and a casual meal. The place is beautifully décor with plants and shelves where you can see the wines. They have delicious steaks, empanadas, and Milanesa. The food might take a while to get served, so make sure you are not in a rush. They accept all payment methods and offer discounts for cash payments.

Opening Hours: 09:00 am to 01:00 am every day.

Contact Details: +54 9 11 5133-0150.

Address: Suipacha 395, C1008 San Nicolas, Cdad. Autónoma de Buenos Aires, Argentina

PLACES TO SHOP

ABASTO DE BUENOS AIRES

Abasto de Buenos Aires is one of the largest shopping malls in the city. It is in a 1930s Art Deco building, with architecture alone worth the visit. There is a wide range of shops, from mid-range retail stores to more unique outlets, and a huge food court with plenty of fast food options and a few sit-down restaurants. The mall has a movie theater, a theme park for kids, and a bowling alley. It is family-friendly as there are children's activities like a zipline. The mall is easy to get to by taxi or public transport.

Opening Hours: 10:00 am to 10:00 pm every day.

Address: Avenida Corrientes 3247, Lavalle 3120, C1193 Cdad. Autónoma de Buenos Aires, Argentina

TIENDA SAN NICOLÁS

Tienda San Nicolás is a dress shop with good prices and friendly staff. Other than dresses, you will also find undergarments and sleepwear for women, such as nightgowns and pajamas.

Opening Hours: 10:15 am to 01:00 pm / 04:00 pm to 07:30 pm from Monday to Friday, 10:00 am to 01:00 pm on Saturday, and closed on Sunday.

Address: Peña 3100, C1425 AVL, Cdad. Autónoma de Buenos Aires, Argentina

PEATONAL LAVALLE

Located near the Obelisk, Peatonal Lavalle is a popular street for tourists. It is perfect for a casual stroll, shopping, and getting something to eat. It has many stores, including clothing, gifts, and souvenirs. It is also a good place for window shopping if you don't feel like buying anything and only want to have fun looking at clothes. However, be cautious about people offering currency exchange in the streets as they might be scammers.

Opening Hours: 09:00 am to 07:30 pm from Monday to Saturday, and closed on Sunday.

Address: Lavalle 1000, C1189 Cdad. Autónoma de Buenos Aires, Argentina

ENTERTAINMENT

Catch the Piazzolla Tango Show with dinner for an authentic Buenos Aires experience.

PIAZZOLLA TANGO SHOW

The Piazzolla Tango Show takes place in Mirador Guemes Gallery, a beautiful historic theater. The show combines classic and modern tango styles with incredible, talented dancers and singers performing it. It is a bit pricey, but the experience is worth it. The food might not be that good, so make sure you eat something before you go to avoid getting hungry.

Contact Details: +54 11 4094-4571

Address: Galería Güemes, Florida 165, C1005 Cdad. Autónoma de Buenos Aires, Argentina

ACCOMMODATIONS

UNIQUE EXECUTIVE CENTRAL HOTEL

Unique Executive Central is a 4-star hotel near Plaza Lorea, Auca Saiayc, and The Obelisk. The hotel provides concierge service, daily housekeeping, and shuttle service for airport transfer at an additional charge. The rooms come with a flat-screen TV with cable channels, a private bathroom with a bath and a hairdryer, a clothes rack, and a socket near the bed. They come with hardwood or parquet floors and a laptop safe. They also have air-conditioning, heating, and free Wi-Fi. There are restaurants nearby, like Stranger and Sushi Station.

Contact Details: +54 11 2078-5140.

Address: Av. Pres. Roque Sáenz Peña 1178, C1035 Cdad. Autónoma de Buenos Aires, Argentina.

HUINID OBELISCO HOTEL

Huinid Obelisco is a clean, modern, and chic hotel with air-conditioned family rooms, a fitness center, and a spa lounge. There is also a coffee house and bar on-site. For disabled guests, the hotel provides rooms with visual aids, a lower bathroom sink, a toilet with grab rails, and wheelchairs. There is free parking, and the rooms have a telephone, TV, and free toiletries. Restaurants nearby include Wok Express and Chaval.

Contact Details: +54 11 6088-0869.

Address: Sarmiento 1431, C1042 Cdad. Autónoma de Buenos Aires, Argentina.

NH BUENOS AIRES LATINO

NH Buenos Aires Latino is a modern hotel just a short walk from the Obelisk and Corrientes Avenue. There are many restaurants, theaters, and shops surrounding the area. You will also find the Colón Opera House, the Pink House, and the subway within walking distance. It is a big hotel with 100 rooms, with connecting rooms available. The rooms have modern, minimalistic interiors with hardwood floors and flower vases. If you are traveling on business, there is a meeting room and lobby if you need a place to work or meet with someone. The hotel also offers an airport shuttle service.

The Pink House.[53]

Contact Details: +54 11 4321-6700.

Address: Suipacha 309, C1008 Cdad. Autónoma de Buenos Aires, Argentina.

SAVOY HOTEL

Savoy is an impressive hotel with comfortable rooms and helpful staff. It is located in the heart of Buenos Aires near Congreso Square and Plaza Lorea. Restaurants nearby include Las Manzanas and El Tropezon. The rooms have dark wood furniture, clean bedding, a minibar, a snack bar, and a desk. Bathrooms have a bidet, free toiletries, towels, and a hairdryer. The hotel has a fitness center where you can get a relaxing massage. It also has facilities for disabled guests, such as wheelchairs and elevators.

Contact Details: +54 11 4370-8000.

Address: Av. Callao 181, C1022AAB Cdad. Autónoma de Buenos Aires, Argentina.

MONSERRAT DISTRICT

Monserrat is one of the oldest and the most captivating neighborhoods in Buenos Aires. Bustling with tourists and government officials, it offers a unique blend of history, culture, and a lively atmosphere. The neighborhood formed with the foundation of Buenos Aires in 1580. Spanish conquistador Juan de Garay arrived with a group of settlers, and the neighborhood gradually developed. The first major construction was the Fort of Juan Baltazar of Austria in 1594, which later became the government house. The arrival of the Jesuits in the 17th century marked another significant chapter. They built the Iglesia de San Ignacio de Loyola, today's oldest church in Buenos Aires. As the population grew, other religious groups arrived, including the Catalan Brotherhood of the Virgin of Monserrat. Their chapel, built in 1769, gave the neighborhood its name.

MAIN ATTRACTIONS

PLAZA DE MAYO

Plaza de Mayo is the beating heart of Buenos Aires. It's a big square comprising two joined older squares in 1884. Back then, they were called Victory Square and May 25th Square. Today, it's known as Plaza de Mayo. Here in Plaza de Mayo, the fight for Argentina's independence began in 1810. Imagine the energy and excitement that filled the air back then. Today, Plaza de Mayo is surrounded by some of Buenos Aires's most famous landmarks.

Plaza de Mayo.[54]

As of the writing of this book, you can visit Plaza de Mayo at any time during your trip. However, please make sure to double-check the opening hours online should there be any slight changes to their schedule.

Address: Av. Hipólito Yrigoyen s/n, C1087 Cdad. Autónoma de Buenos Aires, Argentina

MANZANA DE LAS LUCES

The Manzana de las Luces, known as the Block of Lights, is a must-see for history lovers visiting Buenos Aires. It's one of the city's most important historical areas and home to some of its oldest buildings. One of the attractions is the San Ignacio Church. Built by the Jesuits who settled in the area, it's considered the oldest church in Buenos Aires. Stepping inside feels like traveling to ancient times. Another amazing wonder lies beneath the Manzana de las Luces, where a network of tunnels previously used for two purposes - defense and smuggling - are hidden from sight.

Manzana de las Luces.[55]

As of the writing of this book, the opening hours are Wednesday to Sunday from 12 pm to 7 pm and closed on Monday and Tuesday. However, please make sure to double-check the opening hours online should there be any slight changes to their schedule.

Address: Perú 222, C1067 Cdad. Autónoma de Buenos Aires, Argentina

CAFÉ TORTONI

This historic cafe was founded in 1858 by a French immigrant. It originally opened in a different spot, but in 1880, it moved to the Grand Avenida de Mayo. This broad avenue sits between two important buildings: the Casa Rosada (the pink presidential palace) and the Congress building. Today, Cafe Tortoni is one of Argentina's most well-preserved 19th-century cafes, with marble tables, dark oak paneling lining the walls, and an old-fashioned toilet.

Café Tortoni.[56]

As of the writing of this book, Café Tortoni is open every day from 8 am to 9 pm. However, please make sure to double-check the opening hours online should there be any slight changes to their schedule.

Address: Av. de Mayo 825, C1084 Cdad. Autónoma de Buenos Aires, Argentina

TRANSPORT OPTIONS

- *Buses*
- *Walking*
- *Taxi*

Admire the neo-Gothic grandeur of Palacio Barolo, a high-rise office building, or step inside the historic Café Tortoni, a storied coffeehouse dating back to the 1850s.

Palacio Barolo

Palacio Barolo is an iconic building in Buenos Aires. It blends Gothic, Art Nouveau, and Eclectic architectural styles. It is a 22-story building 100 m tall. It was once the tallest skyscraper in South America. The building is a tribute to Dante Alghieri's The Divine Comedy, the famous Italian poem. You can explore the lobby for free, but you can also join the guided tour. The building has a cocktail bar, Salon 1923, on the 16th floor, where you can enjoy a drink and the fantastic views of the city.

Palacio Barolo.[57]

Opening Hours: 9:00 am to 10:00 pm from Tuesday to Friday, 10:00 am to 9:00 pm from Saturday to Monday.

Address: Av. de Mayo 1370, C1085 Autonomous City of Buenos Aires, Argentina

WHERE TO EAT

VIEJO ALSINA

Viejo Alsina is a cozy restaurant near many hotels in Buenos Aires. It is not the fanciest of places, but the food is tasty and well-priced. The menu includes traditional Argentine dishes like Milanese and grilled chicken. The portions are generous, and the staff go out of their way to make you feel at home, even if you don't speak Spanish. The atmosphere is perfect for a hearty meal after a day of sightseeing.

Opening Hours: 08:00 am to 12:00 am from Monday to Friday, 09:00 am to 12:00 am on Saturday, and closed on Sunday.

Contact Details: +54 11 2003-5300.

Address: C1087AAK, Adolfo Alsina 799, C1087AAK Buenos Aires, Argentina

CENTRO ASTURIANO DE BUENOS AIRES

Centro Asturiano is a Spanish restaurant with a lot of history. It is a popular spot for tourists and locals, with many regulars. The menu includes Spanish dishes, like the seafood paella as a main dish and croquettes and calamari as starters. While the place can get noisy when busy, it is perfect for a large group of friends or family. It is worth a visit if you are in the mood for authentic Spanish cuisine in Buenos Aires.

Opening Hours: 12:00 pm to 03:30 pm / 08:00 pm to 11:30 pm from Tuesday to Saturday, 12:00 pm to 3:30 pm on Sunday, and closed on Monday.

Contact Details: +54 11 4381-1342.

Address: Solís 475, C1078 AAI, Cdad. Autónoma de Buenos Aires, Argentina

JAVI'S PARRILLA RESTAURANT & CAFETERIA

Javi's Parilla is a family-run steakhouse in Buenos Aires, where it is guaranteed to experience great food and excellent service. The top dishes are the ojo de bife and tenderloin steaks. The portions are filling, and the prices are much lower than most steakhouses. The staff is friendly and speaks English, which is a bonus. The atmosphere has an old charm, and they offer you a limoncello at the end of your meal.

Opening Hours: 09:30 am to 09:30 pm from Monday to Friday, 12 pm to 8:30 pm on Saturday, and closed on Sunday.

Contact Details: +54 11 2853-6261.

Address: Av. Belgrano 901, C1091 Cdad. Autónoma de Buenos Aires, Argentina

LA CASA DE CARMEN

La Casa de Carmen is a cozy restaurant run by a kind family that serves delicious homemade food at great prices. It is the kind of place where you feel like you are eating at someone's home because of how cozy, warm, and welcoming it feels. The dishes are traditional and made with recipes passed down from the owner's Spanish family. The menu includes stewed beef, empanadas, and homemade potato cakes. This hidden gem is perfect for an authentic, home-cooked meal with friends or family.

Opening Hours: 11:30 am to 10:00 pm from Monday to Friday, and closed on Saturday and Sunday.

Contact Details: +54 11 4384-9095.

Address: Venezuela 1225, C1095 Cdad. Autónoma de Buenos Aires, Argentina

PLACES TO SHOP

KIOSKO

Kiosko is a grocery shop that sells snacks like chocolates, biscuits, gum, and chips like Pringles.

Opening Hours: 09:00 am to 09:00 pm from Monday to Saturday and 10 am to 1 pm on Sunday.

Address: C1074AAK, Salta 585, C1074AAK Cdad. Autónoma de Buenos Aires, Argentina

CHIC

Chic is a kiosk in Buenos Aires that offers a same-day delivery service and sells chocolates, biscuits, gum, sodas, and Skittles.

Opening Hours: 07:30 am to 11:30 pm from Monday to Saturday, and closed on Sunday.

Address: Salta 477, C1074 AAI, Cdad. Autónoma de Buenos Aires, Argentina

SHOP LA TIENDITA

Shop la Tiendita is a boutique store that sells women's clothes. You can create trendy outfits with their unique blouses, shorts, pants, and dresses.

Opening Hours: 09:00 am to 10:00 pm from Monday to Friday and 10:00 am to 11:00 pm on Saturday and Sunday.

Address: 3 C, Moreno 950, Cdad. Autónoma de Buenos Aires, Argentina

ENTERTAINMENT

The Teatro Astor Piazzolla offers a spectacular evening out. You can enjoy a night filled with live music, talented dancers, and incredible singers. Enjoy delicious food while you experience the magic of Buenos Aires, the legendary Astor Piazzolla, and the passionate world of Tango.

EL QUERANDI TANGO SHOW

El Querandi Tango Show represents a story told through music and dance. It is performed by a live orchestra, four talented dance couples, and two singers every night. The performances will leave you bewildered from start to finish. The venue is full of 20th-century architecture. The show includes food on request, but the main focus is the show as it steals the spotlight.

Opening Hours: 10:00 am to 11:30 pm from Monday to Saturday, 5:00 pm to 11:30 pm on Sunday.

Contact Details: +54 9 11 3848-5242

Address: Perú 322, C1067AAH Cdad. Autónoma de Buenos Aires, Argentina

ACCOMMODATIONS

HTL CITY BAIRES

HTL City Baires is a well-kept, stylish hotel in Buenos Aires, located near La Manzana de Las Luces and Tortoni Café. Restaurants nearby are Terraza del Virrey and Mediterráneo. It is also very close to Moreno and Piedras subway stations. The rooms are clean and chic, styled with dark wood panels, and have air conditioning, a TV with cable channels, and a minibar. The hotel offers a great breakfast and services at an extra charge, such as ironing, dry cleaning, and laundry.

Contact Details: +54 11 7078-0731.

Address: Piedras 303, C1070 Cdad. Autónoma de Buenos Aires, Argentina.

GRAN HOTEL ARGENTINO

Gran Hotel Argentino is a modern, chic hotel in Buenos Aires that offers rooms overseeing the beautiful views of the city. The rooms have parquet floors with a warm color theme of orange, white, and brown, giving you a warm and peaceful vibe to sleep in. Each room includes a safety deposit box, air conditioning, cable TV, and free Wi-Fi. The hotel's central location makes it easy to get around the city, especially with Avenida de Mayo and Piedras subway stations within walking distance. Nearby attractions are The Obelisk, Palacio Barolo, and Cabildo. Restaurants close to the hotel include El Olmo III and El Tablón Guests leave satisfied and pleased with the excellent service and comfortable stay.

Contact Details: +54 11 4334-4001.

Address: Carlos Pellegrini 37, C1009ABA Cdad. Autónoma de Buenos Aires, Argentina.

KEY HOTELS

Key Hotels in Buenos Aires provides guests with a comfortable stay and easy access to historical landmarks and local dining and shopping spots. The rooms are spacious and well-looked-after and have a modern design that is practical yet elegant. Guests love the friendly and attentive staff, who go out of their way to make them feel comfortable and enjoy their stay. There is also a rooftop pool if you want to relax after a long day.

Contact Details: +54 11 4331-6300.

Address: México 840, C1097 Cdad. Autónoma de Buenos Aires, Argentina.

TANGO DE MAYO HOTEL

Tango de Mayo Hotel is centrally located on Mayo Avenue, just 30 m from Palacio Barolo and 200 m from Plaza Lorea. There are also many shops and restaurants nearby, including Federico and Mostaza. The hotel is inside a restored historical building from the early 1900s, with Art Nouveau architecture and large glass windows. Each room has an individual design with intricate handmade details. Some rooms' walls are painted white, some beige, and some have patterned black and white wall art. All rooms have a 42-inch LED TV, a safety box, a private bathroom, and free Wi-Fi. The hotel offers daily housekeeping and a 24-hour front desk service.

Contact Details: +54 11 3221-6500.

Address: Av. de Mayo 1396, C1085 Cdad. Autónoma de Buenos Aires, Argentina.

VIAJERO HOSTEL BUENOS AIRES

Viajero Hostel Buenos Aires offers many facilities, including a seasonal outdoor swimming pool, a garden, a shared lounge, and a terrace. It also has a 24-hour front desk service and free Wi-Fi. All rooms come with bed linens, air conditioning, and a private bathroom with toilet paper. The hostel is adults-only, and there is a designated area for smoking.

It provides activities like karaoke, bike rentals and tours, happy hour, table tennis, and movie nights. The hostel is near Tortoni Café and Plaza de Mayo Square, with nearby restaurants like Un Dos Crepes and Moira-Morena.

Contact Details: +54 9 11 2737-3561.

Address: Venezuela 649, C1095AAM Cdad. Autónoma de Buenos Aires, Argentina.

BALVANERA DISTRICT

Balvanera is a central area of Buenos Aires pulsing with activity. This lively neighborhood offers much to those seeking a dose of local charm and diverse a taste. The neighborhood's history stretches back to 1799, when a chapel was built, and the area attracted residents. It remained a small community outside central Buenos Aires until the 1860s, when the population grew, and Balvanera became part of the city. During the early 1900s, immigrants from various backgrounds arrived, and the neighborhood became known for its working-class character. Balvanera won't disappoint If you desire a cultural scene. A visit to the Museo Casa Carlos Gardel will introduce you to the legendary tango singer Carlos Gardel's legacy, providing a fascinating glimpse into the world of tango and the man who helped make it famous.

MUSEO DEL AGUA Y DE LA HISTORIA SANITARIA

Do you enjoy museums that are a little strange? Then, you might like the Museo del Agua y de la Historia Sanitaria. It's a small museum on the first floor of an ornate building, the Palacio de las Aguas Corrientes. Instead of paintings or statues, this museum has old pipes, pretty tiles, and even unusual toilets. It's a trip back in time to see how Buenos Aires used to work. They have special tours where a guide will show you the secret parts of the building you wouldn't normally see.

Palacio de las Aguas Corrientes.[58]

As of the writing of this book, the opening hours are Monday to Friday from 9 am to 1 pm and 2 pm to 4 pm and closed on Saturday and Sunday. However, please make sure to double-check the opening hours online should there be any slight change to their schedule.

Address: Riobamba 750, C1025ABP Cdad. Autónoma de Buenos Aires, Argentina

MADRES DE LA PLAZA DE MAYO

During a specific time, a military dictatorship ruled the country. Mothers got together and formed a formidable force to learn what happened when their children were taken and never to be seen again. These mothers wouldn't give up. There's a center in Plaza Congreso where you can learn more about this part of Argentina's history. It mainly comprises pictures and old newspapers (as information is scarce), but it is a heart-wrenching monument to see what these mothers went through and their strength. Every Thursday at 3:30 pm, some mothers march around the plaza to protest about what happened.

Plaza Congreso.[59]

As of the writing of this book, Madres de Plaza de Mayo is open Monday to Friday from 9 am to 5 pm and is closed on Saturday and Sunday. However, please make sure to double-check the opening hours online should there be any slight change to their schedule.

Address: Av. Hipólito Yrigoyen 1584, C1089 Cdad. Autónoma de Buenos Aires, Argentina

PLAZA MISERERE

Plaza Miserere is a large square in Buenos Aires and a central meeting spot. You'll likely come across it when in Balvanera. It's next to a train station, Once de Septiembre Station, on the Ferrocarril Domingo Faustino Sarmiento train line (that's a lengthy way to say a big train line). It is one of the main plazas of Buenos Aires and well worth a visit.

As of the writing of this book, you can visit Plaza Miserere at any time during your trip. However, please make sure to double-check the opening hours online should there be any slight change to their schedule.

Plaza Miserere.[60]

Address: Bartolomé Mitre 2819, C1203 Cdad. Autónoma de Buenos Aires, Argentina

TRANSPORT OPTIONS

- *Subte*
- *Buses*
- *Trains*
- *Walking*
- *Taxi*

EXPERIENCES

Join a guided tour for wine and cuisine tasting, visit the Palacio de Aguas Corrientes, and learn to dance tango like the locals.

PALACIO DE AGUAS CORRIENTES

The Museum of Water and Health History, or the Palace of Running Water, is a historic building in Buenos Aires built in the late 1800s to provide the city with clean water. The building's exterior is decorated with over 170,000 glazed tiles and enameled bricks imported from England and Belgium. The entrance is on Calle Riobamba, and you can take guided tours of the building by booking in advance.

Opening Hours: 9:00 am to 1:00 pm and 2:00 pm to 4:00 pm from Monday to Friday.

Address: Riobamba 750, C1025ABP Autonomous City of Buenos Aires, Argentina

WHERE TO EAT

RESTAURANT LA PERLITA

Restaurant La Perlita has great food with generous portions and excellent service. The menu includes the classic Argentine asado, risottos, and shrimp dishes. The restaurant has a classic style with traditional white tablecloths and wooden chairs. The staff is helpful and always ready to give great recommendations. The prices might be a little high, but the portions and quality make them worth it.

Opening Hours: 07:00 am to 01:00 am from Monday to Friday, 8 am to 1 am on Saturday and Sunday.

Contact Details: +54 11 4861-9800.

Address: Av. Jujuy 74, C1083 Cdad. Autónoma de Buenos Aires, Argentina

GRILL GILDO

Grill Gildo is a homey and warm restaurant in Buenos Aires with nostalgic vibes. It has been running since 1928. Going in feels like traveling back in time for its vintage décor and cozy vibes. The menu includes classic Argentine barbecue, empanadas, and a rich lentil stew. The prices are reasonable, and the staff is attentive.

Opening Hours: 08:00 am to 07:00 pm from Monday to Saturday, and closed on Sunday.

Contact Details: +54 11 4861-9667.

Address: Av. Pueyrredón 39, C1032 Cdad. Autónoma de Buenos Aires, Argentina

BELLAGAMBA

Bellagamba is a small restaurant known for its tasty and affordable food. You order at the counter, and then the meal is brought to your table by the waitstaff. The service is quick as you won't wait long to receive your food. The menu includes Argentine comfort food like Milanesa, empanadas, and plates of chicken and beef. There are multiple small picture frames on the walls and a huge Argentine flag in the middle of the restaurant. The place has outdoor seating and doesn't accept reservations.

Opening Hours: 08:00 am to 01:00 am from Sunday to Thursday and 08:00 am to 02:00 am on Friday and Saturday.

Contact Details: +54 11 4951-5833.

Address: Av. Gaona 1537, C1416 DRD, Cdad. Autónoma de Buenos Aires, Argentina

BORGOÑA

Borgoña is a restaurant in Balvanera, Buenos Aires, with friendly service and warm vibes. The prices are reasonable, and the food comes in generous portions. The menu includes traditional Argentine dishes like juicy cuts of meat like the Parillada, Milanesa sandwiches, and homemade cannelloni. The place is family-friendly, so you can bring your kids to enjoy a meal together.

Opening Hours: 09:00 am to 10:30 pm from Monday to Saturday, 11 am to 8:30 pm on Sunday.

Contact Details: +54 11 4387-9147.

Address: Av. Hipólito Yrigoyen 2700, C1090ABD Cdad. Autónoma de Buenos Aires, Argentina

PLACES TO SHOP

PASEO COMERCIAL MISERERE

Paseo Comercial Miserere is a flea market-style shopping mall on Terminal Once in Buenos Aires. It offers many products, but mainly clothing. It is a good, affordable option if you are looking for casual clothing. However, the place could use some improvements regarding organization and aesthetics.

Opening Hours: 09:00 am to 07:00 pm from Monday to Saturday, and closed on Sunday.

Address: La Rioja 70, C1214 ADB, Cdad. Autónoma de Buenos Aires, Argentina

PASEO DEL ONCE

Paseo del Once is a shopping mall in Buenos Aires where you can find everything from clothes and shoes to food and home goods. Prices are generally affordable, but it takes some searching to find the best deals. It is a popular place for wholesale and retail shopping.

Opening Hours: 08:30 am to 08:00 pm from Monday to Saturday, and closed on Sunday.

Address: Av. Rivadavia 2539, C1034ACE Cdad. Autónoma de Buenos Aires, Argentina

SPINETTO SHOPPING CENTER

Spinetto Shopping Center is a practical mall in Buenos Aires. It has a good supermarket on the ground floor and a few small shops that sell clothes. If you are looking for food, there are affordable places nearby, like Coto Restaurant and Mostaza. Locals mostly go there for groceries and quick shopping.

Opening Hours: 08:30 am to 09:00 pm from Sunday to Thursday and 08:30 am to 09:30 pm on Friday and Saturday.

Address: Matheu 240, C1082 Cdad. Autónoma de Buenos Aires, Argentina

GALERÍA DE LA PAZ

Galería de la Paz is a shopping mall in Buenos Aires that mainly sells electronics and clothes.

Opening Hours: 08:00 am to 08:00 pm from Monday to Friday, 08:00 am to 03:30 pm on Saturday, and closed on Sunday.

Address: Galeria la Paz, Av. Corrientes 2314, C1046AAO Cdad. Autónoma de Buenos Aires, Argentina

ENTERTAINMENT

Enjoy a traditional tango show, watching couples dancing gracefully to the soulful music of the bandoneon while you sip on a refreshing drink and bask in the lively atmosphere.

LA VENTANA TANGO SHOW

La Ventana is one of the best Tango shows in Buenos Aires. If you love Tango, don't think twice before choosing this show. The show features traditional Argentine dances skillfully performed by talented dancers, musicians, and singers. You can upgrade and include dinner, which previous guests loved as it is tasty and reasonably priced for the venue. The tour also provides a pickup and drop-off service to and from your hotel.

ACCOMMODATIONS

GRAN HOTEL ORIENTAL

This one-star hotel is located near top destinations in Buenos Aires, like Congreso Square and Plaza Lorea, and subway stations, including Congreso and Callao. It is also surrounded by many restaurants, including El Bagual, Chifan, and La Americana. The hotel offers daily housekeeping, concierge service, and a 24-hour front desk service. The rooms are air-conditioned and non-smoking.

Contact Details: +54 11 4952-3371.

Address: C1039AAB, Bartolomé Mitre 1840, C1039AAB Cdad. Autónoma de Buenos Aires, Argentina.

HOTEL LA BARCA

Hotel La Barca is a great accommodation in Buenos Aires with good value for money. It is in a convenient location near the Alberti subway station. The rooms are clean and comfortable, with free Wi-Fi, a TV, and a private bathroom. The staff are friendly and helpful and offer great advice on what to do and see around the city. The hotel offers breakfast in the room, and there is a kitchen you can use if you need to. Previous guests advise to take a cab instead of walking after dark. Overall, it is a good choice for budget travelers.

Contact Details: +54 11 4942-2767.

Address: Adolfo Alsina 2448, C1090 Cdad. Autónoma de Buenos Aires, Argentina.

AIRES DE TANGO HOSTEL

Aires De Tango Hostel is a comfortable place to stay in a convenient location just a short walk from Congreso Nacional and public transportation. The hostel has six spacious, well-equipped rooms with air conditioning, a TV, a writing desk, and a reading lamp beside the bed. There is also a shared kitchen if you prefer to cook. But, if you don't, you can eat at nearby restaurants like La Perlita and Pertutti. The staff are friendly and offer help whenever you need it.

Contact Details: +54 11 5371-9830.

Address: Bartolomé Mitre 2388, C1039 Cdad. Autónoma de Buenos Aires, Argentina.

HOTEL CENTRAL BUENOS AIRES

Hotel Central Buenos Aires is a budget-friendly accommodation option if you care more about exploring the city. The staff is friendly and helps you if you have any concerns. Rooms have hot water, a fridge, and a microwave. It is not the most luxurious, but the combination of price, location, convenience, and service make it ideal for budget-conscious travelers.

Contact Details: +54 11 4373-8785.

Address: Solís 196, C1078AAD Cdad. Autónoma de Buenos Aires, Argentina.

ALMAGRO DISTRICT

Almagro got its name from a wealthy Spanish landowner, Juan María de Almagro y de la Torre, back in the early 1700s. It is outside the main city and was once a farming area. Around 1900, Almagro became a city neighborhood, growing fast. Many Italians and Basque people from Spain moved there. Today, Almagro is a busy commercial area with plenty of shops, tall apartment buildings, and a population of over 120,000 people. It's considered more down-to-earth and authentic Buenos Aires than some elite neighborhoods nearby.

MAIN ATTRACTIONS

LAS VIOLETAS CAFÉ

Almagro's top spot for tourists is this fancy café, Las Violetas. It has existed for over 125 years, and stepping inside will take you back to a far more pleasant era.

As of the writing of this book, Las Violetas is open every day from 6 am to 1 am. However, please make sure to double-check the opening hours online should there be any slight changes to their schedule.

Address: Av. Rivadavia 3899, C1204 Cdad. Autónoma de Buenos Aires, Argentina

SAN CARLOS CHURCH AND BASILICA

Next door to Las Violetas, you can't miss the impressive San Carlos Borromeo church. Built between 1900 and 1910 in a style that looks like old Roman buildings (Romanesque revival), it's thought to be one of the most beautiful churches in the city. Walk down Pasaje San Carlos if you have a few minutes - it's a cute walkway that runs alongside the church and is only about 50 meters long.

The altar for San Carlos Borromeo.[61]

As of the writing of this book, the Basilica is open every day from 7:30 am to 12 pm and from 5:30 pm to 8 pm. However, please make sure to double-check the opening hours online should there be any slight changes to their schedule.

Address: Av. Hipólito Yrigoyen 3999, C1181 Cdad. Autónoma de Buenos Aires, Argentina

PARQUE CENTENARIO

A park that comes alive at weekends and is a great place to soak up the atmosphere. Young people gather to play music outdoors, and markets sell handmade crafts and vintage books. Beautiful buildings, including the Natural Science Museum, surround the park. This museum is a great place to visit and learn something new - they have shows and exhibitions.

Natural Science Museum in Parque Centenario.[62]

As of the writing of this book, Parque Centenario is open every day from 8 am to 8 pm. However, please make sure to double-check the opening hours online should there be any slight changes to their schedule.

Address: Av. Díaz Vélez 4859, C1405DCD Cdad. Autónoma de Buenos Aires, Argentina

TRANSPORT OPTIONS

- *Taxi*
- *Shuttles*
- *Buses*
- *Subway*
- *Walking*

EXPERIENCES

Visit the Plaza Almagro, the neighborhood's only park, and join the locals in a game of chess, watch carnival troupes play drums and practice their dance routines, visit the Acuña de Figeroa, Almagro's flower market – once one of the largest in Latin America.

HASTA TRILCE

Hasta Trilce is a dinner theater and bar in Buenos Aires that offers a great mix of live music, tasty food, and a cozy bohemian vibe. The bar serves drinks and snacks, including Argentine classics like empanadas, picadas, pizzas, and tapas. The venue has an intimate theater where you can watch local performances, including theater, music, and dance shows.

Opening Hours: 8:00 am to 2:00 am from Sunday to Thursday, 8:00 am to 4:00 am Friday and Saturday.

Contact Details: +54 11 4862-1758

Address: Maza 177, C1206ACC Cdad. Autónoma de Buenos Aires, Argentina

WHERE TO EAT

REGGINA RISTORANTE ALMAGRO

Reggina Ristorante Almagro is an Italian restaurant with a warm ambiance, perfect for any meal of the day. The menu includes fresh pasta dishes, meats, and good vegetarian options. Their top dishes are Lomo al Funghi and chicken empanadas. The service is friendly, attentive, and willing to assist with the menu. There are occasional delays with the food, but the prices are reasonable.

Opening Hours: 07:00 am to 01:00 am every day.

Contact Details: +54 11 4862-2505.

Address: Av. Corrientes 4602, C1195AAS Cdad. Autónoma de Buenos Aires, Argentina

EL SALTEÑO

El Salteño restaurant is known for its hearty Argentine dishes, especially those from the north. It has a tavern-style setting and good, solid food at reasonable prices. The menu includes generous portions of grilled meats, empanadas, and traditional dishes like Locro, which is thick squash stew. The staff is friendly and makes sure you feel welcome. The space is simple and a bit cramped, but the main focus is the hearty food.

Opening Hours: 12:00 pm to 04:00 pm / 08:00 pm to 11:30 pm from Monday to Saturday and 12:00 pm to 04:00 pm on Sunday.

Contact Details: +54 11 4864-8764.

Address: Gascón 578, C1181 Cdad. Autónoma de Buenos Aires, Argentina

EL FUELLE

La Fuelle is a cozy pizza restaurant in Almagro known for its hearty Argentine-style pizzas and casual vibes. It is a place where friends go together to enjoy a relaxing meal. The menu includes classic ham and bell peppers pizza, mushrooms, and provolone cheese pizza, empanadas, hamburgers, and Milanesa. For appetizers, customers recommend trying their Rabas, which are fried squid. If you go in the morning, you can enjoy their croissants and coffee, which are also a hit. The service is friendly and efficient, with waitstaff who make you feel at home. It never disappoints.

Opening Hours: 07:00 am to 01:00 am every day.

Contact Details: +54 11 4983-5777.

Address: Av. Medrano 99, C1178 Cdad. Autónoma de Buenos Aires, Argentina

PLACES TO SHOP

GALERÍA PATAGONIA

Galería Patagonia is a local shopping spot in Almagro with many services and stores. It is more of a service-oriented gallery than a typical mall. It has everything from jewelry stores to hair salons like Ruda Pelo. They have affordable jewelry like surgical steel and other accessories. Several businesses in the mall provide excellent customer care.

Opening Hours: 09:30 am to 08:00 pm from Monday to Friday, 09:30 am to 04:00 pm on Saturday, and closed on Sunday.

Address: Galería Patagonia, Av. Corrientes 3968, C1179 Cdad. Autónoma de Buenos Aires, Argentina

LA TIENDA MINI SHOP

La Tienda Mini Shop in Buenos Aires has a great selection of products, such as stylish accessories, handmade items, trendy clothing, and decorative pieces.

Opening Hours: 09:00 to 08:00 pm from Monday to Saturday, and closed to Sunday.

Address: Francisco Acuña de Figueroa 855, C1180AAO Cdad. Autónoma de Buenos Aires, Argentina

GALPÓN DE ROPA

Galpón de Ropa is a second-hand clothing store in Buenos Aires, great for thrifting. You will find cute and trendy pieces for a good price. Most sizes are available, but there is no fitting room. The store also offers a same-day delivery service. The staff is friendly and helps you look for what you need.

Opening Hours: 10:00 am to 08:00 pm from Monday to Saturday, and closed on Sunday.

Address: Av. Corrientes 3751, C1194AAD Cdad. Autónoma de Buenos Aires, Argentina

OHMYSHOP!

OhMyShop! is a gift shop in Almagro where you will find lovely pieces to buy for your loved ones back home, such as decorative Christmas dolls, mini jewelry boxes, and inflatable pool mattresses for the summer. You will also find cool and practical stuff like portable handheld fans, toothbrushes and toothpaste holders for the bathroom, and a mini makeup and cosmetics fridge.

Opening Hours: 10:00 am to 05:00 pm from Monday to Friday, 10:00 am to 01:00 pm on Saturday, and closed on Sunday.

Address: Av. Juan Bautista Justo 5038, C1416 Cdad. Autónoma de Buenos Aires, Argentina

ENTERTAINMENT

Visit Bar de Roberto on Bulnes 331, a small, cool bar with a local vibe that often has live music. It's a hidden treasure in Almagro and will make you feel like you belong.

ESCAPE GAMES ALMAGRO

Escape Room Almagro is an unforgettable adventure for adrenaline seekers! It has many themed rooms, such as *The Strangers*, *Catalepsy*, and *Relentless Search*. Each is full of surprises, suspense, and unexpected twists and turns. The rooms are designed to make you feel like the main character in the story. The staff is friendly and engages with you to guide you through the experience. The place is perfect for friends or families looking for a fun challenge for a change.

Opening Hours: 10:00 am to 11:30 pm daily.

Contact Details: +54 11 5699-4154

Address: Av. Rivadavia 3862, C1204AAQ Cdad. Autónoma de Buenos Aires, Argentina

ACCOMMODATIONS

CASA UMARE

Casa Umare is a four-star hotel in a convenient location in Buenos Aires near Plaza Serrano Square and Patio Salguero. It is also near Carlos Gardel and Loria subway stations. The rooms are spacious, and the beds are comfortable with clean bedsheets. All units include air conditioning, a TV with satellite channels, a kitchen with a microwave and a kettle, a dining area, and a private bathroom with free toiletries and a bidet. The stay includes a continental breakfast, including fresh pastries and cheese every morning. If you don't feel like eating at the hotel, you can go to restaurants nearby, like Parrilla or Cúrcuma.

Contact Details: +54 11 4861-2030.

Address: Billinghurst 362, C1174ABF Cdad. Autónoma de Buenos Aires, Argentina.

HOTEL AATRAC

Hotel Aatrac is just a short walk from shopping spots like Galpon de Ropa and Abasto de Buenos Aires shopping mall and restaurants like Gratto and Pertutti. The hotel has easy access to public transport, which is perfect for exploring the city. The rooms are peaceful and have air conditioning, free Wi-Fi, and a private bathroom. It also provides a 24-hour front desk service. Room options include double, triple, and quadruple to suit families and friends traveling together. Each room has a TV, safe, and heating.

Contact Details: +54 11 4863-1744.

Address: Av. Córdoba 3418, C1188 Cdad. Autónoma de Buenos Aires, Argentina.

DESTINO REAL HOTEL

Destino Real Hotel is a great choice if you are looking for an affordable stay in Buenos Aires in a convenient location. If you stay there, you will find it easy to get around the city as there are subway and bus stations nearby. The hotel rooms are clean and recently renovated with tiled floors and modern bathrooms. They offer a simple breakfast, including coffee, croissants, cereal, and juice. The staff is friendly and easy on guests, allowing for early check-ins and late check-outs whenever possible. There are minor issues like unreliable Wi-Fi or missing towels. However, the hotel offers good value for money, especially considering the location.

Contact Details: +54 11 6464-4317.

Address: Dr. Tomás Manuel de Anchorena 58, C1170 ABB, Cdad. Autónoma de Buenos Aires, Argentina.

CHAPTER 8

ITINERARIES AND PROGRAMS

Just thinking about your trip to Buenos Aires gets your heart racing. It's normal to feel this way about a new place. The city's infectious energy, a mix of architectural grandeur, historical significance, and a buoyant urban life are enough to overwhelm anyone. Everywhere you turn, there's something to see and loads of fun activities to engage in. However, with over 40 neighborhoods in the city, plazas, and iconic buildings, where do you begin planning your itinerary? Don't worry. This chapter is your one-stop guide for experiencing the perfect Buenos Aires adventure. It is your chance to tailor your trip to your interests, and it offers a shortcut to the best spots.

4-DAY ITINERARY IN MONSERRAT, CENTRAL BUENOS AIRES

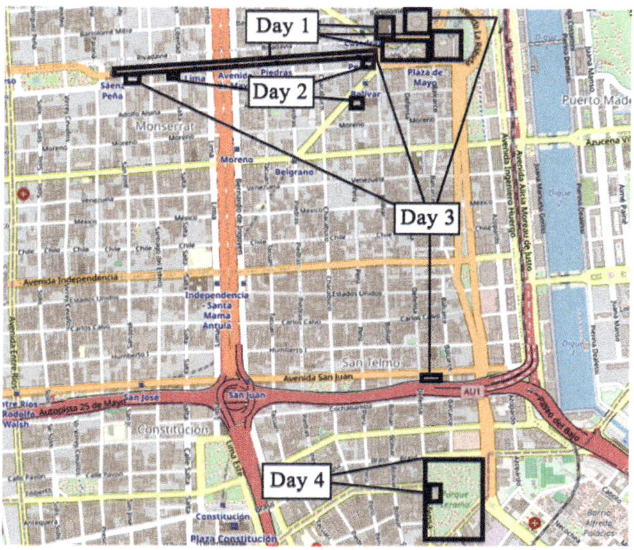

4-day itinerary in Monserrat. [63]

DAY 1: EXPLORE THE HEART OF MONSERRAT

Day 1.

OpenStreetMap Contributors **https://www.openstreetmap.org**

Morning: Begin your journey with a visit to the iconic Plaza de Mayo, the historical and political center of Buenos Aires. Admire the Casa Rosada, the executive mansion, and the President of Argentina's office. Do not miss the chance to take a guided tour inside.

Walk 160 m from Plaza de Mayo to get to the Casa Rosada.

Plaza de Mayo QR Code.

Casa Rosada QR Code.

Afternoon: Head to the Cathedral Metropolitana, where the tomb of General San Martín lies. Afterward, enjoy a leisurely lunch at a nearby café.

Walk 350 m from Casa Rosada to get to the Cathedral Metropolitana.

Cathedral Metropolitana QR Code.

Evening: Stroll down Avenida de Mayo, soaking in the European architecture. Cap off the day with dinner at a traditional Argentine restaurant, followed by a visit to Café Tortoni for coffee and live tango.

Walk 550 m from Cathedral Metropolitana to Café Tortoni.

Address: Av. de Mayo 825, C1084 Cdad. Autónoma de Buenos Aires, Argentina

Avenida de Mayo QR Code.

DAY 2: EXPLORE HISTORY AND CULTURE

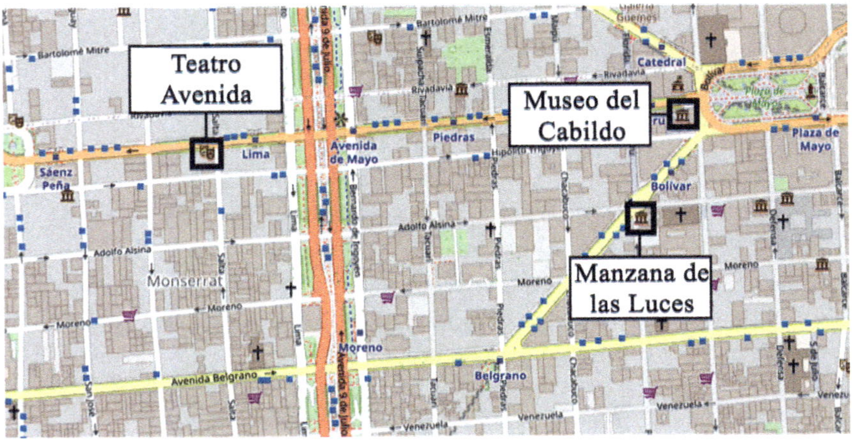

Day 2.[64]

Morning: Visit the Manzana de las Luces for a guided tour to uncover the rich history and underground tunnels of Buenos Aires.

Manzana de las Luces QR Code.

Afternoon: Explore the Museo del Cabildo, offering insights into Argentina's colonial history. Later, indulge in shopping and local cuisine at the Feria de San Telmo, which is especially vibrant on Sundays.

Walk 240 m from the Manzana de las Luces to get to the Museo del Cabildo. To get to Feria de San Telmo, walk 140 m from Museo del Cabildo to 555 Roca Julio A. Presidente Diagonal and take line 24A (a Barracas - IDA) to Avenida Paseo Colon 1080, then walk 300 m.

Address: Defensa 1086, C1065AAT C1065AAT, Cdad. Autónoma de Buenos Aires, Argentina

Museo del Cabildo QR Code.

Evening: Enjoy a contemporary Argentine play at the Teatro Avenida, followed by a late-night snack at one of the traditional pizzerias on Avenida de Mayo.

To get to Teatro Avenida, walk 350 m from Feria de San Telmo to 600 Calvo Carlos metro stop and take line 24A (a Barracas - Vuelta) to 57 Libertad, then walk 160 m.

Teatro Avenida QR Code.

DAY 3: ART AND ARCHITECTURE

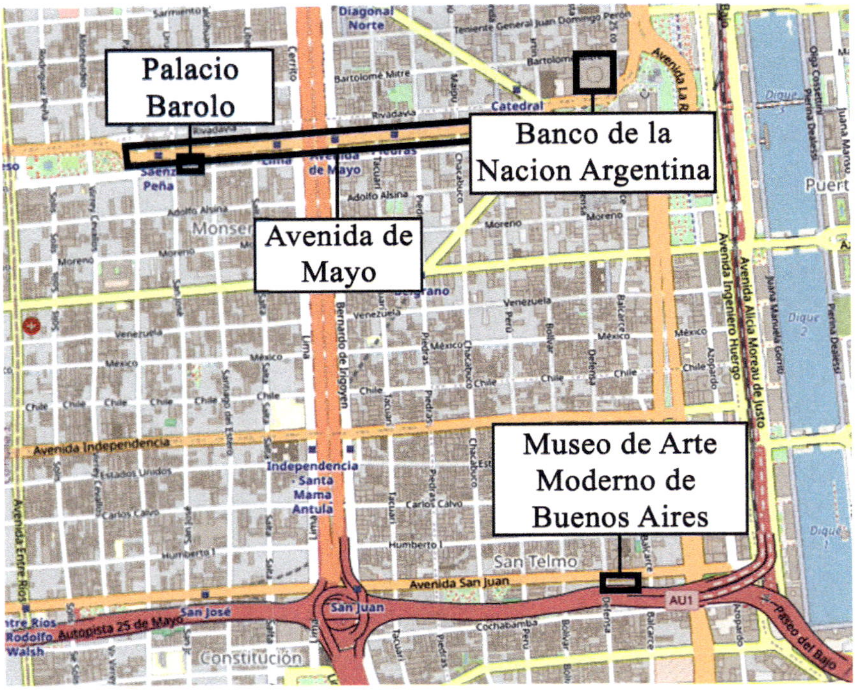

Day 3.[65]

Morning: Start with the Museo de Arte Moderno de Buenos Aires (MAMBA) to admire contemporary art. Then, visit the Banco de la Nación Argentina building to appreciate its architectural grandeur.

Walk 110 m from Museo de Arte Moderno de Buenos Aires to Avenida San Juan 419 bus stop and take bus 126B (a Hospital Ferroviario) to 352 Yrigoyen Hipolito Av., then walk 210 m to get to the Banco de la Nación Argentina.

Museo de Arte Moderno de Buenos Aires QR Code

Banco de la Nación Argentina QR Code.

Afternoon: Lunch in the area, then go to Palacio Barolo, inspired by Dante's Divine Comedy. Book a guided tour to the lighthouse for stunning city views.

Palacio Barolo QR Code.

Evening: Dine in Montserrat, sampling an upscale Argentine grill. Post-dinner, take a leisurely walk along the illuminated Avenida de Mayo.

DAY 4: LEISURE AND REFLECTION

Day 4.[66]

Morning: Visit the Parque Lezama in the neighboring San Telmo district, a perfect place for a relaxed morning. Browse through the local art galleries and artisan shops.

Parque Lezama QR Code.

Afternoon: Enjoy a leisurely lunch at a historic bar in San Telmo. Spend your afternoon visiting the Museo Histórico Nacional to learn more about Argentina's fight for independence.

Museo Histórico Nacional QR Code.

Evening: For your final night, choose a special dinner at a renowned Parrilla in San Telmo or Monserrat, followed by a visit to a local milonga (tango dance hall) to experience the authentic Buenos Aires nightlife.

5-DAY ITINERARY IN RECOLETA, EASTERN BUENOS AIRES

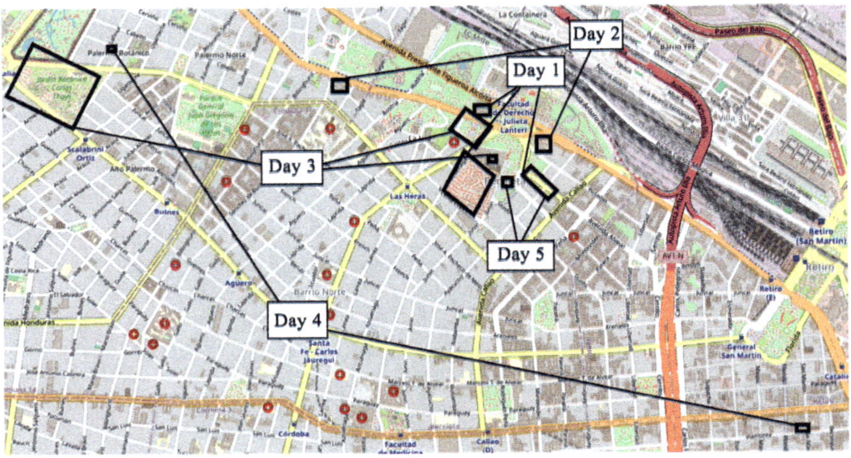

5-day itinerary in Recoleta.[67]

DAY 1: RECOLETA UNVEILED

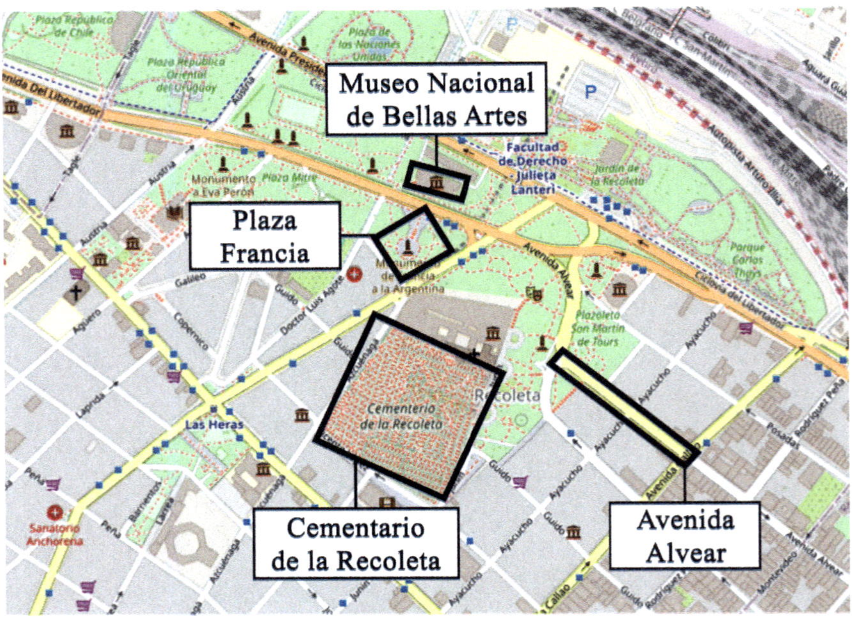

Day 1.[68]

Morning: Start your day with a visit to the elegant Recoleta Cemetery, the final resting place of some of Argentina's most prominent figures, including Eva Perón. Wander through the maze of mausoleums and learn about the history behind each one.

Recoleta Cemetary QR Code.

Afternoon: Take a leisurely stroll along Avenida Alvear, lined with upscale boutiques and beautiful architecture. Stop for lunch at one of the charming cafes in the area, where you can enjoy a classic Argentine meal.

Avenida Alvear QR Code.

Evening: Spend your evening at the Museo Nacional de Bellas Artes, admiring its impressive Argentine and international art collection. Afterward, indulge in a gourmet dinner at one of Recoleta's trendy restaurants, followed by a relaxing evening walk in Plaza Francia.

Walk 750 m from Avenida Alvear to get to the Museo Nacional de Bellas Artes. To get to Plaza Francia, walk 65 m from Museo Nacional de Bellas Artes.

Museo Nacional de Bellas Artes QR Code.

Plaza Francia QR Code.

DAY 2: EXPLORE RECOLETA'S CULTURAL SCENE

Day 2.[69]

Morning: Begin your day with a visit to the striking Palais de Glace, a cultural center that hosts exhibitions, concerts, and events. Explore the exhibits and immerse yourself in Buenos Aires' vibrant arts scene.

Palais de Glace QR Code.

Afternoon: Enjoy a traditional Argentine lunch at one of Recoleta's charming cafes, then head to the nearby Museo Nacional de Arte Decorativo. Marvel at its opulent interiors and extensive decorative arts collection.

Museo Nacional de Arte Decorativo QR Code.

Evening: Dine at a cozy restaurant in Recoleta, savoring delicious Argentine cuisine.

DAY 3: PARKS AND GARDENS OF RECOLETA

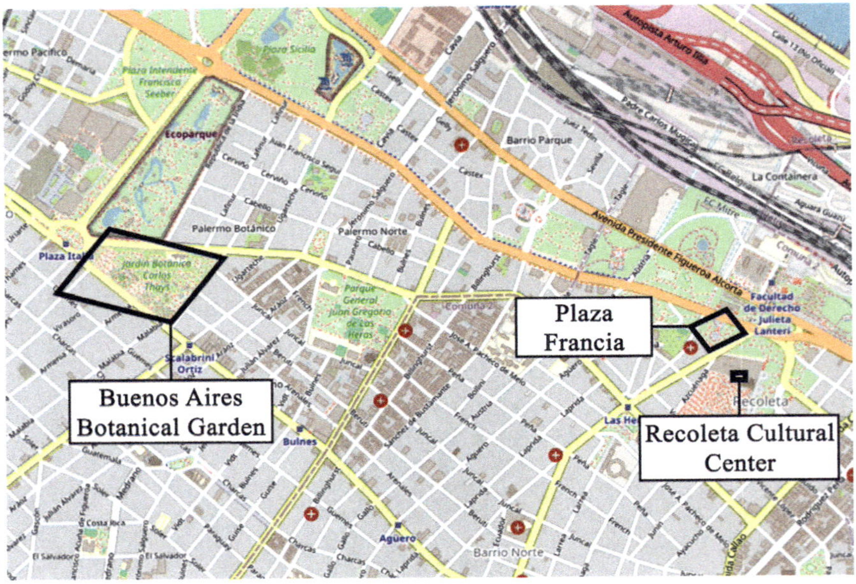

Day 3.[70]

Morning: Spend your morning exploring the lush greenery of the Buenos Aires Botanical Garden, home to a vast array of plant species from around the world. Take a stroll through its winding paths and tranquil ponds.

Buenos Aires Botanical Garden QR Code.

Afternoon: Enjoy a picnic lunch in the scenic surroundings of the nearby Plaza Francia. Relax and soak up the sun while taking in the sights and sounds of Recoleta's bustling streets.

Evening: Head to the Recoleta Cultural Center for an evening of live music or theater. Afterward, dine at a cozy bistro in the neighborhood, sampling Argentine specialties paired with fine wine.

Walk 280 m from Plaza Francia to get to the Recoleta Cultural Center.

Recoleta Cultural Center QR Code.

DAY 4: TAKE A PEEK INTO RECOLETA'S HISTORY AND HERITAGE

Day 4.[71]

Morning: Start your day with a visit to the Museo Nacional de Arte Oriental, housed in a beautiful French-style mansion. Explore its extensive collection of Asian art and artifacts, learning about the cultural connections between Argentina and the East.

Museo Nacional de Arte Oriental QR Code.

Afternoon: Enjoy a leisurely lunch at a traditional parrilla, where you can feast on grilled meats and savory empanadas. Then, visit Museo Evita to learn about the life and legacy of Eva Perón.

Museo Evita QR Code.

Evening: Stop for dinner at a cozy restaurant to enjoy delicious Argentine cuisine.

DAY 5: SHOPPING AND CUISINE EXPERIENCE

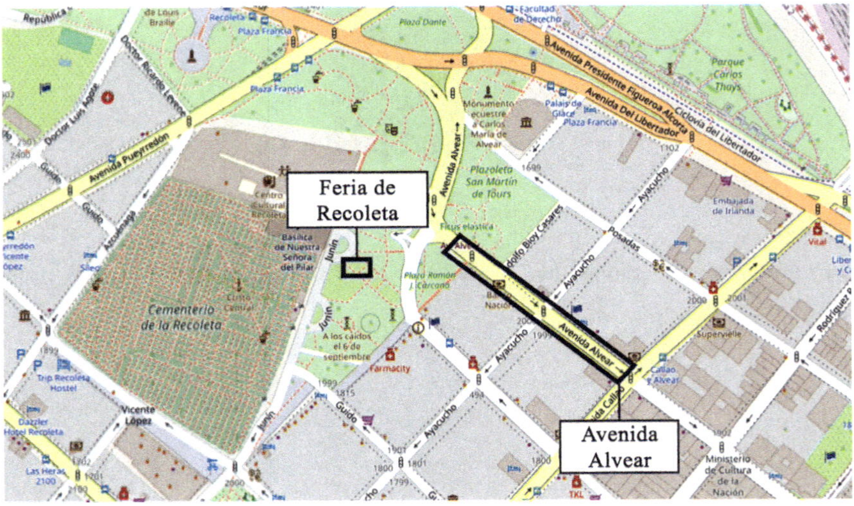

Day 5.[72]

Morning: Spend your morning exploring Recoleta's vibrant street markets, browsing for souvenirs, artisanal crafts, and locally made goods. Don't miss the Feria de Recoleta, held on weekends, for a lively shopping experience.

Feria de Recoleta QR Code.

Afternoon: Treat yourself to a leisurely lunch at one of Recoleta's trendy cafes or bistros, sampling delicious Argentine specialties and sipping a glass of Malbec. Then, indulge in retail therapy at the upscale boutiques along Avenida Alvear.

Evening: Enjoy a memorable dining experience at one of Recoleta's gourmet restaurants, where you can savor innovative Argentine cuisine prepared by talented chefs. After dinner, stroll through the neighborhood, soaking in its sophisticated ambiance.

4-DAY ITINERARY IN PALERMO, NORTHERN BUENOS AIRES

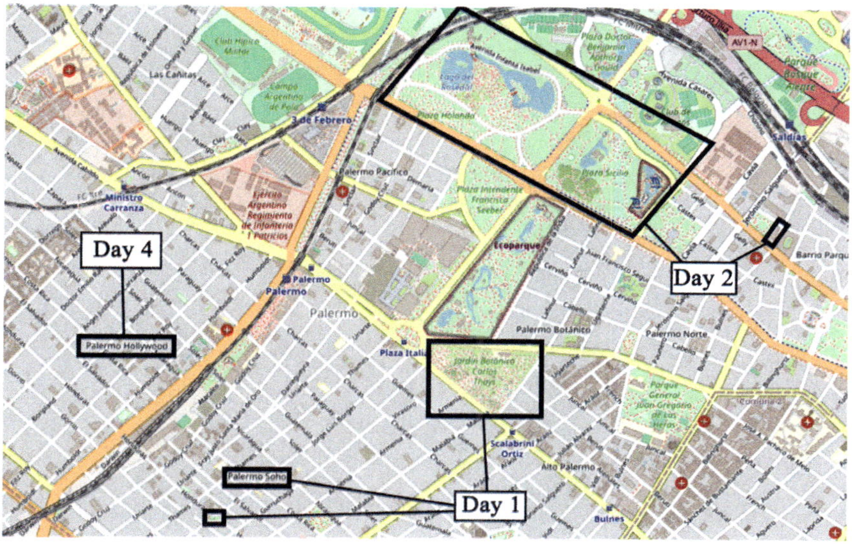

Spend 4 days in Palermo.[73]

DAY 1: PALERMO VIEJO EXPLORATION

Day 1.[74]

Morning: Start your Palermo adventure by wandering through Palermo Viejo, the charming and eclectic neighborhood known for its vibrant street art and trendy boutiques. Begin at Plaza Serrano, a bustling square surrounded by cafes and shops. Explore the area and soak in the local atmosphere.

Plaza Serrano QR Code.

Afternoon: After a delightful morning stroll, treat yourself to a traditional Argentine lunch at one of the many restaurants in Palermo Viejo. Then, head to the nearby Botanical Garden to relax amid lush greenery and exotic plant species.

Evening: As the sun sets, venture to Palermo Soho, a nightlife and entertainment hub. Enjoy dinner at a trendy restaurant offering an Argentine and international cuisine fusion. Afterward, experience the vibrant nightlife of Palermo by visiting a lively bar or club.

To get to Palermo Soho, walk 400 m from the Buenos Aires Botanical Garden to the 2644 Scalabrini Ortiz Raul stop and take bus 110B (a Villa Martelli x Artigas) to 1612 Scalabrini Ortiz Raul Av., then walk 600 m.

Palermo Soho QR Code.

DAY 2: PARKS AND MUSEUMS

Day 2.[75]

Morning: Start your day with a leisurely walk through the expansive Tres de Febrero Park. Enjoy the serene atmosphere as you stroll along tree-lined paths and visit attractions like the Rose Garden and the Planetarium.

Tres de Febrero QR Code.

Afternoon: After a refreshing morning in the park, delve into the cultural side of Palermo by visiting the Museo de Arte Latinoamericano de Buenos Aires

(MALBA). Explore its impressive collection of Latin American art, including works by renowned artists such as Frida Kahlo and Diego Rivera.

To get to Museo de Arte Latinoamericano de Buenos Aires, walk 650 from the Tres de Febrero Park to 3296 Sinclair bus stop and take bus 130A (a La Boca x Munro) to 3896 Salguero Jeronimo, then walk 450 m.

Museo de Arte Latinoamericano de Buenos Aires QR Code.

Evening: Conclude your day with dinner at a traditional Argentine steakhouse and savor the exquisite flavors of local cuisine.

DAY 3: SHOPPING AND GASTRONOMY

Morning: Spend your morning exploring the trendy boutiques and designer stores along Palermo's bustling shopping streets. There's something for every shopper in Palermo, from fashion boutiques to artisanal markets.

Afternoon: Indulge in a culinary adventure by sampling delicious delicacies at one of Palermo's many cafes and restaurants. Whether you crave empanadas, traditional Argentine barbecue, or gourmet pastries, you'll find plenty of options to satisfy your appetite.

Evening: End your day with a culinary experience at a local cooking class and learn to prepare classic Argentine dishes under the guidance of expert chefs. Enjoy the fruits of your labor as you dine on your creations and toast to a memorable day in Palermo.

DAY 4: RELAXATION AND EXPLORATION

Day 4.[76]

Morning/Afternoon: Ease into your last day in Palermo with a leisurely breakfast at a bustling outdoor Palermo cafe. Savor the aroma of freshly brewed coffee and indulge in flaky pastries. Enjoy people-watching, plan your afternoon adventure, or relax and reflect on the amazing memories you've made in Buenos Aires.

Evening: As your time in Palermo draws to a close, take a relaxing evening stroll along the picturesque streets of Palermo Hollywood. This trendy neighborhood boasts a unique charm with its colorful houses and eclectic shops. Find a bistro or cafe that catches your eye and enjoy a delicious final dinner in Buenos Aires. Enjoy the laid-back atmosphere and savor the flavors of Argentinian cuisine one last time.

Palermo Hollywood QR Code.

CHAPTER 9 DAY TRIPS BEYOND THE CITY

Buenos Aires is an amazing city filled with plenty to see and do. However, equally amazing places are just outside the city's border. This section guides you to exploring towns and areas surrounding Argentina's capital city. Get ready for fun day trips and exciting adventures.

TIGRE AND THE PARANÁ DELTA

Moving north from Buenos Aires, the landscape melts away from towering buildings and bustling avenues, unveiling a serene countryside. Lush green fields unfurl as far as the eye can see, filling you with calmness and peace. Arriving in Tigre, you step into a riverside town at the gateway to the awesome Paraná Delta. The gentle murmur of water lapping against the banks mingles with the charm of meandering canals and colonial-style architecture. Tigre is an unusual destination, 32.6 kilometers (20 miles) north of Buenos Aires. This fascinating town sits on several islands within the vast Paraná Delta, a sprawling waterway network covering more than 14,000 square kilometers (or 5,400 square miles).

The Paraná Delta is where the mighty Paraná River, South America's second-longest after the Amazon, meets the Rio de la Plata. This incredible delta is a web of streams and islands, teeming with a variety of exotic plants and animals. Gliding through tranquil canals, you will be surrounded by lush vegetation and native birds darting colorfully from tree to tree. It's a genuinely unforgettable natural wonder.

The Paraná Delta.[77]

TRAVELING FROM BUENOS AIRES TO TIGRE AND PARANÁ DELTA

- **By Bus:** *The bus is a good option to get to Tigre from Buenos Aires, but it's slower and more expensive than the train.*

  Travel Time: Approximately 1 hour 30 minutes (depending on traffic)

  Cost: $1

- **By Mitre Train:** *Taking the Mitre Train is the cheapest and fastest way to get to Tigre. It departs from Retiro station on the Mitre Ramal Tigre line.*

  Travel Time: 50 minutes to 1 hour

  Cost: $1

- **By Taxi:** *Taxis are available in Buenos Aires to take you to Tigre.*

  Travel Time: Approximately 30 minutes

  Cost: $12 to $15

- **By Car:** *You can drive to Tigre from the city via two routes: take the Panamericana highway and the Tigre branch or go straight on Avenida Libertador and enter through Calle Italia.*

  Travel Time: Approximately 45 minutes, depending on traffic

  Cost: $5 to $10

- **By Bicycle:** *Many cyclists in Buenos Aires love cycling to Tigre. The route is beautiful because it follows the river. You can bike there and then catch the train back.*

  Travel Time: 2 to 2.5 hours

  Things to Do and See in Tigre and Paraná Delta

Join a Boat Tour: Once you board a boat, you sign up to explore the Paraná Delta even further. As it reaches the end of its journey, the mighty Paraná reveals a network of channels, streams, and emerald islands. The air is fragrant with the sweet scent of wildflowers, and the melodic calls of birdsong echo through the lush mangrove forests. Sunlight dances on the rippling surface, painting the water lilies that adorn the banks with a warm, golden glow.

Rent a Kayak: Kayaking is the next best thing for a thrilling experience if you are open to a more intimate encounter with this untamed paradise. As you paddle through narrow channels, the rhythm of the water becomes yours. Navigate through emerald tunnels formed by overhanging branches. Each stroke of the paddle takes you deeper into the heart of this tranquil sanctuary.

Visit the Artisanal Market: Back in Tigre, the vibrant artisanal market offers a panorama of locally crafted treasures and experience the region's rich culture. Strike up conversations with artisans, savor delicious homemade treats, and perhaps unearth the perfect memento.

Communities live in areas where a river meets the ocean. They use boats for everything. Kids go to school by ferry, get their mail by boat, and a boat store sells fruits and vegetables at their houses. It's like Venice but in a forest, and it's amazing. Even as you say goodbye to the idyllic landscapes of Tigre and the Paraná Delta, the memories of this day trip will linger, a sweet reverie reminding you of the enduring power of nature's serenity.

SAN ANTONIO DE ARECO

Take a day trip from Buenos Aires to a popular town in Argentina's grassy plains, San Antonio de Areco. It's best to leave early to enjoy the sunrise over the big city. On your way to San Antonio de Areco, you'll see endless fields of golden grass swaying in the wind, rolling hills, and curvy streams. It's a peaceful place, wild and pretty, just like explorers love. The town was built by cowboys (gauchos), and their way of life still exists. The streets are cobblestones, and the buildings are old and made from mud bricks. The main square, the town center, has a beautiful church and big trees for shade. San Antonio de Areco is the place to go if you want to experience the wild beauty of Argentina's cowboy culture. This hidden gem in the plains has historic ranches, silverware workshops, a gaucho museum, and adventures waiting for you.

TRAVELING FROM BUENOS AIRES TO SAN ANTONIO DE ARECO

- **By Bus:** *You can travel from Buenos Aires to San Antonio de Areco by bus. The trip takes about 2 to 2.5 hours. Head to the bus station in Retiro, a neighborhood in Buenos Aires, and look for buses from Chevallier.*

  Travel Time: 2 hours

  Cost: $9 to $15

- **By Taxi:** *Taxis are the fastest option, but also the most expensive. A taxi ride will take up to an hour, depending on the traffic. Ensure to agree on a price before you get in.*

  Travel Time: 1 hour 15 minutes

  Cost: $32 to $49

- **By Car:** *If you're adventurous and have access to a car, you can drive to San Antonio de Areco. The distance is about 118 kilometers, and is a great option to stop and explore the beautiful Pampas countryside along the way.*

  Travel Time: 1 hour 15 minutes

  Cost: $10 to $16

THINGS TO DO AND SEE IN SAN ANTONIO DE ARECO

Visit Historic Estancias: You can visit big ranches (estancias) built long ago and still operational today to show how things used to be in the city. Walking through gardens and courtyards, you'll hear the laughter and music as old as time. You'll get inside knowledge of how real gauchos care for their horses and cows like their families have done for generations.

Join Silver Workshops: If you like crafts, San Antonio de Areco is famous for its silverware. Watch skilled workers turn plain metal into intriguing jewelry and plates. Their hands move smoothly because they love what they do. You can buy unique souvenirs to remember your trip, something shiny that shows the town's history.

Visit Museo Gauchesco Ricardo Güiraldes: No trip to San Antonio de Areco would be complete without seeing the Gaucho Museum (Museo Gauchesco Ricardo Güiraldes). It's filled with fascinating Guacho (Argentina's cowboys) artifacts and information from their clothes to their amazing horse-riding skills. You'll feel like you're there with them, hearing stories of bravery and love that inspired Argentinians for years.

Museo Gauchesco Ricardo Güiraldes.[78]

By the end of the day, you'll be tired but happy. You can eat delicious food at a local restaurant, like savory empanadas and grilled meats (asado). Raise a glass of Malbec wine to celebrate your day full of discoveries and wonders, knowing you'll never forget San Antonio de Areco.

LA PLATA

As you go from Buenos Aires to La Plata, the urban sprawl gradually gives way to open fields and rolling hills, offering a serene backdrop for your adventure. Catch glimpses of quaint towns and picturesque vineyards, adding to the scenic view of the journey. International tourists often overlook La Plata. It looks so much like Buenos Aires it was nicknamed "mini-Buenos Aires."

La Plata was the first planned city in South America. This fascinating fact becomes evident as you explore. The city layout is a well-organized grid featuring wide avenues and numerous parks. Major plazas are connected in a distinctive star-shaped design, making it a delight to navigate on foot. As you explore, admire the beautiful European-style architecture. La Plata has its crown jewel - a stunning neo-Gothic cathedral. However, the city offers more than this architectural masterpiece. Keep reading to discover more.

Traveling from Buenos Aires to La Plata

- **By Bus:** *A bus journey is a budget-friendly and efficient way to reach your destination. It is a perfect choice for people seeking a quick and direct route. The bus trip gives you a window into the local life as you whiz past bustling streets and shops and maybe catch glimpses of the countryside, depending on the route.*

  Travel Time: Approximately 40 minutes

  Cost: $1 - $31

- **By Train:** *The train is a great choice if you want a more leisurely and scenic travel experience. The travel time is slightly longer, so the journey offers a chance to unwind. Relax in a comfortable seat, watch the ever-changing landscape unfold outside your window, and perhaps enjoy a light snack or beverage from the onboard cafe.*

  Travel Time: 1 hour 10 minutes

  Cost: $1

- **By Taxi:** *The fastest option door-to-door, but the most expensive. A taxi ride takes about the same time as the bus but will cost you more.*

  Travel Time: 35 minutes

  Cost: $17 to $22

- **By Shuttle:** *A shuttle bus service runs from Cerrito y Santa Fe to Plaza Rocha in La Plata. It is a good option if you have luggage or want a more comfortable ride than a regular bus.*

  Travel Time: 1 hour

  Cost: $2

- **By Car:** *The distance to La Plata is about 56 kilometers, and the trip should take around the same time as a taxi.*

  Travel Time: 35 minutes

  Cost: $5 to $8

THINGS TO DO AND SEE IN LA PLATA

The La Plata Neo-Gothic Cathedral: Arriving in La Plata, you'll be wowed by the imposing silhouette of its neo-Gothic cathedral. It's an unmissable cathedral. This massive church looks like Europe's grand old cathedrals. The building began in 1885, but it took a long time to complete - the tall towers weren't completed until 1999 - almost a century of building. The inside is as impressive. You'll be greeted by beautiful stained-glass windows casting colorful lights everywhere. The floors are polished granite, so shiny you can almost see your reflection. Don't forget to explore the outside - the spires are breathtaking, reaching high into the sky. A museum in the basement tells the story of how they built this giant cathedral. Your ticket to the museum lets you take an elevator ride to the top of one of the towers, and from there, you can see the whole city spread out below you.

Catedral de la Plata.[79]

Visit the Museo de La Plata: The cathedral is only the beginning of your La Plata exploration. Next on your itinerary is a visit to the Natural Science Museum, a treasure trove of knowledge housed within a majestic building reminiscent of a bygone era. Inside, you're transported through time and space, from the dawn of the universe to the wonders of the natural world. Exhibits showcasing fossils and minerals and interactive displays bring science to life in an educational and entertaining way, making it a must-see destination for visitors of all ages.

Casa Curutchet: La Plata has another must-see spot if you're an architecture buff, Casa Curutchet. This unique house was designed by the world-famous architect Le Corbusier, who created many groundbreaking designs worldwide. Casa Curutchet is one of only two buildings he built in North and South America. Casa Curutchet is a striking example of modern architecture, a style that broke away from traditional designs. It's a building with clean lines, lots of open space, and windows stretching from floor to ceiling built around a tree in the middle of the house. The tree might seem strange, but it's part of Le Corbusier's brilliant design. He believed buildings should connect with nature, and a tree growing inside the house brings the outdoors indoors. The house is a prime example of Le Corbusier's "Five Points of Architecture." These were his ideas about what makes a perfect modern building.

Casa Curutchet.[80]

After experiencing the main attractions in La Plata, explore the city's unique layout, characterized by its diagonal avenues crisscrossing like a giant's footprint across the landscape. Strolling along these broad thoroughfares, you're treated to panoramic views of tree-lined streets, charming cafes, and historic landmarks at every turn. The city's layout is a work of art designed to enhance its surroundings' beauty and create harmony between nature and architecture.

LUJÁN

Luján, a city west of Buenos Aires, is a must-visit for anyone interested in Argentinian history and culture. The city's history dates back to its founding in 1755. Originally called the "Village of Luján," it's one of the oldest settlements near Buenos Aires and significant in the province's history. It wasn't until the late 1800s that the city's most famous landmark took shape - the Basilica of Luján. Today, with its two towers reaching almost 350 feet high, it's a massive structure holding hundreds of worshippers. The beautiful rose-stone Basilica is well-known, attracting pilgrims from all over Argentina. Every September, gauchos (Argentina's famous cowboys) make a memorable trip to the church. In October, a huge pilgrimage takes place where up to a million young people walk from Buenos Aires (about 43 miles) to visit the Basilica. Located on the Luján River, the city offers plenty to do beyond the Basilica. However, there's no doubt that this grand church is the main attraction, drawing visitors who come to pay their respects or fulfill a pilgrimage promise.

Traveling from Buenos Aires to Luján

- **By Bus:** *If speed and affordability are your top priorities, then the bus is a fantastic choice. Buenos Aires Colectivos offers frequent departures, with buses leaving every 20 minutes from Jujuy Av. So you won't wait too long to get on your way.*

  Travel Time: 1 hour 25 minutes

  Cost: $1

- **By Car:** *Enjoy the freedom of the open road - driving to Luján can be a great option. The distance is manageable at 72.3 kilometers, and the travel time should be like a taxi ride. This option allows you to stop if you see something interesting or take a more scenic route. It can be a more cost-effective option if you have an efficient car and travel with several people.*

  Travel Time: 50 minutes

  Cost: $6 to $10

- **By Train:** *The train can be a good choice if you enjoy train travel and don't mind a slightly longer journey. However, it's not a direct route. Take a train from Liniers station to Moreno first, then transfer to another train for the final leg to Luján.*

  Travel Time: 2 hours 50 minutes

  Cost: $1

- **By Taxi:** *If you're short on time and getting there quickly is your main concern, then a taxi is the answer. A taxi ride is the fastest option. However, with speed comes a hefty price tag. Taxi fares are usually on the high side.*

  Travel Time: 50 minutes

  Cost: $22 to $30

THINGS TO DO AND SEE IN LUJÁN

Basilica of Our Lady of Lujan: The Basilica, a towering beacon of faith, emerges from the horizon like a sentinel guarding the town's soul. The front of this giant church is adorned with intricate carvings and soaring spires, indicating centuries of devotion and architectural prowess. Once you enter through the imposing front doors, you'll be enveloped in an aura of reverence as shafts of sunlight filter through stained glass windows, casting colorful patterns on the marble floors. People whisper prayers quietly inside, and you can hear soft, religious music. Every corner of the basilica exudes an aura of sanctity, from the ornate altars adorned with flickering candles to the towering statue of Our Lady of Luján, the patroness of Argentina, cradled in a mantle of gold.

Basilica of Our Lady of Lujan.[81]

The Luján Zoo: Adjacent to the basilica is the Luján Zoo. In this sanctuary, the wonders of nature converge with the delights of family entertainment. Lush gardens, meandering pathways, and diverse creatures from around the globe await discovery. From the lions' majestic roar to the monkeys' playful antics, each encounter is a symphony of sights and sounds igniting the imagination and fostering a deeper appreciation for the natural world. Families stroll hand in hand, their laughter mingling with the birds chirping and the rustle of leaves, forging cherished memories against the backdrop of exotic fauna.

Visit the Centro Cultural Islas Malvinas: It used to be the operations center for the former Officers' Casino of the 7th Infantry Regiment. Now, it's a cool place for art, music, and contemporary movements. The old brick buildings are renovated, and rooms exhibit paintings and other artwork by local artists from La Plata and Argentina. Continuous events, like movie nights and dance shows, are held, so there's always something fun to see or do.

Centro Cultural Islas Malvinas.[82]

As the day draws to a close and the sun dips below the horizon, you can leave Luján with a heart full of wonder and your spirit uplifted. If all you wanted was to experience solace in the sanctuary of the basilica or to delight in the wonders of the zoo, a day trip to Luján promises an unforgettable experience.

BONUS CHAPTER: USEFUL SURVIVAL PHRASES

Unlike some tourist destinations where English is spoken widely, Buenos Aires proudly wears its Spanish-speaking heart on its sleeve. You may not know a single Spanish word, but don't let that discourage you. While exploring the busy streets of Argentina's capital city there are ways to make things work. You might be surprised by how many people understand and speak basic English in the most popular tourist areas. Menus might have translations, and you can likely find your way around by pointing and gesturing.

This would work until you go beyond the usual tourist hotspots and unlock a new side of Buenos Aires. Here, your basic English might not take you as far. Learning a few key Spanish phrases, even only greetings, basic questions, and numbers, can transform your experience. Imagine ordering a delicious plate of "bife ancho" (a juicy ribeye steak) with the confidence of a local or asking for directions to a hidden tango show with a friendly smile. These small interactions bridge the language gap and allow you to connect with the heart and soul of Buenos Aires. So, embrace the challenge, learn a few basic phrases, and prepare to be amazed by the magic that unfolds when you connect with the city on its terms – in Spanish.

BASIC SPANISH PHRASES

Here are common words and phrases and their phonetic pronunciations:

- *Hello - Hola (OH-lah)*
- *Goodbye - Adiós (ah-DYOS)*
- *Please - Por favor (por fah-VOR)*
- *Thank you - Gracias (GRAH-syahs)*
- *Yes - Sí (see)*
- *No - No (noh)*
- *Excuse me / I am sorry - Perdón / Lo siento (per-DON / loh SYEN-toh)*

GREETINGS

- *Hello/Hi - ¡Buenas! (BWEH-nas)*
- *Greetings - ¡Saludos! (sah-LOO-dohs)*
- *Welcome - ¡Bienvenido! (bee-en-ben-EE-doh)*
- *Good morning – Buenos días (BWEH-nos DEE-as)*
- *Good afternoon - Buenas tardes (BWEH-nas TAR-des)*
- *Good night / Good evening - Buenas noches (BWEH-nas NO-chehs)*

GOODBYES

- *Goodbye - Adiós (ah-dee-OS)*
- *See you later - Hasta luego (AAS-ta loo-AYE-go)*
- *See you soon - Hasta pronto (AAS-ta PRON-toh)*
- *See you - Nos vemos (nos BAY-mos)*
- *Have a good day - ¡Qué tengas un buen día! (keh TEN-gahs oon bwen DEE-ah)*

NUMBERS

- *One - Uno (OO-noh)*
- *Two - Dos (dohs)*
- *Three - Tres (trehs)*
- *Four - Cuatro (KWAH-troh)*
- *Five - Cinco (SEEN-koh)*
- *Six - Seis (seys)*
- *Seven - Siete (SYEH-teh)*
- *Eight - Ocho (OH-choh)*
- *Nine - Nueve (NWEH-veh)*
- *Ten - Diez (DYEH-th)*

DAYS OF THE WEEK

- *Monday - Lunes (LOO-nes)*
- *Tuesday - Martes (MAR-tes)*
- *Wednesday - Miércoles (myer-KOH-les)*
- *Thursday - Jueves (HWEH-ves)*
- *Friday - Viernes (VYER-nes)*
- *Saturday - Sábado (SAH-ba-doh)*
- *Sunday - Domingo (doh-MEEN-go)*

PHRASES FOR SMALL TALK

INTRODUCTIONS

- *How are you? - ¿Cómo estás? (koh-MOH ehs-TAHS)*
- *How's it going? - ¿Qué tal? (keh TAHL)*
- *Nice to meet you - Mucho gusto (MOO-choh GOOS-toh)*
- *What's your name? - ¿Cómo te llamas? (koh-MOH teh YAH-mahs)*
- *My name is... - Me llamo... (meh YAH-moh)*
- *Delighted/Pleased to meet you - Encantado (en-kahn-TAH-doh) if you're talking to a male, and Encantada (en-kahn-TAH-dah) if you're talking to a female*
- *How has your day been? - ¿Cómo ha ido tu día? (koh-MOH ah EE-doh too DEE-ah)*
- *What are you doing? - ¿Qué haces? (keh AH-sehs)*
- *Where are you from? - ¿De dónde eres? (deh DON-deh EH-res)*
- *I am from... - Soy de... (soy deh)*
- *Everything alright? - ¿Todo bien? (TOH-doh byen)*
- *I'm fine, thanks - Estoy bien ¡Gracias! (eh-STOY bee-en GRA-see-aas)*
- *And you? - ¿Y tú? (ee-too)*
- *I have to go - Tengo que irme (TEN-goh keh EER-meh)*
- *Take care - Cuídate (kwee-DAH-teh)*

TALKING ABOUT HOBBIES AND INTERESTS

- *I like to... - Me gusta (meh GOOS-tah)*
- *Listen to music - Escuchar música (es-koo-CHAR MOO-see-kah)*
- *Play sports - Hacer deporte (AH-ser deh-POR-teh)*
- *Cook - Cocinar (ko-see-NAR)*
- *Read books - Leer libros (le-ER LEE-bros)*
- *Do you have any hobbies? - ¿Tienes algún pasatiempo? (TYEH-nes AHL-goon pah-sah-TYEM-poh)*

TALKING ABOUT SPORTS

- *I like sports - Me gustan los deportes (meh goos-TAHN lohs deh-POR-tes)*
- *Do you like sports? - ¿Te gustan los deportes? (teh goos-TAHN lohs deh-POR-tes)*
- *What's your favorite sport? - ¿Cuál es tu deporte favorito? (kwahl ehs too deh-POR-teh fah-VOH-ree-toh)*
- *Are you a fan of a team? - ¿Eres fanático de algún equipo? (EH-res fah-NAH-tee-koh deh AHL-goon eh-KEE-poh)*
- *Do you play any sports? - ¿Practicas algún deporte? (PRAHK-tee-kahs AHL-goon deh-POR-teh)*
- *Do you follow the Olympics? - ¿Sigues los Juegos Olímpicos? (SEE-gwes lohs HWEH-gos oh-LEEM-pee-kos)*

TALKING ABOUT FOOD

- *Do you know a good restaurant nearby? - ¿Conoces algún buen restaurante cercano?*
- *I like the local food - me gusta la comida local*
- *What's your favorite food? - ¿Cuál es tu comida favorita?*
- *I am vegetarian - Soy vegetariana(feminine) or Soy vegetariano(masculine)*

PHRASES FOR RESTAURANTS

- *Hello - Buenas tardes. (BWE-nas TAR-des)*
- *Can you give me the menu, please? - ¿Puede darme el menú, por favor? (PWE-de DAR-meh el meh-NOO, por fah-VOR?)*
- *What is today's special? - ¿Cuál es el plato del día? (KWAL es el PLAH-toh del DEE-ah?)*
- *I would like to order... - Quiero pedir... (KYEH-roh peh-DEER...)*
- *I would like a... (for drinks) - Me gustaría un/una... (meh goos-TAH-ree-ah oon/oo-nah...)*
- *Could we have some water, please? - ¿Podríamos tener agua, por favor? (poh-DREE-ah-mohs teh-NEHR AH-gwah, por fah-VOR?)*
- *I am allergic to... - Soy alérgico/a a... (soy al-EHR-hee-koh/kah ah...)*
- *I am vegetarian - Soy vegetariano/a (soy veh-heh-tah-ree-AH-noh/nah)*
- *Do you have a vegetarian option? - ¿Tienen opción vegetariana? (TYEH-nehn ohp-see-YOHN veh-heh-tah-REEAH-nah?)*
- *Do you accept credit cards? - ¿Aceptan tarjetas de crédito? (ah-sehp-TAN tar-HEH-tas deh KREH-dee-toh?)*
- *I am satisfied - Estoy satisfecho/a (ehs-TOY sah-tees-FEH-choh/chah)*
- *The food was delicious, thank you. - La comida estaba deliciosa, gracias. (lah koh-MEE-dah ehs-TAH-bah deh-lee-SYOH-sah, GRAH-syahs.)*
- *The check, please - La cuenta, por favor (lah KWEN-tah, por fah-VOR)*

PHRASES FOR SHOPPING

- *I'm going shopping - Me voy de compras (meh voy deh KOM-prahs)*
- *Where is the nearest shopping center? - ¿Dónde está el centro comercial más cercano? (DOHN-deh ehs-TAH el SEN-tro koh-mer-SYAL mahs ser-KAH-noh)*
- *I want something like this - Quiero algo como esto (KYEH-roh AHL-goh KOH-moh EHS-toh)*
- *How much does this cost? - ¿Cuánto cuesta esto? (KWAN-toh KWES-ta ES-to)*
- *I don't have cash - no tengo efectivo (noh TEN-goh eh-fehk-TEE-voh)*

- *Do you accept credit cards? - ¿Aceptan tarjetas de crédito? (ah-sehp-TAHN tar-HEH-tas deh KREH-dee-toh?)*
- *Can I try this on? - ¿Puedo probármelo? (PWEH-doh proh-BAHR-meh-loh?)*
- *Do you have this in a different color/size? - ¿Tienen esto en otro color/talla? (TYEH-nehn EHS-toh en O-troh koh-LOHR/TAH-yah?)*
- *Where are the fitting rooms? - ¿Dónde están los probadores? (DOHN-deh ehs-TAHN lohs proh-bah-DOH-res?)*
- *Is there a discount on this item? - ¿Hay algún descuento en este artículo? (eye ahl-GOON dehs-KWEHN-toh ehn EHS-teh ahr-TEE-koo-loh?)*
- *Can you help me find...? - ¿Puede ayudarme a encontrar...? (PWEH-deh ah-yoo-DAHR-meh ah ehn-kohn-TRAHR...?)*
- *Can I get a receipt, please? - ¿Puede darme un recibo, por favor? (PWEH-deh DAR-meh oon reh-SEE-boh, por fah-VOR)*
- *This is too expensive - Esto es demasiado caro (EH-stoh es deh-mah-SYA-doh KAH-roh)*
- *I'm just looking, thank you - Solo estoy mirando, gracias. (SOH-loh ehs-TOY meer-AHN-doh, GRAH-syahs)*
- *I'll take it - Me lo/la llevo (Meh loh/lah YEH-vo)*

PHRASES FOR USING PUBLIC TRANSPORT

- *I am going to... - Voy a... (voy ah)*
- *How much is a ticket to...? - ¿Cuánto cuesta un billete para...? (KWAN-toh KWES-tah oon bee-YEH-teh PAH-rah)*
- *Where can I buy the ticket? - ¿Dónde puedo comprar el billete? (DON-deh PWAY-doh kom-PRAR el bee-YEH-teh)*
- *Where is the nearest bus station? - ¿Dónde está la estación de autobuses más cercana? (DON-deh ehs-TAH la es-ta-SYON deh ow-toh-BOO-ses mahs ser-KAH-nah)*
- *What time does the bus leave? - ¿A qué hora sale el autobús? (ah keh OH-rah SAH-leh el ow-toh-BOOS)*
- *Where is the nearest train station? - ¿Dónde está la estación de tren más cercana? (DON-deh ehs-TAH la es-ta-SYON deh tren mahs ser-KAH-nah)*

- *Where can I get a taxi going to...? - ¿Dónde puedo tomar un taxi para...? (DOHN-deh PWEH-doh toh-MAR oon TAHK-see PAH-rah...?)*
- *Can you take me to the Airport? - ¿Puedes llevarme al aeropuerto? (PWAY-des yeh-VAR-meh al ah-eh-roo-PWER-toh)*
- *How much will that cost? - ¿Cuánto costará? (KWAN-toh kos-ta-RAH)*
- *Is it far from here? - ¿Está lejos de aquí? (ehs-TAH LEH-hos deh ah-KEE)*
- *What time does the train leave? - ¿A qué hora sale el tren? (ah keh OH-rah SAH-leh el tren)*

PHRASES FOR EMERGENCIES

- *Help me, please - Ayúdame, por favor (ah-YOO-dah-meh, por fah-VOR)*
- *Call an ambulance! - Llama a la ambulancia! (YAH-mah ah lah ahm-boo-LAHN-see-ah)*
- *There is a fire! - Hay un incendio (eye oon een-THEN-dee-oh)*
- *I am injured - Estoy herido (ehs-TOY eh-REE-doh)*
- *I need a doctor - Necesito un médico (neh-seh-SEE-toh oon MEH-dee-koh)*
- *Can you help me? - ¿Puede ayudarme? (PWEH-deh ah-yoo-DAR-meh?)*
- *I am lost - Estoy perdido/a (ehs-TOY pehr-DEE-doh/dah)*
- *I need to find... - Necesito encontrar... (neh-seh-SEE-toh ehn-kohn-TRAR...)*
- *I don't understand - No entiendo (noh ehn-TYEN-doh)*
- *I have allergies - Tengo alergias (TEN-goh ah-lehr-HEE-ahs)*
- *I have lost my passport - He perdido mi pasaporte (eh pehr-DEE-doh mee pah-sah-POR-teh)*
- *I lost my bag in the taxi - Perdí mi bolso en el taxi (pehr-DEE mee BOHL-soh ehn ehl TAHK-see)*
- *My wallet has been stolen - Me han robado la cartera (meh ahn roh-BAH-doh lah kahr-TEH-rah)*
- *Where is the bathroom? - ¿Dónde está el baño? (DON-deh es-TAH el BAH-nyo?)*

CULTURAL TIPS ON POLITE INTERACTIONS AND COURTESY GESTURES

- *Greet shopkeepers and service staff with "Buenos días/tardes" (Good morning/afternoon) when entering the store or shop.*
- *Make eye contact and greet people with a handshake or a kiss on the cheek (for close friends/family) when meeting.*
- *Speak slowly and clearly if your Spanish is limited. Porteños appreciate the effort.*
- *Dress modestly when going out as porteños take pride in their appearance.*
- *Be patient in restaurants and shops as service can sometimes be slower-paced.*
- *Try local cuisine like asado (barbecue), empanadas, and "dulce de leche."*
- *Don't be overly loud in public; it's considered rude and insulting.*
- *Don't rush interactions or transactions - take your time and be polite.*
- *Don't point with your finger at the locals. It can be insulting - use an open-hand gesture instead.*
- *Don't enter churches or religious sites without appropriate modest clothing covering shoulders and knees.*
- *Don't be overly demonstrative with public displays of affection. No one wants to see your private business in public.*

APPENDIX

- *Artisanal Market - mentioned in chapter 9.*
- *Acuña de Figeroa - mentioned in chapter 7.*
- *Almagro District - mentioned in chapter 7.*
- *Almagro's shopping scene - mentioned in chapter 7.*
- *Alma y Fuego - mentioned in chapter 6.*
- *Argentine Parrilla - mentioned in chapter 8.*
- *Asado - mentioned in Chapter 1.*
- *Avenida Avellaneda - mentioned in chapter 6.*
- *Avenida Corrientes - mentioned in chapter 7.*
- *Avenida del Libertador - mentioned in chapter 8.*
- *Avenida Rivadavia - mentioned in chapter 6.*
- *Balvanera District - mentioned in chapter 7.*
- *Balvanera's shopping scene - mentioned in chapter 7.*
- *Banco de la Nación - mentioned in chapter 8.*
- *Barracas District - mentioned in chapter 4.*
- *Barracas's shopping scene - mentioned in chapter 4.*
- *Barrancas de Belgrano - mentioned in chapter 3.*
- *Barrio Chino - mentioned in chapter 3.*
- *Basilica of Our Lady of Luján - mentioned in chapter 9.*
- *Batucada Area - mentioned in chapter 6.*
- *Belgrano District - mentioned in chapter 3.*
- *Boat Tour - mentioned in chapter 9.*
- *Bohemian atmosphere - mentioned in chapter 5.*
- *Borgoña - mentioned in chapter 7.*
- *Bosques de Palermo - mentioned in chapter 3.*
- *Boulevard Ramón Falcón - mentioned in chapter 6.*

- *Buenos Aires International Festival of Independent Cinema (BAFICI) - mentioned in chapter 1.*
- *Caballito Day - mentioned in chapter 6.*
- *Caballito District - mentioned in chapter 6.*
- *Caballito's shopping scene - mentioned in chapter 6.*
- *Café San Juan - mentioned in chapter 5.*
- *Café Tortoni - mentioned in chapter 7.*
- *Calle Lanín - mentioned in chapter 4.*
- *Caminito - mentioned in chapter 4.*
- *Casa Curutchet - mentioned in chapter 9.*
- *Casa Rosada - mentioned in chapter 8.*
- *Cathedral Metropolitana - mentioned in chapter 8.*
- *Centro Asturiano de Buenos Aires - mentioned in chapter 7.*
- *Cementerio de la Recoleta - mentioned in chapter 5.*
- *Centro Cultural Islas Malvinas - mentioned in chapter 9.*
- *Ciudad Universitaria - mentioned in chapter 3.*
- *Defensa Street - mentioned in chapter 5.*
- *Distrito Tecnológico - mentioned in chapter 4.*
- *Dada Bistró - mentioned in chapter 5.*
- *Edificio Kavanagh - mentioned in chapter 5.*
- *El Burladero - mentioned in chapter 5.*
- *El Centro - mentioned in chapter 7.*
- *El Puente Alsina - mentioned in chapter 4.*
- *Estadio Monumental - mentioned in chapter 3.*
- *Five Points of Architecture - mentioned in chapter 9.*
- *Floralis Genérica - mentioned in chapter 5.*
- *Florida Street - mentioned in chapter 5.*
- *Floresta District - mentioned in chapter 6.*

- *Palermo Hollywood - mentioned in chapter 8.*
- *Palermo Soho - mentioned in chapter 8.*
- *Parque Centenario - mentioned in chapter 7.*
- *Parque Lezama - mentioned in chapter 8.*
- *Parque Tres de Febrero - mentioned in Chapter 1.*
- *Parque Centenario - mentioned in chapter 6.*
- *Parque Patricios District - mentioned in chapter 4.*
- *Parque Patricios's shopping scene - mentioned in chapter 4.*
- *Parque de los Niños - mentioned in chapter 3.*
- *Parque de los Patricios - mentioned in chapter 4.*
- *Paseo de la Costa - mentioned in chapter 3.*
- *Pasaje San Carlo - mentioned in chapter 7.*
- *Planetarium - mentioned in chapter 8.*
- *Plaza Almagro - mentioned in chapter 7.*
- *Plaza Ejército de los Andes - mentioned in chapter 6.*
- *Plaza Miserere - mentioned in chapter 7.*
- *Plaza Velez Sarsfield - mentioned in chapter 6.*
- *Plaza de Mayo - mentioned in chapter 7.*
- *Plaza Dorrego - mentioned in chapter 5.*
- *Plaza Rocha - mentioned in chapter 9.*
- *Plaza San Martín - mentioned in chapter 5.*
- *Porteños - mentioned in chapter 1.*
- *Puerto Madero District - mentioned in chapter 5.*
- *Puente de la Mujer - mentioned in chapter 5.*
- *Quinta de Olivos - mentioned in chapter 3.*
- *Recoleta District - mentioned in chapter 5.*
- *Reserva Ecológica Costanera Sur - mentioned in chapter 5.*
- *Retiro District - mentioned in chapter 5.*

- *River Plate Stadium - mentioned in chapter 3.*
- *Rodizio Puerto Madero - mentioned in chapter 5.*
- *Rosedale (rose garden) - mentioned in chapter 1.*
- *San Antonio de Areco - mentioned in chapter 9.*
- *San Carlos Church & Basilica - mentioned in chapter 7.*
- *San Nicolás District - mentioned in chapter 7.*
- *San Nicolás shopping scene - mentioned in chapter 7.*
- *Sanctuary of San Cayetano - mentioned in chapter 6.*
- *San Telmo District - mentioned in chapter 5.*
- *Santuario Virgen de los Milagros de Pompeya - mentioned in chapter 4.*
- *Superclásico - mentioned in chapter 1.*
- *Silver Workshops - mentioned in chapter 9.*
- *Tango Argentino - mentioned in chapter 1.*
- *Tango Festival and World Tango Championship - mentioned in Chapter 1.*
- *Teatro Avenida - mentioned in chapter 8.*
- *Teatro Colón - mentioned in chapter 7.*
- *Teatro Colón's Production Workshops - mentioned in chapter 4.*
- *Teatro Gran Rivadavia - mentioned in chapter 6.*
- *Tigre and the Paraná Delta - mentioned in chapter 9.*
- *Torre Monumental - mentioned in chapter 5.*
- *Tower of the English - mentioned in chapter 5.*
- *Traveling From Buenos Aires to La Plata - mentioned in chapter 9.*
- *Traveling From Buenos Aires to Luján - mentioned in chapter 9.*
- *Traveling From Buenos Aires to San Antonio de Areco - mentioned in chapter 9.*
- *Traveling From Buenos Aires to Tigre and Paraná Delta - mentioned in chapter 9.*
- *Vélez Sársfield - mentioned in chapter 6.*

CONCLUSION

This guidebook has taken you on a virtual journey through Buenos Aires, a city overflowing with character in every neighborhood. It has invited you to wander through its streets and quiet corners, helping you discover hidden gems in every corner. From the energetic Palermo neighborhood to the refined elegance of Recoleta, each neighborhood has its unique allure, waiting for you to explore and create memories. Now, it's time to turn those dreams into unforgettable experiences.

In Palermo, lose yourself in the beauty of its parks and gardens and join locals for leisurely strolls and picnics. San Nicolás is calling your name with its busy streets, grand buildings, and famous landmarks like the Obelisco. Barracas reveals the city's industrial past through colorful murals and renovated warehouses, while Floresta charms with its tranquil atmosphere and leafy streets. In Recoleta, you can explore the opulent Recoleta Cemetery, home to the resting places of Argentina's elite, and indulge in the neighborhood's upscale boutiques and cafes.

You can bask in the warmth of Buenos Aires' splendor, where history and culture come together in a perfect mix. Everywhere in Buenos Aires, you'll feel the warmth of the city's beauty. Look for hidden treasures like the colorful street art in La Boca or the charming cafes in San Telmo. On the lively Avenida Corrientes, you can experience the city's theater scene and treat yourself to a delicious traditional Argentine steak dinner. Head to the peaceful Tigre Delta, where you can find lush greenery and calm waterways if you need a break from the hustle and bustle.

With each neighborhood offering its unique charm and attractions, there's never a dull moment in Buenos Aires. Whether exploring the bohemian vibe of San Telmo, marveling at the modern architecture of Puerto Madero, or soaking up the sun along the waterfront in La Boca, every experience promises to be unforgettable.

Thanks to this awesome guide, you're geared up for your trip to Buenos Aires. No more stressing about how to get around – the guide gives clear directions on navigating airports and using public transportation. It is jam-packed with suggested itineraries, so you can create the perfect trip, whether you want to relax in the numerous parks or explore the sights. You got a bonus section with essential Spanish phrases. Even if you can't speak the language fluently, knowing a few basic words will greatly help. Saying "thank you" or "hello" to the locals will make the trip more enjoyable and create a connection.

Now, you have no excuse. So, don't hesitate any longer. Pack your bags, book your flights, and prepare to embark on an adventure of a lifetime in Buenos Aires. With its endless possibilities for exploration and discovery, this vibrant city is sure to enchant and captivate you at every turn.

Here's another book by Captivating Travels that you might like

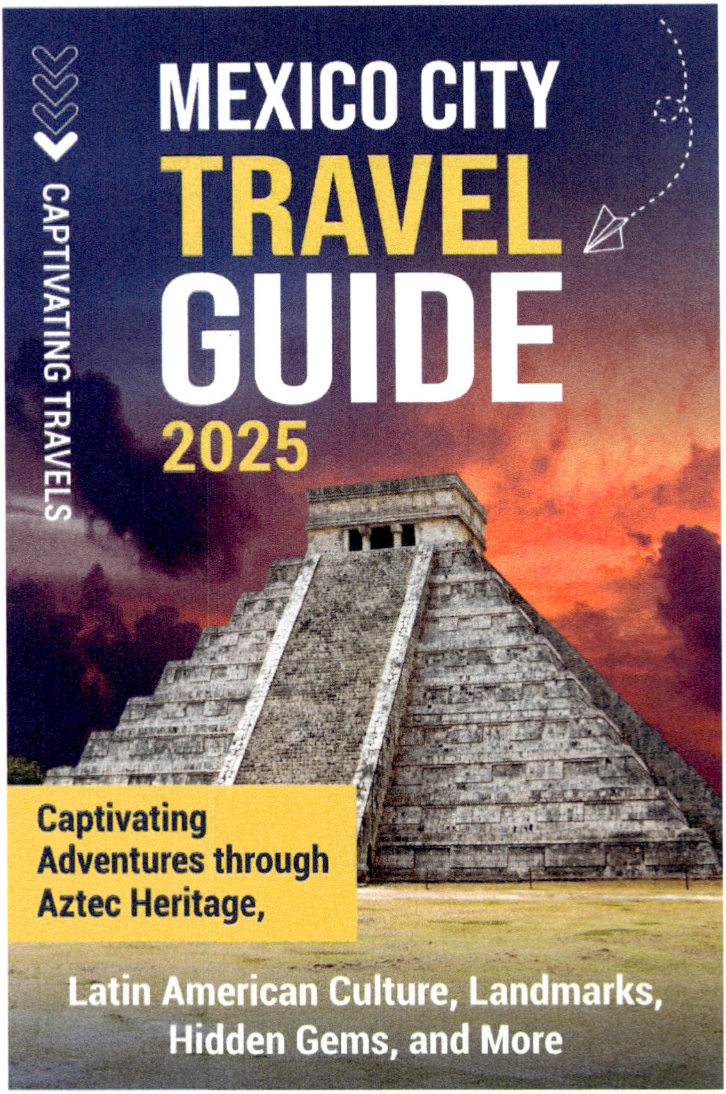

Welcome Aboard, Discover

Your Limited-Time Free Bonus!

Hello, traveler! Welcome to the Captivating Travels family, and thanks for grabbing a copy of this book! Since you've chosen to join us on this journey, we'd like to offer you something special.

Check out the link below for a FREE Ultimate Travel Checklist eBook & Printable PDF to make your travel planning stress-free and enjoyable.

But that's not all - you'll also gain access to our exclusive email list with even more free e-books and insider travel tips. Well, what are you waiting for? Click the link below to join and embark on your next adventure with ease.

Access your bonus here: https://livetolearn.lpages.co/checklist/

Or, Scan the QR code!

REFERENCES

25 Best Things to Do in Buenos Aires (Argentina) - The Crazy Tourist. (2019, April 30). The Crazy Tourist. https://www.thecrazytourist.com/25-best-things-buenos-aires-argentina/

7 days in Buenos Aires Itinerary: day-by-day Guide. (2023, October 23). BetterTravel. https://bettertravel.ai/itineraries/buenos-aires-argentina-7-days-itinerary

A Newcomer's Guide to Buenos Aires Neighborhoods | Mente Argentina Blog. (2022, June 22). Mente Argentina. https://www.menteargentina.com/blog/neighborhoods-in-buenos-aires/

A.R.A. Sarmiento Frigate museum ship. (2016, July 15). Official English Website for the City of Buenos Aires. https://turismo.buenosaires.gob.ar/en/otros-establecimientos/ara-sarmiento-frigate-museum-ship

Abeele, B. V. (2011, August 9). Best milongas in Buenos Aires. Tanguito, Argentine Tango Academy. https://www.tanguito.co.uk/tango-culture/milonguear-in-bs-as/best-milongas-in-buenos-aires/

Agusciin. (2008, November 5). Balvanera. Agusciin's Blog. https://agusciin.wordpress.com/balvanera/

Alex. (2016, August 5). Discovering The Best Places for Skateboarding in Buenos Aires, Argentina. Vamospanish.com. https://vamospanish.com/discover/skateboarding-buenos-aires-argentina/

Alex. (2023, December 4). Historic Buenos Aires: Uncovering the City's Past Historical Insights | VAMOS OBSERVER. Vamospanish.com. https://vamospanish.com/magazine/lifestyle/historic-buenos-aires-uncovering-the-citys-past-historical-insights/

Alex. (2023, October 20). Exploring La Plata, Buenos Aires: A Perfect Day Trip for Culture. Vamospanish.com. https://vamospanish.com/discover/la-plata-buenos-aires-day-trip/

Almagro - Gringo in Buenos Aires. (2010, February 8). Www.gringoinbuenosaires.com. https://www.gringoinbuenosaires.com/neighborhood-guides/almagro/

Almagro-Balvanera-San Nicolás. (2008, November 4). Trabajo Interdisciplinario. https://tpeje2.wordpress.com/almagro/

Anda. (2020, May 14). The Most Interesting Neighborhoods to Visit in Buenos Aires. Travel Notes & Beyond. https://travelnotesandbeyond.com/buenos-aires-neighborhoods/

Ande. (2012, May 25). Buenos Aires Neighborhoods: Almagro Attractions. Wander Argentina. https://wander-argentina.com/almagro-places-of-interest/

Angel, M. (2023, August 10). Plaza San Martin Peru Guide: History, Facts, Maps, and Tours - Evolution Treks Peru. Www.evolutiontreksperu.com. https://www.evolutiontreksperu.com/peru/tourist-attraction/plaza-san-martin/

Araoz, G. (2021, January 6). Full Digital Nomad Guide to Buenos Aires, Argentina. Digital Nomad World. https://digitalnomads.world/city-guide/buenos-aires/

Austin, C. (2019). 10 Top Tourist Attractions in Buenos Aires. Touropia. https://www.touropia.com/tourist-attractions-in-buenos-aires

Botanical Garden. (2016, September 9). Official English Website for the City of Buenos Aires. https://turismo.buenosaires.gob.ar/en/atractivo/botanical-garden

Bradley. (2022, February 7). Tigre | Buenos Aires | The gateway to the Paraná Delta. Bwd Vacations. https://www.bwd-vacations.com/travelog/tigre-buenos-aires-the-gateway-to-the-parana-delta/

Brown, C. (2019, December 10). Ministro Pistarini (Ezeiza) Airport Guide. TripSavvy. https://www.tripsavvy.com/ministro-pistarini-ezeiza-airport-guide-4778627

Buenos Aires Airport (EZE) | The Main Airport in Buenos Aires. (2019, September 4). Buenos Aires International Airport (EZE). https://buenos-aires-international-airport.com/

Buenos Aires to Tigre - 6 ways to travel via train, bus, taxi, car, and Uber. (2023). Rome2rio. https://www.rome2rio.com/s/Buenos-Aires/Tigre

Carey, L. (2017, August 24). An Insider's Guide To Ciudad Universitaria... Culture Trip. https://theculturetrip.com/north-america/mexico/articles/an-insiders-guide-to-ciudad-universitaria-mexico-city

Centennial Park (Parque Centenario). (2021, January 20). Free Tour Buenos Aires. https://www.buenosairesfreewalks.com/batips/centennial-park-parque-centenario/

Cheung, P. (2021, September 29). 121 Common Spanish Phrases For Travelers - Swap Language Blog. Swap Language Blog. https://swaplanguage.com/blog/121-common-spanish-phrases-for-travelers/

Cieri, J. L. (2024, February 4). Distrito Tecnológico: razones del auge inmobiliario que mantiene esta zona del sur porteño. Infobae. https://www.infobae.com/economia/2024/02/04/distrito-tecnologico-razones-del-auge-inmobiliario-que-mantiene-esta-zona-del-sur-porteno/

Claudia. (2022, June 16). Best Way To Get From EZE Airport To Buenos Aires: 5 Options. Myadventuresacrosstheworld.com. https://myadventuresacrosstheworld.com/eze-airport-to-buenos-aires/

Daniel, E. (n.d.). THE FLORESTA NEIGHBORHOOD BUENOS AIRES ARGENTINA. Turismoenelmundo. https://www.turismoenelmundo.com/en/the-floresta-neighborhood-buenos-aires-argentina/

David, A. (2019, August 16). A Practical Guide to Buenos Aires (Part I: Getting Settled). Adam David. https://www.adam-david.me/a-practical-guide-to-buenos-aires-part-i-getting-settled/

Dearsley, B. (2023, December 28). 12 Top Tourist Attractions & Places to Visit in Buenos Aires. Www.planetware.com. https://www.planetware.com/tourist-attractions-/buenos-aires-arg-cf-ba.htm.

Deasy, K. (2017, June 20). Recoleta Cemetery What to Know About the... Culture Trip. https://theculturetrip.com/south-america/argentina/articles/recoleta-cemetery-what-to-know-about-the-worlds-best-cemetery

Dehesa, J. (n.d.). https://guide.en-vols.com/en/adresse/the-bosque-de-palermo-or-the-citys-green-lung/, https://guide.en-vols.com/en/adresse/the-bosque-de-palermo-or-the-citys-green-lung/. Envols. https://guide.en-vols.com/en/adresse/the-bosque-de-palermo-or-the-citys-green-lung/#/search@23.0714579

Dejtiar, F. (2017, July 11). The History of One of the Best Theaters in the World: Teatro Colón in Buenos Aires. ArchDaily. https://www.archdaily.com/875370/the-history-of-one-of-the-best-theaters-in-the-world-teatro-colon-in-buenos-aires

Discover Floresta. (2010, December 10). ¿Qué Sé Yo, Argentina? https://queseyoargentina.wordpress.com/2010/12/10/discover-floresta/

Ediney. (2019, March 7). Buenos Aires Aeroparque Jorge Newbery Airport - Spotting Guide. Spotterguide.net. https://www.spotterguide.net/planespotting/south-america/argentina/buenos-aires-aeroparque-aep-sabe/

Ellie. (2023, October 10). How to spend 4 days in Buenos Aires: A first-time itinerary. This Remote Corner. https://thisremotecorner.com/buenos-aires-itinerary/

Erin. (2023, September 6). The Perfect 3 Days in Buenos Aires Itinerary by a Local. Https://Solsalute.com/. https://solsalute.com/blog/3-days-in-buenos-aires-itinerary/

Estadio de Boca Juniors, La Bombonera. (2013, February 14). Sitio Oficial de Turismo de La Ciudad de Buenos Aires. https://turismo.buenosaires.gob.ar/es/otros-establecimientos/estadio-de-boca-juniors-la-bombonera

Famous People From Buenos Aires, Argentina & Celebs Born In Buenos Aires. (2023). Www.thefamouspeople.com. https://www.thefamouspeople.com/buenos-aires-1280.php

Floralis Generica. (2013, August 13). Atlas Obscura. https://www.atlasobscura.com/places/floralis-generica

French, D. (2023, January 11). 12 Amazing Day Trips from Buenos Aires: The Best Additions to Your Vacation. Our French Travels. https://ourfrenchtravels.com/12-best-day-trips-from-buenos-aires/

Garcia Mancelo, I. (2023, February 2). Museo Nacional de Bellas Artes - Precios y horarios, Buenos Aires. Www.disfrutabuenosaires.com. https://www.disfrutabuenosaires.com/museo-nacional-bellas-artes

Glenn. (2024, May 3). How getting from Ezeiza Buenos Aires airport to Buenos Aires. Secrets of Buenos Aires. https://secretsofbuenosaires.com/how-get-from-or-go-to-the-international-airport-ezeiza-to-buenos-aires/

Gobierno, D. (2017a, January 27). Parque de los Niños. Official English Website for the City of Buenos Aires. https://turismo.buenosaires.gob.ar/en/atractivo/parque-de-los-ni%C3%B1os

Gobierno, D. (2017b, August 3). Barrancas de Belgrano. Official English Website for the City of Buenos Aires. https://turismo.buenosaires.gob.ar/en/atractivo/barrancas-de-belgrano

Gonchissa. (2020, August 10). Barrancas de Belgrano. MiBsAs.com. https://www.mibsas.com/en/belgrano-canyons/

Gonzalez, D. (2018, December 10). The most epic day trips from Buenos Aires you need to take. Matador Network. https://matadornetwork.com/destinations/south-america/argentina/buenos-aires/day-trips/

Harwicz, A. (2018, August 29). Ariana Harwicz's Buenos Aires: A Life In Stories. Culture Trip. https://theculturetrip.com/south-america/argentina/articles/ariana-harwiczs-buenos-aires-a-life-in-stories

Historic cafes In Buenos Aires. (2017, August 31). Official English Website for the City of Buenos Aires. https://turismo.buenosaires.gob.ar/en/article/historic-cafes

How to get to Tigre from Buenos Aires | Buenos Aires Free Walks. (2016, August 16). Free Tour Buenos Aires. https://www.buenosairesfreewalks.com/barrios/tigre-en/how-to-get-to-tigre-from-buenos-aires/

Iñiguez, A. (2023, May 14). La historia de Cora Kavanagh y su emblemático edificio en Buenos Aires. ArchDaily En Español. https://www.archdaily.cl/cl/1000854/la-historia-de-cora-kavanagh-y-su-emblematico-edificio-en-buenos-aires

Inside Barrio Boliviano: A Food Tour of Mercado Andino de Liniers. (2016, August 17). Pick up the Fork. https://pickupthefork.com/2016/08/17/inside-barrio-boliviano-a-food-tour-of-mercado-andino-de-liniers/

Krier, J. (2024, January 16). 3 Days in Buenos Aires: The Perfect Buenos Aires Itinerary - Road Affair. Road Affair. https://www.roadaffair.com/best-buenos-aires-itinerary/

Mancebo, I. G. (2023, February 2). Buenos Aires neighborhoods and districts - Areas of Buenos Aires. Www.introducingbuenosaires.com. https://www.introducingbuenosaires.com/neighborhoods-districts

Manebo, I. G. (2023, February 2). History of Buenos Aires - Past, present, and future of the city. Www.introducingbuenosaires.com. https://www.introducingbuenosaires.com/history

Mara. (2023, December 29). The Ultimate Guide: 100+ Useful Spanish Phrases For Travel That You Need To Know! Sololingual. https://www.sololingual.com/travel-phrases/spanish-phrases-for-travel

Maria. (2023, July 17). 4 Days in Buenos Aires - A Local's Perfect Itinerary. Go Ask a Local. https://goaskalocal.com/blog/4-day-buenos-aires-itinerary

Martinez, I. (2019, April 8). Santuario de la Beata Virgen del Rosario de Pompeya. Visitar Pompeya. https://www.visitarpompeya.com/santuario-virgen-del-rosario/

McKinnon, P. (2019, November 18). The Guide to Visiting La Boca. Very Nice Travels. https://verynicetravels.com/argentina/2019/1/10/la-boca

Meeuwesen, J. (2018, May 7). 15 Best Day Trips from Buenos Aires. The Crazy Tourist. https://www.thecrazytourist.com/15-best-day-trips-buenos-aires/

Minister, C. (2008, March 17). What Should Everyone Know About the History of Buenos Aires? ThoughtCo. https://www.thoughtco.com/the-history-of-buenos-aires-2136353

Moss, C. (2018, November 23). Barracas, Buenos Aires: the neighborhood guide. CN Traveller. https://www.cntraveller.com/gallery/barracas-buenos-aires-neighbourhood-guide

Museo de Calcos y Escultura comparada. (2020, September 15). La Guía de Buenos Aires. https://www.laguiadebuenosaires.com/que-ver/museos/museo-de-calcos-y-escultura-comparada/

Nick. (2013, April 30). Day Trips from Buenos Aires: Tigre, the Paraná Delta, and the Tren de la Costa. Vaya Adventures. https://www.vayaadventures.com/blog/tigre-the-parana-delta-and-the-tren-de-la-costa/

Nicki. (2023). The ULTIMATE ITINERARY for 10 days in Buenos Aires. Www.youtube.com. https://www.youtube.com/watch?v=61LN3RkLQ0o

Nicki. (2023, March 15). BALVANERA: Buenos Aires Neighborhoods Guide -. Nickipoststravelstuff.com. https://nickipoststravelstuff.com/balvanera/

Notable People of Buenos Aires: Exploring the City's Icons. (2023). Yolopedia.com. https://www.yolopedia.com/argentina/buenos-aires/notable-people

Parra, R. (2021, April 8). 100+ Words and Phrases Related to Transportation in Spanish. Homeschool Spanish Academy. https://www.spanish.academy/blog/100-words-and-phrases-related-to-transportation-in-spanish/

Puerto Madero - Gringo in Buenos Aires. (2010, February 27). Www.gringoinbuenosaires.com. https://www.gringoinbuenosaires.com/neighborhood-guides/puerto-madero/

Raes, V. (2017, August 2). 25 Best Things to Do in Buenos Aires (Argentina). The Crazy Tourist. https://www.thecrazytourist.com/25-best-things-buenos-aires-argentina

Rebecca. (2016, October 10). Buenos Aires. Nomad Secrets. https://nomad-secrets.com/buenos-aires/

Rebecca. (2022, February 19). La Plata: A Great Day Trip From Buenos Aires - Becci Abroad. Becci Abroad. https://becci.dk/la-plata-day-trip-buenos-aires/

Rebecca. (2022, September 22). The Local's Guide to 3 Days in Buenos Aires Itinerary (2024). Rebecca and the World. https://www.rebeccaandtheworld.com/3-days-in-buenos-aires-itinerary/

Rebecca. (2024, April 17). What to Do in Buenos Aires: 25 Best Things to Do. Rebecca and the World. https://www.rebeccaandtheworld.com/what-to-do-in-buenos-aires-argentina/

Restaurant Spanish: The Only Phrases You Need to Know. (2018, October 5). Happy Hour Spanish. https://www.happyhourspanish.com/restaurant-spanish-the-only-phrases-you-need-to-know/

Sabine. (2017, September 24). Day trip from Buenos Aires: discover San Antonio de Areco. BESABINE. https://www.besabine.com/en/day-trip-from-buenos-aires-discover-gaucho-village-of-san-antonio-de-areco/

Sadlowski, A. (n.d.). Plaza Dorrego Review - Buenos Aires Argentina - Sights. Fodor's Travel. https://www.fodors.com/world/south-america/argentina/buenos-aires/things-to-do/sights/reviews/plaza-dorrego-111089

Salazar, M. (2024, January 15). Essential Spanish restaurant phrases in Spain | CIEE. Www.ciee.org. https://www.ciee.org/go-abroad/college-study-abroad/blog/essential-spanish-restaurant-phrases-spain

San Telmo market. (2016, September 8). Official English Website for the City of Buenos Aires. https://turismo.buenosaires.gob.ar/en/atractivo/san-telmo-market

Sarah & Kris. (2024, February 15). One Day in Buenos Aires Itinerary. Jetsetting Fools. https://jetsettingfools.com/a-one-day-itinerary-for-buenos-aires/

Sarlo, B. (2018, April 1). Why Buenos Aires Is Not Paris by Beatriz Sarlo. Words without Borders. https://wordswithoutborders.org/read/article/2018-04/april-2018-argentina-buenos-aires-is-not-paris-beatriz-sarlo-becker-tomasin/

Shelley, L. (2023, May 2). Floralis Genérica | 5 Amazing Things To Know About The Giant Steel Flower In Buenos Aires» Travel-Stained. Travel Stained. https://travel-stained.com/the-floralis-generica/

Soheilylangroud, I. (2023, January 27). A guide to Ezeiza International Airport (EZE). Blacklane Blog. https://blog.blacklane.com/travel/a-guide-to-ezeiza-international-airport/

Summer, E. (2021, March 1). San Martin Square. LimaEasy. https://www.limaeasy.com/lima-guide/lima-culture-guide/plazas-city-squares/san-martin-square

Tomašević, A. (2021, September 23). Buenos Aires Jorge Newbery Airport (EZE) - Passenger Info & Transport. GetByBus Blog. https://getbybus.com/en/blog/buenos-aires-jorge-newbery-airport/

Vare, F. J. (2018, May 24). Get Going! Spanish Transportation Vocabulary for People in a Hurry. Www.fluentu.com. https://www.fluentu.com/blog/spanish/spanish-transportation-vocabulary/

Visit Buenos Aires: The Ultimate Buenos Aires City Guide. (2018, February 4). Https://Solsalute.com/. https://solsalute.com/blog/guide-buenos-aires/

Vyve, L. V. (2023, December 7). 100 Common Spanish Phrases To Survive Any Situation. Effortless Conversations. https://effortlessconversations.com/learn-spanish/common-spanish-phrases/

Walks, F. (2016, May 5). Walk of Vicente López | Free Walks Buenos Aires. Free Tour Buenos Aires. https://www.buenosairesfreewalks.com/batips/walk-of-vicente-lopez/

Wandell, B. (2023, July 10). The Perfect 3 and 5-Day Buenos Aires Itinerary (2024 Guide). Worldly Adventurer. https://worldlyadventurer.com/buenos-aires-itinerary/

Wehrmeijer, K.-J. (2021, August 18). Parque de los Niños. Buenos Aires Free Walks; Buenos Aires Free Walks. https://www.buenosairesfreewalks.com/spanish/que-hacer-buenos-aires/parque-de-los-ninos/

Welcome to Parque Centenario! (2018, January 8). Mente Argentina Blog. https://www.menteargentina.com/blog/welcome-to-parque-centenario/

What to do in Barracas. (2021, May 31). Free Tour Buenos Aires. https://www.buenosairesfreewalks.com/barrios/barracas/what-to-do-in-barracas/

What to do in Belgrano. (2021, May 3). Buenos Aires Free Tour. https://ba-freetour.com/what-to-do-in-belgrano/

What to do in Lujan. (2023, March 20). Free Tour Buenos Aires. https://www.buenosairesfreewalks.com/what-to-do/what-to-do-in-lujan/

Wick, T. (2006, September 20). Buenos Aires History. Buenos Aires Argentina Travel Guide. https://tangotours.wordpress.com/buenos-aires-history/

Wieteska, A. (2019, January 21). 3 Days in Buenos Aires: Perfect First-Timer's Itinerary. Roam and Thrive. https://roamandthrive.com/best-things-to-do-in-buenos-aires/

Wood, G. (2023, April 21). 102 Essential Spanish Phrases for Traveling - Rosetta Stone. Rosetta Stone. https://blog.rosettastone.com/102-essential-spanish-phrases-for-traveling/

Wood, M. (2021, July 14). Buenos Aires Travel Guide. Travel + Leisure. https://www.travelandleisure.com/travel-guide/buenos-aires

Wyrick, R. (2023, June 30). 47 Facts about BUENOS AIRES. Facts.net. https://facts.net/world/cities/47-facts-about-buenos-aires/

IMAGE SOURCES

1 *TheDarkFear, CC BY-SA 4.0 <https://creativecommons.org/licenses/by-sa/4.0>, via Wikimedia Commons: https://commons.wikimedia.org/wiki/File:Wikivoyage_Buenos_Aires_Map_ES.svg*

2 *Deensel, CC BY 2.0 <https://creativecommons.org/licenses/by/2.0>, via Wikimedia Commons https://commons.wikimedia.org/wiki/File:Puerto_Madero,_Buenos_Aires_(40689219792).jpg*

3 *Manticora87, CC BY-SA 4.0 <https://creativecommons.org/licenses/by-sa/4.0>, via Wikimedia Commons https://commons.wikimedia.org/wiki/File:Tango_Porte%C3%B1o.jpg*

4 *Unknown author, CC BY-SA 3.0 NL <https://creativecommons.org/licenses/by-sa/3.0/nl/deed.en>, via Wikimedia Commons https://commons.wikimedia.org/wiki/File:Alfredo_Di_St%C3%A9fano_1962.jpg*

5 *Flickr user: flvouz https://www.flickr.com/photos/flavouz/397882988/, CC BY 2.0 <https://creativecommons.org/licenses/by/2.0>, via Wikimedia Commons https://commons.wikimedia.org/wiki/File:EZE_airport.jpg*

6 *Roberto Fiadone, CC BY-SA 4.0 <https://creativecommons.org/licenses/by-sa/4.0>, via Wikimedia Commons https://commons.wikimedia.org/wiki/File:Barrio_Chino_Belgrano_Buenos_Aires_entrada.jpg*

7 *Fulviusbsas, CC BY-SA 4.0 <https://creativecommons.org/licenses/by-sa/4.0>, via Wikimedia Commons https://commons.wikimedia.org/wiki/File:MuseoLarreta2.jpg*

8 *Roberto Fiadone, CC BY-SA 4.0 <https://creativecommons.org/licenses/by-sa/4.0>, via Wikimedia Commons https://commons.wikimedia.org/wiki/File:Barrancas_de_Belgrano_faroles.jpg*

9 *ProtoplasmaKid, CC BY-SA 4.0 <https://creativecommons.org/licenses/by-sa/4.0>, via Wikimedia Commons https://commons.wikimedia.org/wiki/File:Parque_de_la_Memoria,_Buenos_Aires_-_7.JPG*

10 *Attribution-ShareAlike 2.5 Generic CC BY-SA 2.5 <https://creativecommons.org/licenses/by-sa/2.5/deed.en> https://commons.wikimedia.org/wiki/File:Parque_Tres_de_Febrero.jpg*

11 *kara brugman, Attribution-NonCommercial-NoDerivs 2.0 Generic, CC BY-NC-ND 2.0* <https://creativecommons.org/licenses/by-nc-nd/2.0/> https://www.flickr.com/photos/hyperbolation/3093015023

12 *Ted McGrath, Attribution-NonCommercial-ShareAlike 2.0 Generic , CC BY-NC-SA 2.0* <https://creativecommons.org/licenses/by-nc-sa/2.0/ > https://www.flickr.com/photos/time-to-look/49998189421

13 *Stefano Vigorelli, Attribution-ShareAlike 4.0 International, CC BY-SA 4.0* <https://creativecommons.org/licenses/by-sa/4.0/deed.en> https://commons.m.wikimedia.org/wiki/File:Estadio_Monumental,_Buenos_Aires_ARG.jpg

14 *Roberto Fiadone, CC BY-SA 4.0* <https://creativecommons.org/licenses/by-sa/4.0>, *via Wikimedia Commons* https://commons.wikimedia.org/wiki/File:Reserva_Ecol%C3%B3gica_Ciudad_Universitaria-Costanera_Norte,_Buenos_Aires_06.jpg

15 *Erikao, CC BY-SA 3.0* <https://creativecommons.org/licenses/by-sa/3.0>, *via Wikimedia Commons* https://commons.wikimedia.org/wiki/File:Plaza_Libertad,_Balcarce.JPG

16 *Lombardia1, CC BY-SA 4.0* <https://creativecommons.org/licenses/by-sa/4.0>, *via Wikimedia Commons* https://commons.wikimedia.org/wiki/File:Paseo_de_la_Costa_en_Vicente_L%C3%B3pez2.jpg

17 *English: Taken by the uploader, w:es:Usuario:BarcexEspañol: Tomada por w:es:Usuario:Barcex, CC BY-SA 3.0* <http://creativecommons.org/licenses/by-sa/3.0/>, *via Wikimedia Commons* https://commons.wikimedia.org/wiki/File:Buenos_Aires_-_Barracas_-_Calle_Lan%C3%ADn_-_20071215o.jpg

18 *Roberto Fiadone, CC BY-SA 4.0* <https://creativecommons.org/licenses/by-sa/4.0>, *via Wikimedia Commons* https://commons.wikimedia.org/wiki/File:Museo_de_Escultura_Comparada_Ernesto_de_la_C%C3%A1rcova_01.jpg

19 *Auxi84, CC BY-SA 3.0* <https://creativecommons.org/licenses/by-sa/3.0>, *via Wikimedia Commons* https://commons.wikimedia.org/wiki/File:Iglesia_Parroquial_San_Antonio_Mar%C3%ADa_Claret.JPG

20 *Ted McGrath, Attribution-NonCommercial-ShareAlike 2.0 Generic, CC BY-NC-SA 2.0* <https://creativecommons.org/licenses/by-nc-sa/2.0/ > https://www.flickr.com/photos/time-to-look/49845352908

21 *Julia Sumangil, CC BY-SA 4.0 <https://creativecommons.org/licenses/by-sa/4.0>, via Wikimedia Commons https://commons.wikimedia.org/wiki/File:La_Bombonera_football_stadium.jpg*

22 *Wally Gobetz, Attribution-NonCommercial-NoDerivs 2.0 Generic, CC BY-NC-ND 2.0 <https://creativecommons.org/licenses/by-nc-nd/2.0/> https://www.flickr.com/photos/wallyg/7848409072*

23 *Roberto Fiadone, CC BY-SA 4.0 <https://creativecommons.org/licenses/by-sa/4.0>, via Wikimedia Commons https://commons.wikimedia.org/wiki/File:Escuela_Pedro_de_Mendoza,_Museo_Benito_Quinquela_Mart%C3%ADn,_Escultura_Antonio_Oriana.jpg*

24 *Nicolasrnphoto, CC BY 3.0 <https://creativecommons.org/licenses/by/3.0>, via Wikimedia Commons https://commons.wikimedia.org/wiki/File:ParqueDeLosPatricios-1.jpg*

25 *Tecnópolis Argentina, CC BY 2.0 <https://creativecommons.org/licenses/by/2.0>, via Wikimedia Commons https://commons.wikimedia.org/wiki/File:Tecn%C3%B3polis_desde_el_cielo.jpg*

26 *Mikelzubi, CC BY-SA 3.0 <https://creativecommons.org/licenses/by-sa/3.0>, via Wikimedia Commons https://commons.wikimedia.org/wiki/File:Casa_de_Gobierno_de_Buenos_Aires_(La_Plata_1).JPG*

27 *Roberto Fiadone, CC BY-SA 4.0 <https://creativecommons.org/licenses/by-sa/4.0>, via Wikimedia Commons https://commons.wikimedia.org/wiki/File:Santuario_Nuestra_Se%C3%B1ora_del_Rosario_de_Pompeya,_Buenos_Aires_01.jpg*

28 *Dario Alpern, CC BY-SA 3.0 <https://creativecommons.org/licenses/by-sa/3.0>, via Wikimedia Commons https://commons.wikimedia.org/wiki/File:Pasarela_peatonal_del_Puente_Alsina_2.jpg*

29 *Maximiliano Buono, CC BY-SA 2.0 <https://creativecommons.org/licenses/by-sa/2.0>, via Wikimedia Commons https://commons.wikimedia.org/wiki/File:Puente_de_la_Mujer_Woman%27s_bridge,_Puerto_Madero,_Buenos_Aires_(32029221153).jpg*

30 *Horacio patrone, CC BY-SA 4.0 <https://creativecommons.org/licenses/by-sa/4.0>, via Wikimedia Commons https://commons.wikimedia.org/wiki/File:RESERVA_ECOLOGICA_COSTANERA_SUR_.RECS.jpg*

31 *Wally Gobetz, Attribution-NonCommercial-NoDerivs 2.0 Generic, CC BY-NC-ND 2.0 <https://creativecommons.org/licenses/by-nc-nd/2.0/ > https://www.flickr.com/photos/wallyg/8015939528*

32 *Gino Lucas Turra, CC BY-SA 3.0 <https://creativecommons.org/licenses/by-sa/3.0>, via Wikimedia Commons https://commons.wikimedia.org/wiki/File:Fuente_de_las_Nereidas.jpg*

33 *Gobierno de la Ciudad Autónoma de Buenos Aires, CC BY 2.5 AR <https://creativecommons.org/licenses/by/2.5/ar/deed.en>, via Wikimedia Commons https://commons.wikimedia.org/wiki/File:Colecci%C3%B3n_de_Arte_Amalia_Lacroze_de_Fortabat.jpg*

34 *Carlos Figueroa Rojas, CC BY-SA 4.0 <https://creativecommons.org/licenses/by-sa/4.0>, via Wikimedia Commons https://commons.wikimedia.org/wiki/File:Museo_Nacional_de_Bellas_Artes,_Santiago_20230311.jpg*

35 *Ted McGrath, Attribution-NonCommercial-ShareAlike 2.0 Generic, CC BY-NC-SA 2.0 <https://creativecommons.org/licenses/by-nc-sa/2.0/ > https://www.flickr.com/photos/time-to-look/49934794117*

36 *Kreepin Deth, CC BY-SA 4.0 <https://creativecommons.org/licenses/by-sa/4.0>, via Wikimedia Commons https://commons.wikimedia.org/wiki/File:Catedral-Bas%C3%ADlica_de_Nuestra_Se%C3%B1ora_del_Pilar_(Front).jpg*

37 *Josefito123, CC BY-SA 4.0 <https://creativecommons.org/licenses/by-sa/4.0>, via Wikimedia Commons https://commons.wikimedia.org/wiki/File:Mercado_San_Telmo,_Buenos_Aires_20181103_170613.jpg*

38 *Jorge Láscar, Attribution 2.0 Generic, CC BY 2.0, <https://creativecommons.org/licenses/by/2.0/> https://www.flickr.com/photos/jlascar/4728829963*

39 *Julia Sumangil, CC BY-SA 4.0 <https://creativecommons.org/licenses/by-sa/4.0>, via Wikimedia Commons https://commons.wikimedia.org/wiki/File:Plaza_San_Mart%C3%ADn_(Buenos_Aires)_02.jpg*

40 *https://commons.wikimedia.org/wiki/File:Argentina-01792_-_Torre_Monumental_(49004695478).jpg*

41 *Martín A. Aurand, CC BY-SA 4.0 <https://creativecommons.org/licenses/by-sa/4.0>, via Wikimedia Commons https://commons.wikimedia.org/wiki/File:Edificio_Kavanagh_04.jpg*

42 Andrzej Otrębski, CC BY-SA 4.0 <https://creativecommons.org/licenses/by-sa/4.0>, via Wikimedia Commons https://commons.wikimedia.org/wiki/File:Buenos_Aires_Palacio_Paz_3.jpg

43 https://commons.wikimedia.org/wiki/File:Laguna_y_fuente_Parque_Centenario,_Buenos_Aires.jpg

44 Roberto Fiadone, CC BY-SA 4.0 <https://creativecommons.org/licenses/by-sa/4.0>, via Wikimedia Commons https://commons.wikimedia.org/wiki/File:MACN24021402.JPG

45 ProtoplasmaKid, CC BY-SA 4.0 <https://creativecommons.org/licenses/by-sa/4.0>, via Wikimedia Commons https://commons.wikimedia.org/wiki/File:Mercado_del_Progreso_-_Interior_4.jpg

46 Humberto.García, CC BY-SA 3.0 <https://creativecommons.org/licenses/by-sa/3.0>, via Wikimedia Commons https://commons.wikimedia.org/wiki/File:Templo_de_San_Cayetano_01.jpg

47 Frank Vincentz, CC BY-SA 3.0 <http://creativecommons.org/licenses/by-sa/3.0/>, via Wikimedia Commons https://commons.wikimedia.org/wiki/File:Santa_Cruz_-_Virgen_de_las_Nieves_07_ies.jpg

48 Roblespepe, CC BY-SA 4.0 <https://creativecommons.org/licenses/by-sa/4.0>, via Wikimedia Commons https://commons.wikimedia.org/wiki/File:Estadio_Amalfitani_-_Jaguares_2019.jpg

49 Dgpmas, CC BY-SA 4.0 <https://creativecommons.org/licenses/by-sa/4.0>, via Wikimedia Commons https://commons.wikimedia.org/wiki/File:Iglesia_San_Cayetano..jpg

50 Gobierno de la Ciudad Autónoma de Buenos Aires, CC BY 2.5 AR <https://creativecommons.org/licenses/by/2.5/ar/deed.en>, via Wikimedia Commons https://commons.wikimedia.org/wiki/File:Panorama_Teatro_Col%C3%B3n.jpg

51 Sebastianalmaraz, CC BY-SA 4.0 <https://creativecommons.org/licenses/by-sa/4.0>, via Wikimedia Commons https://commons.wikimedia.org/wiki/File:ObeliscoBA2015.2.jpg

52 Luis Argerich, CC BY 2.0 <https://creativecommons.org/licenses/by/2.0>, via Wikimedia Commons https://commons.wikimedia.org/wiki/File:Corrientes_Buenos_Aires_at_Night.jpg

53 *Phil Whitehouse from London, United Kingdom, CC BY 2.0 <https://creativecommons.org/licenses/by/2.0>, via Wikimedia Commons https://commons.wikimedia.org/wiki/File:Casa_Rosada_(2051973489).jpg*

54 *Gobierno de la Ciudad Autónoma de Buenos Aires, CC BY 2.5 AR <https://creativecommons.org/licenses/by/2.5/ar/deed.en>, via Wikimedia Commons https://commons.wikimedia.org/wiki/File:View_of_Plaza_de_Mayo.jpg*

55 *User:Roberto Fiadone, CC BY-SA 3.0 <http://creativecommons.org/licenses/by-sa/3.0/>, via Wikimedia Commons https://commons.wikimedia.org/wiki/File:Manzana_de_las_Luces_vista_desde_arriba.jpg*

56 *Unknown author, CC BY-SA 2.5 <https://creativecommons.org/licenses/by-sa/2.5>, via Wikimedia Commons https://commons.wikimedia.org/wiki/File:Cafe_Tortoni_-_interior.jpg*

57 *Alienlanus, CC BY-SA 3.0 <https://creativecommons.org/licenses/by-sa/3.0>, via Wikimedia Commons https://commons.wikimedia.org/wiki/File:Palacio_Barolo.JPG*

58 *Roberto Fiadone, CC BY-SA 4.0 <https://creativecommons.org/licenses/by-sa/4.0>, via Wikimedia Commons https://commons.wikimedia.org/wiki/File:Palacio_de_Aguas_Corrientes,_Buenos_Aires_03.jpg*

59 *Tim Adams from San Francisco, CC BY 2.0 <https://creativecommons.org/licenses/by/2.0>, via Wikimedia Commons https://commons.wikimedia.org/wiki/File:Plaza_del_Congreso_in_Buenos_Aires,_Argentina_(15755494427).png*

60 *Beatrice Murch from Buenos Aires, Argentina, CC BY 2.0 <https://creativecommons.org/licenses/by/2.0>, via Wikimedia Commons https://commons.wikimedia.org/wiki/File:Plaza_Miserere_at_Springtime_(5184910265).jpg*

61 *Gabriel Sozzi, CC BY-SA 4.0 <https://creativecommons.org/licenses/by-sa/4.0>, via Wikimedia Commons https://commons.wikimedia.org/wiki/File:Altar_de_san_Carlos_Borromeo_-_Bas%C3%ADlica_Mar%C3%ADa_Auxiliadora_y_San_Carlos.JPG*

62 *Erico Valadares, CC BY-SA 3.0 <https://creativecommons.org/licenses/by-sa/3.0>, via Wikimedia Commons https://commons.wikimedia.org/wiki/File:MACN24021402.JPG*

63 *OpenStreetMap Contributors https://www.openstreetmap.org*

64 OpenStreetMap Contributors https://www.openstreetmap.org

65 OpenStreetMap Contributors https://www.openstreetmap.org

66 OpenStreetMap Contributors https://www.openstreetmap.org

67 OpenStreetMap Contributors https://www.openstreetmap.org

68 OpenStreetMap Contributors https://www.openstreetmap.org

69 OpenStreetMap Contributors https://www.openstreetmap.org

70 OpenStreetMap Contributors https://www.openstreetmap.org

71 OpenStreetMap Contributors https://www.openstreetmap.org

72 OpenStreetMap Contributors https://www.openstreetmap.org

73 OpenStreetMap Contributors https://www.openstreetmap.org

74 OpenStreetMap Contributors https://www.openstreetmap.org

75 OpenStreetMap Contributors https://www.openstreetmap.org

76 OpenStreetMap Contributors https://www.openstreetmap.org

77 Ted McGrath https://www.flickr.com/photos/time-to-look/49951820171

78 Roberto Fiadone, CC BY-SA 4.0 <https://creativecommons.org/licenses/by-sa/4.0>, via Wikimedia Commons https://commons.wikimedia.org/wiki/File:Parque_Criollo_y_Museo_Gauchesco_Ricardo_G%C3%BCiraldes_05.jpg

79 Bando daval, CC BY-SA 4.0 <https://creativecommons.org/licenses/by-sa/4.0>, via Wikimedia Commons https://commons.wikimedia.org/wiki/File:CATEDRAL_de_LA_PLATA,_ARGENTINA.jpg

80 Roberto Fiadone, CC BY-SA 4.0 <https://creativecommons.org/licenses/by-sa/4.0>, via Wikimedia Commons https://commons.wikimedia.org/wiki/File:Casa_Curutchet_18.jpg

81 Luis Argerich from Buenos Aires, Argentina, CC BY 2.0 <https://creativecommons.org/licenses/by/2.0>, via Wikimedia Commons https://commons.wikimedia.org/wiki/File:Luj%C3%A1n_-_Bas%C3%ADlica_de_Nuestra_Se%C3%B1ora_de_Luj%C3%A1n_-_200807e.jpg

82 *Ministerio de Cultura de la Nación Argentina, CC BY-SA 2.0 <https://creativecommons.org/licenses/by-sa/2.0>, via Wikimedia Commons https://commons.wikimedia.org/wiki/File:Chicos_de_barrios_populares_visitaron_el_Museo_Malvinas_e_Islas_del_Atl%C3%A1ntico_Sur_(15350147666).jpg*

Printed in Great Britain
by Amazon

58595090R10145